The Literary Language of Shakespeare

The Literary Language of Shakespeare

Second edition

S. S. HUSSEY

Longman
London and New York

Longman Group UK Limited,
Longman House, Burnt Mill,
Harlow, Essex CM20 2JE, England
and Associated Companies throughout the world

Published in the United States of America
by Longman Publishing, New York

First edition © Longman Group Limited 1982
Second edition © Longman Group UK Limited 1992

First published 1982
Second edition 1992

British Library Cataloguing-in-Publication Data

A catalogue record for this book is available from the British Library

Library of Congress Cataloging-in-Publication Data

Hussey, S. S., 1925–
    The literary language of Shakespeare / S.S. Hussey. — 2nd ed.
        p.   cm.
    Includes index.
    ISBN 0–582–08770–8
    1. Shakespeare, William, 1564–1616—Style.   2. Shakespeare,
William, 1564–1616—Language.   3. English language—
Early modern, 1500–1700—Style.   I. Title.
    PR3072.H86   1992
    822.3'3—dc20   91–39942
                                                                         CIP

Set by 5 in 10/12 Linotron Bembo Roman

Printed in Malaysia by VP

Contents

Preface to the Second Edition

A proper appreciation of any great writer must begin with his language. Why does he put it in that particular way at that particular point in the play? To say that a writer is great because he exploits the linguistic conventions of his age is to risk a truism. Yet the further back we go, the greater the risk of partial or unsound literary judgements, simply because those conventions may be unfamiliar or even unrecognised. Although we cannot be sure what Shakespeare's own speech was like (any more than we can Chaucer's), we can distinguish, from his own work and that of his fellow Elizabethans, a number of accepted styles in use around the turn of the century. From these Shakespeare selects to achieve a range of characterisation, description or conversation far beyond that of even the best of his contemporaries. Since they are norms, he can also deliberately deviate from these styles to produce a type of language remarkable simply because it is so unexpected in that particular context.

Those words appeared in the Preface to the first edition of this book in 1982 and, to my mind, they remain as true now as they were then. Ten years on, understanding what Shakespeare says has become even more difficult for the beginner. There are, of course, books on Shakespeare's language which illustrate in detail the main features of his vocabulary, grammar, syntax and phonology. What they do not attempt is to demonstrate how these same features achieve the stylistic effects they do. Naturally enough, much writing on Shakespeare has appeared in the last decade and I have tried to take account of some of this. 'New historicism' lies behind some of my remarks on *Henry V*, but ultimately I find this approach to Shakespeare (and its later development, 'cultural materialism') disappointing since its emphasis on discontinuity and contradiction, its determination to see Shakespeare as not merely challenging but so often subversive, leads to an incomplete reading of several plays. Feminist critics seem unable at present to decide whether Shakespeare held more enlightened views about women than his contemporaries or whether he simply conformed to a male-orientated cultural ideology. I believe the approach through gender will ultimately prove more rewarding than many new-historicist readings, but in both a lot of the criticism is still at the stage of manifesto and thematic study rather than of detailed application to individual plays or groups of plays: it sometimes (feminist readings especially) shows an unhealthy absorption in its own critical terminology. What is more encouraging in other recent work is the increasing attempt to consider Shakespeare's style not just in a traditional literary-critical manner but also from the point of view of Renaissance views about language and, latterly, by using some of the techniques of pragmatic theory. I hope this introductory book may help to further such studies.

There are revisions in all parts of the book, but the major changes are a greater concern with theatrical conditions in Chapter 1, the incorporation of some of the material in the original final chapter into a new section, 'Sonnets and Soliloquies', in Chapter 8, and the completely new final chapter which gives a brief reading of four plays (*Henry V*, *As You Like It*, *Macbeth* and *The Winter's Tale*) in which I suggest some of the benefits of adopting the approaches discussed in earlier chapters. I have tried to acknowledge the work of those critics I have found most helpful and I owe a great deal to both my teachers and my students. Three special debts must be mentioned here: to Dr Tony Gilbert for the stimulus of sharing with him courses on Shakespeare's language; to Professor Tom Craik for his detailed comments on (and corrections to) the first edition; and to Messrs Longman for their care and courtesy in encouraging and producing the book.

List of Abbreviations

Shakespeare is quoted from the New Penguin edition, where available, otherwise from the Signet edition (for *TA, MWW, TC, TNK, Hen VIII*). The suggested dates of composition are based on those in the Oxford *Complete Works* (1986) and are sometimes conservative. But it is the probable order of plays rather than exact dating which is important for my argument.

TGV	*The Two Gentlemen of Verona 1591* (?)
1 Hen VI	*1 Henry VI 1592*
2 Hen VI	*2 Henry VI 1591*
3 Hen VI	*3 Henry VI 1592*
R III	*Richard III 1592*
VA	*Venus and Adonis 1593*
RL	*The Rape of Lucrece 1593*
TA	*Titus Andronicus 1593*
CE	*The Comedy of Errors 1594*
TS	*The Taming of the Shrew 1594*
LLL	*Love's Labour's Lost 1594–5*
R II	*Richard II 1595*
RJ	*Romeo and Juliet 1595*
MND	*A Midsummer Night's Dream 1595*
KJ	*King John 1595–6*
MV	*The Merchant of Venice 1596–7*
1 Hen IV	*1 Henry IV 1597*
MWW	*The Merry Wives of Windsor 1597*
2 Hen IV	*2 Henry IV 1598*
MA	*Much Ado About Nothing 1599*
Hen V	*Henry V 1599*

JC	*Julius Caesar* 1599
Ham	*Hamlet* 1600
AYLI	*As You Like It* 1600
TC	*Troilus and Cressida* 1601
TN	*Twelfth Night* 1601
AW	*All's Well That Ends Well* 1604
MM	*Measure for Measure* 1604 (?)
Oth	*Othello* 1604
Tim	*Timon of Athens* 1604 (?)
KL	*King Lear* 1605 (?)
Mac	*Macbeth* 1606
AC	*Antony and Cleopatra* 1606
Cor	*Coriolanus* 1608
Per	*Pericles* 1608 (?)
Cym	*Cymbeline* 1610
WT	*The Winter's Tale* 1611
Temp	*The Tempest* 1611
TNK	*The Two Noble Kinsmen* 1613
Hen VIII	*Henry VIII* 1613

For Joyce

CHAPTER ONE
Is this Shakespeare's language?

SHAKESPEARE'S ROOTS

What the 'real' language of Shakespeare – his own language – was like, we will probably never completely know. He came to London from Stratford before 1592, in which year he was sufficiently established for his fellow writer Robert Greene, embittered by poverty and ill-health, to attack him in print:

> . . . an upstart Crow, beautified with our feathers, that with his *Tygers heart wrapt in a Players hide*, supposes he is as well able to bumbast out a blanke verse as the best of you: and being an absolute *Iohannes fac totum*, is in his owne conceit the onely Shake-scene in a countrie.[1]

In the middle of a long speech in *3 Henry VI* (possibly performed the same year) York calls the Queen a "tiger's heart wrapped in a *woman's* hide!" (I. iv. 137). There is no firm evidence for dating any of his plays before 1590–1. He was not a university man, as were many of his contemporaries: Marlowe, Greene and Nashe, for instance. His father, indeed, although a prominent Stratford citizen and merchant, was perhaps illiterate – at least, he signed documents with his mark. There is a tradition that, in his earlier years, William was a schoolmaster 'in the country'. From a literary point of view this is so much more attractive, if less romantic, than the other story which has him holding horses outside the theatre. Certainly his first plays already exhibit a close knowledge of rhetorical devices of the kind found in contemporary school textbooks, but this of course is not proof. It is possible to make informed guesses at many of the circumstances of Shakespeare's career,[2] but several tantalising questions must remain unanswered. Did his wife and children stay at Stratford? If so, perhaps he visited them fairly regularly; he

1

certainly retained some business connections in the town. Yet he lived in London, close to the theatres in which he worked, first in Bishopsgate near the Theatre and later on the Bankside near the Globe in Southwark. He acted in plays as well as wrote them (Greene's attack is on both the player and the playwright). Tradition has it that he played Adam in *As You Like It* and the Ghost in *Hamlet*; he certainly appeared in at least two of Ben Jonson's plays. So, whatever Warwickshire may have contributed to his own language, he was presumably understood on the London stage.

We might have hoped for more from Christopher Sly, the drunken Warwickshire tinker who, in the Induction to *The Taming of the Shrew*, is persuaded that he is a "lord indeed" and, in the country house, "wrapped in sweet clothes", surrounded by attentive servants, "wanton pictures" and music sweeter than that of Apollo or caged nightingales, dreams he sees a play, "a kind of history", performed by the sort of strolling players who might have captivated the young Shakespeare. But although the local names are present (Wincot was four miles from Stratford and a Sara Hacket was baptised there in 1591):

> What, would you make me mad? Am not I Christopher Sly, old Sly's son of Burton-heath, by birth a pedlar, by education a cardmaker, by transmutation a bear-herd, and now by present profession a tinker? Ask Marian Hacket, the fat ale-wife of Wincot, if she know me not. If she say I am not fourteen pence on the score for sheer ale, score me up for the lyingest knave in Christendom.
>
> (Ind. II. 16–23)

indications of specifically Warwickshire language are disappointingly absent, as they are from the further Sly scenes found in *The Taming of the Shrew*.

The large *Oxford English Dictionary (OED)* is compiled almost entirely from printed accounts for Shakespeare's time and its localisations for dialect words are usually very tentative. We lack a Tudor and Stuart dictionary of the kind which might provide more extensive (and more recently documented) coverage over a more limited period. We can, however, get a little help from Warwickshire documents, such as the parish accounts recording the detailed spending by public officers. These are valuable because they are clearly localised and dated, and for most of the seventeenth century they are not influenced by the spread of standard English which reduces their linguistic usefulness later. Two examples quoted by Dr Hilda Hulme, who has made a special study of these records,[3] will illustrate the kind of help they can give in appreciating Shakespearean usage. In *The Merry*

Wives of Windsor (IV. iii. 8), the retainers of a suspicious-sounding German duke wish to hire horses from the Host of the Garter inn. The Host replies:

> They shall have my horses, but I'll make them pay; I'll sauce them. They have had my house a week at command. I have turned away my other guests. They must come off. I'll sauce them. Come.

The *OED* interprets *to pay sauce* as 'to pay dearly', but can only date this usage between 1678 and 1718. Even if we turn to *As You Like It* (III. v. 67) where Rosalind says

> If it be so, as fast as she answers thee with frowning looks, I'll sauce her with bitter words.

we still only perceive the metaphor of an unexpectedly hot seasoning. The parish accounts of Solihull (Warwickshire) for 1666, however, contain the following record:

> Thomas Palmer & my selfe went before to vew the timber & caused sawers to look on it. 0–0–4
> Another time I took 2 Carpenters to looke on it and to saw it & I found ye sauce worse then the meat. 0–0–8

Surely, as Dr Hulme remarks, one would expect to pay less for the sauce than for the meat, just as the churchwardens expected to pay less (not more) to the carpenters than to the real wood cutters, the *sawers*. Hence the meaning can be elaborated from 'to pay dearly' to 'to pay more than you expected'. The furious Host of the Garter is determined to obtain his revenge by deliberate overcharging. Again, the accounts of the Stratford Corporation for 1582–3 read

> Payd to davi Jones and his companye for his pastyme at Whitsontyde xii s iii d.

where *pastyme* is clearly not merely 'entertainment' but some kind of dramatic entertainment. When Gertrude, worried about Hamlet's melancholia, asks (III. i. 15):

> Did you assay him/To any pastime?

it is natural that Rosencrantz and Guildenstern should at once think of actors:

> Madam, it so fell out that certain *players*/We o'er-raught on the way.

This is fascinating, and shows how quite usual words could acquire a special use so that a joke or an extra layer of meaning becomes apparent. Yet it is inevitably limited in its extent, nor do we know how widespread these dialectal usages were. Did they seem, to London audiences, simply 'country' as opposed to 'normal' usage and not Warwickshire dialect at all?

SHAKESPEARE'S TEXT

In one way, however, the Elizabethan play-text may come between Shakespeare's own language and the modern reader. It is natural for the latter to assume that the text he reads is in all respects – act and scene division, lineation, spelling and punctuation – what Shakespeare wrote. An author today will correct his own proofs (or at least designate a responsible person to do it for him) so that the published version of the work will represent what author and editor have agreed should appear. But we have no fair copies of the plays which are demonstrably in Shakespeare's own hand. The first collected edition, the First Folio, was published in 1623, seven years after Shakespeare's death, and was compiled by two of his fellow-actors and business associates, John Heminges and Henry Condell. A volume of 'collected works' by the author himself was a rarity at that time, and drama was perhaps not thought of as sufficient of a literary form to justify such care and exactness. Ben Jonson, whose interest in language is shown by his English-Latin grammar (covering pronunciation, morphology and syntax) and whose reputation was very dear to him, is the exception in issuing in 1616 the first volume of the *Workes of Beniamin Jonson*. When a playwright sold his play to a company he ceased to be responsible for it. The company in turn tended not to publish unless they needed the money or unless the play was no longer a box-office success, for publication might mean a production by a rival company.

The First Folio (F1) contains thirty-six of Shakespeare's plays, sixteen of them appearing in print for the first time. The Sonnets, *Venus and Adonis* and *The Rape of Lucrece* are not included, and *Pericles* was added in the 1664 copy of the Folio. But during Shakespeare's lifetime, seventeen plays were published in quarto and a quarto text of *Othello* appeared in 1622. The sheets of a quarto are printed on both sides and folded twice to give eight pages per gathering (or quire); in a folio each sheet is folded only once. The quarto versions which are reasonably accurate are known as 'good' quartos and the six which are seriously corrupt, textually, are called 'bad' quartos. *Hamlet* and

Romeo and Juliet exist in both good and bad quartos, as well as in F1. In their address "To the great Variety of Readers", Heminges and Condell claim that their texts are greatly superior to previous bad quartos and indeed represent Shakespeare's own version:

> where (before) you were abus'd with diuerse stolne, and surreptitious copies, maimed, and deformed by the frauds and stealthes of iniurious imposters, that expos'd them; euen those, are now offer'd to your view cur'd, and perfect of their limbes; and all the rest, absolute in their numbers, as he conceiued them.

This is frankly advertising copy; in fact the quality of a text available to the printer, whether of F1 or of any quarto, varied considerably. Shakespeare, no doubt, had his original rough copy (or 'foul papers') and this sometimes seems to lie not far below some of the good quartos. In these, the stage directions are often of a 'literary' nature, of the kind which might assist the author's memory rather than be of great use to the producer, and the designation of minor characters shows that Shakespeare was thinking of the type of character rather than of an individual. The stage-direction at I. i. 69 of *Titus Andronicus*, for example, after listing the characters who actually enter at that point, concludes "and others as many as can be"; just how many can be decided later by the producer. In the stage-directions of the quarto of *Much Ado*, Dogberry and Verges are sometimes given their proper names, sometimes called "Constable" and "Headborough", and sometimes (IV. ii) "Kemp" and "Cowley", the actors for whom the parts were written. The printer might at best receive a fair copy of the authorial manuscript, like those made for some of the plays in F1 by Ralph Crane, a professional scribe, who probably produced the copy for *The Tempest*, the first play in F1 and which is well set out, and others such as *The Winter's Tale* and *The Two Gentlemen of Verona*. His copies have full division into acts and scenes, although few stage directions, and one of his identifying features is his extensive use of brackets and hyphens.

The other source of printer's copy was the theatre prompt-book. The importance of the prompt-book was legal. It contained the authorisation of the Master of the Revels. He was an official subordinate to the Lord Chamberlain and licensed scripts for performance; sometimes he censored them too. The company was thus given legal protection. Major revisions in a prompt-text were unlikely after the play had been licensed, otherwise it might need to be re-submitted. The prompter (or book-keeper), as well as tidying up the stage-directions, especially marking entrances and exits, might himself make interpolations or cuts, perhaps for a particular performance or to reduce the size of a travelling company through the elimination of minor characters. The Folio text of *Richard II*, for example, was printed from a quarto that had been checked against a theatre copy. Its stage-directions are therefore businesslike, indicating entrances and exits clearly. One of the most uncompromising (yet perfectly adequate) stage directions in Shakespeare is that which begins Act II of *Pericles*: "Enter Pericles, wet." The F1 text of *King John*, on the other hand, has infrequent stage-directions and these are not conspicuously theatrical in character; it was probably set up from a copy of an authorial manuscript.

Where we are fortunate enough to possess both the Folio and a quarto text, we can use one to throw light on the other, but even so they may vary considerably. The quarto of *Henry V* omits the prologue, choruses and epilogue; the F1 text of *Hamlet* omits one of the soliloquies, "How all occasions . . .". Some bad quartos were probably put together illegally ("stolne and surreptitious copies") by one or two of the actors. Their attempts at memorial reconstruction of the whole play show a good recollection of the parts these actors themselves played, but with a tendency to fill out the lines less clearly remembered. Here is the opening of the best-known of all Hamlet's soliloquies as it appears in the bad Q1:

> To be, or not to be, I there's the point
> To Die, to sleepe, is that all? I all:
> No, to sleepe, to dreame, I mary there it goes,
> For in that dreame of death, when wee awake,
> And borne before an euerlasting Iudge,
> From whence no passenger euer retur'nd,
> The vndiscouered country, at whose sight
> The happy smile, and the accursed damn'd.

If an actor was responsible for this, it was certainly not Hamlet himself who would have remembered better.

The bad quarto of *2 Henry VI* is entitled "The First part of the Contention betwixt the two famous Houses of Yorke and Lancaster, with the death of the good Duke Humphrey: And the banishment and death of the Duke of Suffolke, and the Tragicall end of the proud Cardinall of Winchester, with the notable Rebellion of Iacke Cade: And the Duke of Yorkes first claime unto the Crowne", and it contains echoes of Marlowe's *Edward II* and *Arden of Feversham*. Yet bad quartos are far from useless. Occasionally they include stage directions, absent from better texts but telling us something of how the scene may have been played. Against F1's brief "Enter Ophelia distracted", Q1 of *Hamlet* has "Enter Ofelia playing on a Lute, and her haire downe singing" (IV. v. 21). Elizabethan ladies arranged their elaborate coiffures on a wire frame; the hair down is a conventional sign of madness. At the close of II. v. of *Romeo and Juliet*, the Nurse sends Juliet off to Friar Laurence's cell where there "stays a husband to make you a wife". The Friar counsels patience and moderation, but at II. vi. 15 Q1 has "Enter Juliet somewhat fast, and embraceth Romeo". By the end of this short scene the Friar is convinced: "Come, come with me, and we will make short work."

But what about a situation in which the comparative textual value of Folio and quarto(s) is unclear? The 1608 quarto of *King Lear* contains about 300 lines not in F1 which in its turn includes some 100 lines not in the quarto. These differences go far beyond mere variations in phraseology. Did Lear die believing Cordelia was still alive? The Folio suggests he did:

> Why should a Dog, a Horse, a Rat haue life,
> And thou no breath at all? Thou'lt come no more,
> Neuer, neuer, neuer, neuer, neuer.
> Pray you vndo this Button. Thanke you Sir,
> Do you see this? Looke on her. Looke her lips,
> Looke there, looke there.
>
> (V.iii.306–11)

But the quarto (which, incidentally, prints the speech as prose) omits the last two lines of the Folio text:

> Why should a dog, a horse, a rat of life and thou no breath at all.
> O thou wilt come no more, neuer, neuer, neuer, pray you vndo this
> button, thank you sir. O, o, o, o.

The *O, o, o, o* is the usual indication of a long-drawn-out death-cry on stage. So this is probably an actor's interpolation. But of what? Lear's own dying groans or a realisation that Cordelia is in fact dead (in which latter case he would of course be looking at Cordelia)? If our modern stage direction (at 256) reads "Enter Lear with Cordelia dead in his arms", this does not solve the puzzle, for *dead* was added by the eighteenth-century editor Nicholas Rowe. Until recently the assumption was that both F1 and Q of *King Lear* are corrupted versions of Shakespeare's own lost manuscript; the editor consequently produced a composite text with the better features of both. But might not the play have been revised *in the light of theatrical experience*? Q1 would then be the original and F1 the revised version. Once stated, the proposition seems eminently reasonable, although it might not have been the case with very many other plays. Both versions of *King Lear* are therefore included in the recent Oxford Shakespeare.

A printer, then, might receive copy of widely different kinds: the author's working copy, his 'foul papers'; a fair copy of the author's final version handed over to the theatre company which would then own it; the promptbook, the version prepared for acting by the prompter; a version memorially reconstructed by one or more actors; or, of course, scribal copies of any of these. But even if he received good copy, he might himself contribute some errors, either through carelessness, or through a desire to correct apparent nonsense, or to achieve a typographically tidy page. The first kind is comparatively easy to spot and rectify, the second and third more difficult to detect because they may produce a plausible reading. Not only writing but also spelling was a personal matter (as may be seen from the quotations and titles above) and contracted forms, not marked by punctuation as now, were frequent. Furthermore, the printing of a text may have been divided between two or more compositors working simultaneously and each with his own idiosyncrasies. Clearly, a knowledge of the palaeographical and linguistic habits of Shakespeare's age is an indispensable part of the modern editor's equipment. We have some knowledge of a few typically Shakespearean spellings, largely from his contribution to the play of *Sir Thomas More*. This play, in a unique manuscript and originally written in one hand, perhaps in the mid 1590s, was augmented and corrected by five other hands, one of which is thought to be Shakespeare's. He contributed the early part of Act II, scene iii, in which More pacifies the citizens, and, less certainly, More's soliloquy which opens Act III, scene i.

Where F1 is printed from a good quarto, textual criticism is correspondingly easier, but in any event the task of reconstructing what Shakespeare actually wrote is far less hopeless than some of the above remarks may have suggested. Printers, prompters, scribes and unauthorised actors may all have helped to obscure what Shakespeare intended, but we now have a far better knowledge of Elizabethan handwriting, stage conditions, the whole printing process (even to the extent of identifying scribes such as Ralph Crane and individual compositors from their linguistic mannerisms and minor damage to their typefaces) and, finally, contemporary language than our predecessors had. The editor will supply act and scene division where these are either not marked or demonstrably erroneous, silently regularise speech prefixes (Lady Macbeth for "Lady" and Armado for "Braggart"), correct mislineation and verse printed as prose, supply stage-directions and indicate locale. He will almost always use modern punctuation. Elizabethan punctuation, especially in the quartos, is less than today's reader is accustomed to and frequently rhetorical in its aim (as an aid to the actor speaking the lines) rather than grammatical (for the convenience of the reader). The amount and the style of modern punctuation is important, for punctuation is itself a form of interpretation; the editor is himself contributing here to the way we understand the text. In his aim of reconstructing as closely as possible what Shakespeare wrote, the editor should remember that Shakespeare at times wrote below his best and should resist any temptation to remove every awkwardness of expression. He must always give his reasons for his choice between variant but possible readings. In this book I quote from the New Penguin edition which provides a sound text and the evidence on which that text is based. The later volumes of the Arden edition (especially *Hamlet*, *Troilus and Cressida* and *Richard III*) are valuable, as are the editions of such plays as have appeared in the Oxford and New Cambridge series. I have checked difficult readings against the Complete Oxford Shakespeare (edited by S. Wells and G. Taylor, 1986) and the same editors' *William Shakespeare*: *A Textual Companion* (1987).

Shakespeare, as we are increasingly and properly reminded nowadays, wrote for the stage.[4] Of the Elizabethan playwrights he seems to have been unusual, perhaps unique, in the closeness of his relationship with a single company, the King's (earlier the Chamberlain's) Men. Jonson and Webster, for instance, wrote for several companies. Shakespeare was actor (although there is no record of his acting after 1603), shareholder and resident dramatist to them. The sharers, usually some ten or twelve in number, were the most important members of the company and others of the troupe were their employees. They acted as a syndicate, owning the playscripts, costumes and properties and, in the case of Shakespeare's company, the Globe playhouse, although it was more usual for the company to rent the theatre. They shared both expenses and profits and in the eyes of the law they *were* the company. The playing strength of the King's Men was perhaps fifteen or sixteen, so doubling was often necessary. Women's parts were played by boy actors. Long runs were virtually unknown – Middleton's *A Game at Chess* ran for an exceptional nine days – and the number of plays in repertory must have been many more than with a modern company. Most theatres were public playhouses, open amphitheatres with galleries surrounding the pit; they held perhaps 3000. Plays were performed in daylight, in the early afternoon, with no curtain to signify the end of a scene (notice how Shakespeare takes care to introduce his characters or get them off stage, and even to clear the whole stage, as at the end of *Hamlet*), no lights to dim, no spotlight to focus on an important character. Costume and language become important means of identification. In 1608 the company took over the lease of the indoor, *private*, Blackfriars, catering for an audience of some 750, all seated at substantially higher prices. Presumably this meant, in the main, performances at the Globe in summer and at Blackfriars in winter. There was certainly an audience for both theatres, although there is some dispute as to its composition. London's population had doubled, from 100,000 to 200,000, between 1580 and 1600 and was to double again by 1650. At the height of his career, therefore, Shakespeare was supplying plays regularly for two different kinds of theatre, with a repertory which was constantly changing and probably with modification of some plays for different performances. There were also performances at court – perhaps as many as ten or twelve a year – and at great houses. It was a busy life, but it was a company whose capabilities he knew intimately and this must have meant that the language was designed for the players he knew would speak it, for example when one kind of clown, Will Kempe, gave way to the very different Robert Armin.

Our modern texts, therefore, represent a reasonable approximation to what Shakespeare wrote. In most cases it will no doubt be what he actually wrote, although we cannot always be sure just what the words sounded like on stage (there was certainly a good deal of punning, for example) or how closely drama recaptured the spoken idiom. Drama selects from the language of its time, and although it may approach colloquial English more than do other kinds of writing, it has also of necessity to concentrate its material more than, say, the narrative poem or the novel. In any case, none of Shakespeare's sources were great works in their own right and few were drama, so a change of genre took place as well. And the essence of drama is to sound spontaneous, to be spoken as if it were *not* written. The features of the spoken language it contains will be partly deliberate and partly unconscious. And the poem or novel exists on the printed page; we can see it, although of course different readers respond to it differently. The script of a play, however, is "only the plan for a series of events. The events must be produced by actors and technicians in the presence of an audience."[5] And we cannot reconstitute ourselves into the Globe audience. For all these reasons this book perforce deals with the *literary* language of Shakespeare.

Notes and References

1. 'A Groats-worth of Wit', in *Life and Complete Works of Robert Greene*, ed. A. B. Grosart (New York, 1964), p. 144.
2. See further, Honigmann (1985).
3. Hulme (1962), pp. 45–46, 337–38. For *sauce*, compare *Dr Faustus*, I.iv.11–12.
4. I am indebted to Bentley (1984); Gurr (1980) and in Andrews (1985) II, pp. 107–28; and Gurr and Orrell (1989).
5. Urkowitz (1980), p. 18.

CHAPTER TWO
The expanding vocabulary

ENGLISH AND OTHER LANGUAGES

By the final quarter of the sixteenth century (Shakespeare was born in 1564), English had been vindicated as a language able to produce good writing in both prose and verse. It was still occasionally felt to be 'rough', 'unpolished', 'uneloquent' (the standard of comparison, expressed or implied, always being Latin) but not so often as hitherto. Yet it was still considered incapable of expressing much by way of abstract, philosophical or scientific ideas. More had composed *Utopia* in Latin in 1516. It was translated into German in 1524, into Italian by 1548 and into French by 1550, but not into English (by Ralph Robinson) until 1551 – by which time More was dead. Erasmus, More's friend and arguably the most learned European man of his day, visited England but never bothered to learn English; were their conversations in Latin? English was not yet a subject in grammar schools, Latin emphatically was. Harvey, who demonstrated the circulation of the blood in the early seventeenth century, lectured to the Royal College of Physicians on his discovery in English but recorded his results in Latin. Isaac Newton (died 1727) wrote all his scientific works in Latin. The first description of a game of cricket (early eighteenth century) is also in Latin.

But by the middle of the sixteenth century it was becoming possible to view things rather differently, and it is easy to see some of the reasons why. Firstly, to write in English becomes one more manifestation of a growing patriotism. Although Roger

Ascham had lamented in his preface to *Toxophilus* ('the archer') in 1545:

> . . . as for the Latin or greke tonge, euery thyng is so excellently done in them, that none can do better: In the Englysh tonge contrary, euery thinge in a manner so meanly, bothe for the matter and handelynge, that no man can do worse.[1]

he nevertheless writes his book on this English matter, in the English tongue, for Englishmen. By 1582, in the *Elementarie* of Richard Mulcaster (Spenser's schoolmaster), this had become:

> For is it not in dede a mervellous bondage, to becom servants to one tung for learning sake, the most of our time, with losse of most time, whereas we maie have the verie same treasur in our own tung, with the gain of most time? our own bearing the joyfull title of our libertie and fredom, the Latin tung remembring us of our thraldom and bondage? I love Rome, but London better, I favor Italie, but England more, I honor the Latin, but I worship the English.

and again:

> But why not all in English, a tung of it self both depe in conceit and frank in deliverie? I do not think that anie language, be it whatsoever, is better able to utter all arguments, either with more pith, or greater planenesse, then our English tung is, if the English utterer be as skilfull in the matter, which he is to utter: as the foren utterer is.[2]

Puttenham's *Arte of English Poesie* was published in 1589. This is essentially a rhetorical textbook, but Puttenham was a patriot too. His second chapter has the heading "That there may be an Art of our English Poesie as well as there is of the Latine and Greeke", and he gives English definitions (which often sound amusing to us) of the Latin and Greek names for the figures of rhetoric. Even in *Utopia* More had advocated that children "be taught learning in their own native tongue".

Secondly, there was a demand from an increasingly literate public to share in the fruits of the Renaissance. London was a large city by European standards (although Paris, Naples and Constantinople were larger) with a population between 150,000 and 200,000. It has been estimated that between one-third and one-half of the population of Shakespeare's London could read. Noblemen's sons were now going to university, and the study of the liberal arts was no longer simply a training in scholastic method (with a career in the church in mind) but had been restored to its original connection with public affairs. It aimed to make a man more able and more cultured, a rounded personality:

. . . though I lacke Authoritie to give counsell, yet I lacke not good
will to wisshe, that the yougthe in England, speciallie Ientlemen,
and namelie nobilitie, shold be by good bringing up, so grounded in
judgement of learninge, so founded in love of honestie, as, whan they
shold be called forthe to the execution of great affaires, in service
of their Prince and contrie, they might be hable, to use and to order,
all experiences, were they good were they bad, and that, according to
the square, rule and line of wisdom, learning and vertue.

(Ascham, *The Schoolmaster*)[3]

As Ophelia saw Hamlet:

O what a noble mind is here o'erthrown!
The courtier's, soldier's, scholar's, eye, tongue, sword,
Th'expectancy and rose of the fair state,
The glass of fashion and the mould of form,
Th'observed of all observers, quite, quite down!

(III.i.151–5)

or as Sir Philip Sidney must have seemed to his contemporaries:
aristocrat, statesman, parliamentarian, traveller in Europe, friend of
the Queen, author, and finally soldier, dying heroically on a foreign
field at the age of thirty-two. But before university came the grammar
school. Stratford had had an endowed school since the 1480s and
William Harrison (*Description of England*, 1577) noted that "there are
not many corporate towns now under the Queen's dominion that
hath not one grammar school at the least with a sufficient living for
a master and usher appointed to the same".[4] Shakespeare, however,
did not proceed to university. Instead, at eighteen, he married Anne
Hathaway (who was twenty-six and pregnant) in 1582.

Printing, brought to England by Caxton in 1476, had so far
developed by the end of the sixteenth century that middlemen begin
to appear in the publishing trade. Printing, too, was not simply a great
economic factor in the spread of books; since all copies of a printed
text were substantially the same, it acted as a great stabiliser of the
forms of the language, especially the grammar. Something similar to
the rapid spread of books in Renaissance England we have ourselves
seen (although on a considerably larger scale) in the 'paperback
explosion' following the Second World War. We should, however,
remember that the Elizabethans valued the classics not only – not even
mainly – for their style but for their subject-matter: they wanted to
know what earlier writers had had to say about government, ethics
or warfare. So the rush of translations in the later sixteenth and the
earlier seventeenth century is not surprising: Caesar, Cicero, Livy,
Tacitus, Seneca, Virgil, Horace, Ovid, Sallust, Plutarch, Aristotle,
and, above all, the struggle over the translation of the Bible into

English which culminated in the Authorised Version of 1611. Some of these translations, such as North's Plutarch (1579) or Golding's Ovid (1565), we know that Shakespeare used.

Yet as translations increase in number and the monopoly of Latin for learning begins to be broken, so the deficiencies in English stand out more. Ralph Lever, in his *Art of Reason* (1573) expressed the situation succinctly; for him there were "more things than there are words to express things by". The act of translation, indeed, focuses the problem. If English is deficient – or even thought to be deficient – in words for a particular concept, what can the translator do? Not surprisingly he often borrowed from the language of the book he was translating and so added to the enormous number of foreign words (especially Latin words) coming into English at this time. Since so many of these words enter English through writing, it is natural that they frequently seem more learned and unusual than earlier medieval borrowings from Scandinavian and from French which had made their way into English via the spoken word.

Not everyone welcomed this influx of foreign words with enthusiasm. Extreme opposition to loan-words is seen in Sir John Cheke's translation of St Matthew's gospel where he uses such coinages as *hunderder* (centurion in the Authorised Version), *biwordes* (parables), *foresayer* (prophet), *uprising* or *gainrising* (resurrection) and *crossed* (crucified) to avoid the introduction of a Latin-derived word. But although Cheke (an excellent Latin scholar himself) wanted an English "unmixt and vnmangeled with borrowing of other tunges", even he allowed for a minimum of necessary borrowing. Cheke's Cambridge circle included Ascham, Sir Thomas Smith, Sir Walter Haddon and Thomas Wilson whose *Art of Rhetoric* (first published 1553 but revised 1560) was in all probability known to Shakespeare. Wilson lamented:

> And thus we see that poore simple men are much troubled, and talke
> oftentimes they know not what for lacke of wit, and want of Latine
> and French, whereof many of our strange wordes full often are deriued.
> Those therefore that will eschue this folly, and acquaint themselues with
> the best kind of speech, must seeke from time to time such wordes
> as are commonly receiued, and such as properly may expresse in plaine
> maner, the whole conceipt of their minds.[5]

George Gascoigne (1542–77) went still further:

> . . . the most auncient English wordes are of one sillable, so that the
> more monasyllables that you use, the truer Englishman you shall seeme,
> and the lesse you shall smell of the Inkehorne.

and later in the same work, *Certayne notes of Instruction concerning the making of verse or ryme in English*:

> . . . asmuche as may be, eschew straunge words, or obsoleta & inusitata, unless the Theame do give just occasion; marie in some places a straunge worde doth drawe attentive reading, but yet I woulde have you therein use discretion.[6]

The opponents of these Latin newcomers dubbed them 'inkhorn' or 'inkpot' terms[7] and often made their point through parody, such as the frequently quoted plea for preferment to a benefice in Wilson's *Art of Rhetoric*, or this extract from Samuel Rowlands's *Signior Word-Monger, the Ape of Eloquence*:

> As on the way I itinerated,
> A rural person I obviated,
> Interrogating time's transition
> And of the passage demonstration.
> My apprehension did ingenious scan
> That he was merely a simplician;
> So when I saw he was extravagant,
> Unto the obscure vulgar consonant,
> I bade him vanish most promiscuously,
> And not contaminate my company.

The parody, however, is sometimes not so very much more preposterous than the actual. Andrew Borde began the preface to his *Breuiary of Healthe* (1552):

> Egregious Doctors and masters of the eximious and Archane Science of Physicke, of your Urbanitie exasperate not your selues against mee, for making of this little volume of Physick. Considering that my pretense is for an vtilitie and a common wealth. And this is not only, but also I doe it for no detriment but for a preferment of your laudable science, that euery man shuld esteeme, repute and regard the excellent faculty. And also you to be extolled and highly preferred, that hath and doth studie, practise and labor this said Archane Science, to the which none inartious persons, can nor shal attaine to the knowledge: yet notwithstanding fooles and insipient persons, yea and many the which doth think themselues wise (the which in this faculty be fools indeed) wil enterprise to smatter . . .

Naturally there was a compromise, and the more thoughtful critics advocated a kind of controlled borrowing where words are adopted only if they fill a gap in the native language and not merely because they *sound* impressive.[8] George Pettie argues that English has always borrowed words:

> And though for my part I vse those [borrowed] words as litle as any, yet I know no reason why I should not vse them, and I finde it a fault in my selfe that I do not vse them: for it is in deed the ready way

to inrich our tongue, and make it copious, and it is the way which all tongues haue taken to inrich them selues: For take the Latine woordes from the *Spanish* tongue, and it shall be as barren as most part of their Countrey; take them from the *Italian*, and you take away in a manner the whole tongue; take them from the *Frenche*, and you marre the grace of it: yea take from the Latine it selfe the woordes deriued from the *Greeke*, and it shall not be so flowing and flourishing as it is. Wherefore I marueile how our english tongue hath cracke it[s] credite, that it may not borrow of the Latine as well as other tongues: and if it haue broken, it is but of late, for it is not vnknowen to all men how many woordes we haue fetcht from thence within these few yeeres, which if they should be all counted inkepot termes, I know not how we should speake any thing without blacking our mouthes with inke: for what woord can be more plaine then this word *plaine* and yet what can come more neere to the Latine? what more manifest then *manifest*? and yet in a manner Latine: What more commune then *rare* or less rare then *commune*, and yet both of them coming of the Latine? But you wyll say, long vse hath made these woords curraunt: and why may not vse doo as much for these woords which we shall now deriue? Why should not we doo as much for the posteritie, as we haue receiued of the antiquitie? and yet if a thing be of it selfe ill, I see not how the oldnesse of it can make it good, and if it be of it selfe good, I see not how the newnesse of it can make it naught: Wherevpon I infer, that those woords which your selues confesse, by vse to be made good, are good the first time they are vttered, and therefore not to be iested at, nor to be misliked.

(Preface to *The Civile Conuersation of M. Steeuen Guazzo*, 1581)[9]

Puttenham makes the same point:

. . . seruing aptly, when a man wanteth to expresse so much vnles it be in two words, which surplussage to auoide, we are allowed to draw in other words single; and asmuch significatiue: this word *significatiue* is borrowed of the Latine and French, but to vs brought in first by some Noble-mans Secretarie, as I thinke, yet doth so well serue the turne, as it could not now be spared: and many more like vsurped Latine and French words: as, *Methode, methodicall, placation, function, assubtiling, refining, compendious, prolixe, figuratiue, inueigle*. A terme borrowed of our common Lawyers, *impression*, also a new terme, but well expressing the matter, and more than our English word. These words, *Numerous, numerositee, metricall, harmonicall*, but they cannot be refused, specially in this place for description of the arte. Also ye finde these words, *penetrate, penetrable, indignitie*, which I cannot see how we may spare them, whatsoeuer fault wee finde with Ink-horne termes: for our speach wanteth wordes to such sense so well to be vsed: yet in steade of *indignitie*, yee haue vnworthinesse: and for *penetrate*, we may say *peerce*, and that a French terme also, or *broche*, or enter into with violence, but not so well sounding as *penetrate*. Item, *sauage*, for wilde: *obscure*, for darke. Item these words, *declination, delineation, dimention*, are scholasticall termes in deede, and yet very proper. But peraduenture (& I could bring a reason for it)

many other like words borrowed out of the Latin and French, were
not so well to be allowed by vs, as these words, *audacious*, for bold:
facunditie, for eloquence: *egregious*, for great or notable: *implete*, for
replenished: *attemptat*, for attempt: *compatible*, for agreeable in nature,
and many more.[10]

Puttenham's list of indispensable words, however, contains a few
(*placation, assubtiling, numerositee, implete*) which we seem no longer
to need, and he objects to *audacious, egregious*, and *compatible*, all of
which we have kept. Time itself has shown which are necessary,
but 'necessary' (as Puttenham saw) must be allowed to include
synonyms, for it is this extensive Renaissance borrowing (following
the considerable influx of French words into Middle English) that has
given English so many groups of words, the first native English, the
second borrowed French, and the third borrowed Latin:

end	finish	conclude
rise	mount	ascend
goodness	virtue	probity
ask	question	interrogate
two	second	dual
fire	flame	conflagration
fear	terror	trepidation

In some cases the French and the Latin borrowings are from the same
root but entered English at different times:

sicker	sure	secure
kingly	royal	regal

This greatly increases the semantic *density*, although only in the case
of a loan-word that has no real synonym in current English does it
do much to increase semantic *range*. It is easy for native speakers
of present-day English to discover contexts in which one of the
group of three would be more likely to occur than either of the
other two, but difficult sometimes to be sure of such semantic
shading in earlier periods. Pettie called borrowing "the ready way
to inrich our tongue, and make it copious" and *copious* is the favourite
Elizabethan description of a style whose lexis draws considerably on
such synonyms or near-synonyms, often in doublets or triplets, to
help provide dignity and sonority. (In the same way, copious syntax
is balanced, complex, but, above all, controlled.) Examples abound
in Elizabethan prose:

> But now that we may lift up our eyes (as it were) from the footstool
> to the throne of God, and leaving these natural, consider a little the
> state of heavenly and divine creatures; touching Angels which are spirits
> immaterial and intellectual, the glorious inhabitants of those sacred pal-
> aces, where nothing but light and blessed immortality, no shadow of

matter for tears, discontentments, griefs, and uncomfortable passions to work upon, but all joy, tranquillity, and peace, even for ever and ever doth dwell; as in number and order they are huge, mighty, and royal armies: so likewise in perfection of obedience unto that law, which the Highest, whom they adore, love, and imitate, hath imposed upon them, such observants they are thereof, that our Saviour himself being to set down the perfect idea of that which we are to pray and wish for on earth, did not teach to pray or wish for more than only that here it might be with us, as with them it is in heaven.

(Hooker, *Laws of Ecclesiastical Polity* (1593), Book I)[11]

Let me wither and wear out mine age in a discomfortable, in an unwholesome, in a penurious prison, and so pay my debts with my bones, and recompense the wastefulness of my youth, with the beggary of mine age; let me wither in a spital under sharp, and foul, and infamous diseases, and so recompense the wantonness of my youth, with that loathsomeness in mine age: yet, if God withdraw not his spiritual blessings, his grace, his patience, if I can call my suffering his doing, my passion his action, all this that is temporal, is but a caterpillar got into one corner of my garden, but a mildew fallen upon one acre of my corn; the body of all, the substance of all is safe, as long as the soul is safe. But when I shall trust to that, which we call a good spirit, and God shall deject, and impoverish, and evacuate that spirit, when I shall rely upon a moral constancy, and God shall shake, and enfeeble, and enervate, destroy and demolish that constancy; when I shall think to refresh myself in the serenity and sweet air of a good conscience, and God shall call up the damps and vapours of hell itself, and spread a cloud of diffidence, and an impenetrable crust of desperation upon my conscience; when health shall fly from me, and I shall lay hold upon riches to succour me, and comfort me in my sickness, and riches shall fly from me, and I shall snatch after favour, and good opinion, to comfort me in my poverty; when even this good opinion shall leave me, and calumnies and misinformations shall prevail against me; when I shall need peace, because there is none but thou, O Lord, that should stand for me, and then shall find, that all the wounds that I have, come from thy hand, all the arrows that stick in me, from thy quiver; when I shall see, that because I have given myself to my corrupt nature, thou hast changed thine; and because I am all evil towards thee, therefore thou hast given over being good towards me; when it comes to this height, that the fever is not in the humours, but in the spirits, that mine enemy is not an imaginary enemy, fortune, nor a transitory enemy, malice in great persons, but a real, and an irresistible, and an inexorable, and an everlasting enemy, the Lord of hosts himself, the Almighty God himself, the Almighty God himself only knows the weight of this affliction, and except he put in that *pondus gloriæ* , that exceeding weight of an eternal glory, with his own hand, into the other scale, we are weighed down, we are swallowed up, irreparably, irrevocably, irrecoverably, irremediably.

(Donne, Sermon preached at St Paul's, 29 January 1626)[12]

Hooker's sentence (there is only a single sentence in the Hooker extract and only two in the longer Donne passage) contains, for example, the groups *heavenly and divine; tears, discontentments, griefs and uncomfortable passions; joy, tranquillity and peace; adore, love and imitate.* Donne, whose approach is even more expansive (more copious) not only has such groups as *discomfortable . . . unwholesome . . . penurious; sharp and foul and infamous; deject and impoverish and evacuate; shake and enfeeble, and enervate, destroy and demolish,* but is able to balance the groups against one another: *my suffering his doing, my passion his action; wounds . . . from thy hand . . . arrows . . . from thy quiver,* until the whole reaches its climax with those four adverbs which come crashing down at the end of the paragraph. Yet in one of the passages previously held up to ridicule, Borde groups *eximious and Archane; esteeme, repute and regard; extolled and highly preferred; studie, practise and labour; fooles and insipient persons.* But Borde simply elaborates because three words are more impressive than one, and heaps one elaboration upon another. Hooker and Donne write of great matters in an appropriately dignified style. Their doublets (especially Hooker's) are not so much difficult words needing elucidation as a means of adding weight to the sentence. Their examples are better spaced within the passage. They are also not merely synonyms, since frequently the last member adds a new dimension to the group: "huge, mighty and *royal*"; "sharp and foul and *infamous* diseases".

THE IMPACT OF BORROWING

The debate over the *amount* of borrowing into the English vocabulary is perhaps the first extensive critique of the language by its native speakers. Yet the problem itself was not a new one. In the morality play *Mankind*, dated 1465–70, Mercy rhymes *denomynacyon* and *communycacyon*, to which New Gyse immediately retorts "Ey, ey! Your body ys full of Englysch Laten."[13] Choice of an appropriate vocabulary for his translations had exercised Caxton at the end of the fifteenth century:

> And that comyn Englysshe that is spoken in one shyre varyeth from another. . . . Certaynly it is harde to playse every man bycause of dyversite and chaunge of langage. For in these dayes every man that is in ony reputaycon in his countre, wyll utter his commynycacyon and matters in suche maners and termes that fewe men shall understonde theym. And som honest and grete clerkes have been wyth me, and desired me to wryte the moste curyous termes that I coude fynde. And thus bytwene playn rude and curyous I stande abasshed.
>
> (*Preface to Eneydos*, 1490)[14]

Caxton had been worried about two things: variation between regional dialects and the intelligibility of both *curious* and *playn rude* terms. The first was, by the Renaissance, no longer such a problem, for, by the mid sixteenth century it is evident that some form of southern speech (later defined by Puttenham as "the usual speech of the Court, and that of London and the shires lying about London within 60 miles and not much above") was a mark of good birth and good education. Even in the north and 'far west', men might be sufficiently educated to *write* good southern English even if they spoke in dialect (as Sir Walter Raleigh is supposed to have done in 'broad Devonshire'). Caxton's second problem, the number of 'curious' terms to be used, was essentially the same as that facing Renaissance writers; indeed, Caxton has his own doublets within this short passage (*dyversite and chaunge; commynycacyon and maters; maners and termes*). The 'aureate' language of one particular fifteenth-century literary style had, in all probability, paved the way for more extensive – and more Latinate – borrowing later. Lydgate (c. 1370–c. 1450), who wrote twice as much as Shakespeare and three times as much as Chaucer, and whose all–inclusive mind demonstrates a real talent for elaboration, seems to have been the first to use in English such words as *abuse, adjacent, capacity, circumspect, combine, credulity, delude, depend, disappear, equivalent, equipollent, excel, facundious* ('eloquent'), *fructyf* ('fertile'), *obumbred* ('overshadowed'). Even this short list shows the same mixture of necessary and merely outlandish terms.[15]

It is not always realised how widespread are the effects of wholesale borrowing of words in the Renaissance. It might be fanciful, yet not altogether wrong, to view it as another aspect of their willingness to experiment, the spirit that sent them exploring across half the world. Another manifestation of borrowing, especially from the classical languages, is the enormous growth of scientific and medical terminology in English. (Before the sixteenth century most scientific works were written in Latin.) One could have *smallpox* by 1518, *scurvy* by 1565, *mumps* by 1598 and *rheumatism* by 1601. (Shakespeare uses *rheum* which had been in the language from 1377 and which meant a cold in the head – compare French *enrhumé*.) Scientific borrowings are found more extensively in the seventeenth century: *acid* (1626), *apparatus* (1628), *calculus* (1672), *electric* (1646, but *electrical* from 1635), *focus* (1656), *laboratory* (1605), *logarithm* (1616), *microscope* (1656), *specimen* (1610). Also in the early seventeenth century appear the first English dictionaries, although Latin/English, French/English, Italian/English and Spanish/English dictionaries were all in existence by 1600. The first purely English dictionaries were of *hard* words, principally those which had been borrowed into English in the last generation and were therefore most in need of elucidation. This is clear from the title-page of what is usually recognised as the first real English dictionary, *A Table Alphabeticall*, by Robert Cawdrey, a schoolmaster, in 1604:

> A Table Alphabeticall, conteyning and teaching the true writing, and understanding of hard usuall English wordes, borrowed from the Hebrew, Greeke, Latin or French, etc.
> With the interpretation therof by plaine English words gathered for the benefit and helpe of Ladies, Gentlewomen, or any other unskilful persons. Whereby they may the more easilie and better understand many hard English wordes, which they shall heare or read in Scriptures, Sermons, or elsewhere, and also be made able to use the same aptly themselves . . .

or that of Henry Cockerham's *The English Dictionarie* (1623, which had its twelfth and final edition in 1670 and was the first to include the word 'dictionary' in its title):

> The English Dictionarie: or, An Interpreter of hard English Words. Enabling as well Ladies and Gentlewomen, young Schollers, Clarkes, Merchants, as also Strangers of any Nation, to the vnderstanding of the more difficult Authors already printed in our Language, and the more speedy attaining of an elegant perfection of the English tongue, both in reading, speaking and writing. Being a Collection of some thousands of words, neuer published by any heretofore. [16]

How to impress your friends.

Shakespeare possibly introduced some 600 words into English, excluding compounds. The true number may be rather less than this, since he has always been the best-recorded English author and earlier uses of words attributed to him by the *Oxford English Dictionary* turn up quite regularly. Two excellent articles by Brian Garner consider his Latinate coinages and Latin-Saxon hybrids (where the stem belongs to one language and the prefix or suffix to the other). [17] He points out that the borrowings into English (mostly Latinate) reached a climax during Shakespeare's career and afterwards levelled off somewhat. Among the many words that, so far as is known, Shakespeare was the first to use are *abstemious, accommodation, admirable, comply, counterpart, educate, fixture, generous, pendant, pious, quarrelsome, supervise* and *tranquil*. Others are compounds: *dog-weary, fancy-free, lack-lustre, over-credulous, sharp-toothed, wide-skirted*. He seems especially fond of compound adjectives with a participle (especially a past participle) as second element. Spenser before him and Keats, Hopkins and Dylan Thomas after him have similarly formed compound adjectives of this kind where the compression in the participle preserves some of the action of the verb; the alternative might have been a more lengthy simile.[18] The poet and dramatist are less concerned with new objects and more concerned with new ways of looking at existing objects, hence the large number of compound adjectives. Several of Shakespeare's coinages have since disappeared, such as *aidance*, *besort*, *commixture*, *deceptious*, *precurse* and *rubious*.[19] Language seems to operate a kind of sieve where words which do not fulfil a need in the vocabulary eventually drop through. Some of the words first attributed to Shakespeare are hybrids, for example *dislike*, *employer*, *intermingle*, *resound*, *surname*, *undervalue*, and no less than 93 first instances of words beginning with *un-*. Again many of these, especially the more obviously 'poetical', have been lost, amongst them *bemonster*, *disroot*, *outprize*, *subduement* and *trans-shape*. Garner points out that scholarly Renaissance writers by and large avoided hybrids and that most of the comparatively few in the Authorised Version date from the thirteenth or fourteenth centuries. Fortunately Shakespeare was an exception.

But how can we know which words seemed strange to an audience in 1600? The largest *Oxford English Dictionary* gives the etymology of words in English since 1100 and dated contexts for their use. It is also the prime source of evidence for semantic change (see below). The single-volume *Oxford Dictionary of English Etymology* lists the etymology of the word, the century – not the actual date – of its adoption, and major subsequent shifts of meaning. A reliable Concordance (the best is the one by Marvin Spevack) cites the frequency of use in Shakespeare, and dictionary and concordance, used in conjunction, will provide a fair estimate of how unusual the word might have seemed to his audience. The Shakespearean context may be the best help of all. Does the word seem to need definition, by linking it with a simpler synonym or even by paraphrase?

One classical word in a passage of mainly native diction may out-weigh every other word in the passage because of its rarity, specialised sense, or sheer incongruity in that context. Etymological statistics, based on the sheer number of words borrowed, are therefore of only limited value. Shakespeare is far from being the only Elizabethan to realise the value of a strategically-placed borrowing:

> Whenas in silks my Julia goes,
> Then, then (methinks) how sweetly flows
> That *liquefaction* of her clothes.
>
> (Herrick, *Upon Julia's Clothes*)

> When love, with one another so

Interinanimates two souls . . .

(Donne, *The Ecstasy*)

Annihilating all that's made
To a green thought in a green shade.

(Marvell, *The Garden*)

Sweet spring, full of sweet days and roses,
A box where sweets *compacted* lie . . .

(Herbert, *Virtue*)

but he perhaps realised it more often than most. He is careful to
position such borrowed Latinate words within the line where they
coincide with heavy stress and thus achieve maximum emphasis. In
practice this often means near the beginning of the line:

Wouldst thou be windowed in great Rome and see
Thy master thus: with pleached arms, bending down
His *corrigible* neck, his face subdued
To *penetrative* shame?

(*AC* IV.xiv.72–5)

    This hand of yours requires
A *sequester* from liberty, fasting and prayer,
Much *castigation*, exercise devout.

(*Oth* III.iv.39–41)

By *decimation* and a tithed death –
If thy revenges hunger for that food
Which nature loathes – take thou the destined tenth,

(*Tim* V.iv.31–3)

(where *decimation* is glossed by "tithed" and "destined tenth") or at
the end of the line:

Holla your name to the *reverberate* hills

(*TN* I.v.261)

Requickened what in flesh was *fatigate*

(*Cor* II.ii. 115)

With thy sharp teeth this knot *intrinsicate*
Of life at once untie.

(*AC* V.ii.303–4)

(*intrinsicate* is further emphasised by making it split the noun phrase
knot of life and by placing it after the noun, not before it, the position
which adjectives usually fill in English)

The multitudinous seas *incarnadine*

(*Mac* II.ii. 62)

(a word which Davenant, in his version of the play, was insensitive
enough to replace by "add a tincture to").

24

If there is a heavy mid-line pause, the Latinate word sometimes immediately precedes that:

> Of all these bounds, even from this line to this,
> With shadowy forests, and with champains riched,
> With plenteous rivers, and wide-skirted meads,
> We make thee lady. To thine and Albany's issues
> Be this *perpetual*.
>
> (*KL* I.i.63–7)

> Which, when I know that boasting is an honour
> I shall *provulgate*. (F reads *promulgate*)
>
> (*Oth* I.ii.20–1)

> Now boast thee, death, in thy possession lies
> A lass *unparalleled*.
>
> (*AC* V.ii.314–15)

or, less often, immediately follows it:

> Whilst I awhile *obsequiously* lament
> Th' untimely fall of virtuous Lancaster.
>
> (*R III* I.ii.3–4)

> which imports at full,
> By letters *congruing* to that effect,
> The present death of Hamlet.
>
> (*Ham* IV.iii.65–7)

My point about the single Latinate word standing out from a passage whose diction is otherwise not especially remarkable may be illustrated from the best-known soliloquy in *Hamlet* where the hero is considering the consequences of suicide. He asks who would bear the trials and tribulations of public life

> When he himself might his *quietus* make
> With a bare bodkin.
>
> (III.i.75–6)

Quietus is a technical word from accountancy; in the concluding couplet of Sonnet 126 it collocates with *audit*. And this Latin loan in *Hamlet* achieves something not only of the mystery but also of the finality of death: the red line is ruled across the page and the account is closed.[20] But with a bare *bodkin*, a word possibly of Celtic origin, is as far removed from Latin as you can get. Or take *Pericles*, which has been described as "a text full of confusion and with a clumsiness and poverty of language unrivalled in the Shakespeare canon".[21] Critics now seem to agree that Acts I and II are, with the possible exception of a very few passages, unlikely to represent Shakespeare's work but that Acts III, IV and V show a marked improvement in dramatic style. And there, although the language still seems below Shakespeare's best, the Latinisms increase. At the beginning of Act V, in which Pericles is to be restored to Marina, it is appropriate that the diction should become more elevated:

> HELICANUS Our vessel is of Tyre; in it the King,
> A man who for this three months hath not spoken
> To anyone, nor taken sustenance
> But to *prorogue* his grief.
> LYSIMACHUS Upon what ground is his *distemperature*?
>
> (*Per* V.i.21–5)

As with sorrows in *Hamlet*, or as in the passages from Hooker and Donne cited earlier, Shakespeare's Latin borrowings sometimes come not singly but in battalions. They are frequently doublets:

> That all the treasons for these eighteen years
> *Complotted and contrived* in this land
> Fetch from false Mowbray their first head and spring.
>
> (*R II* I.i.95–7)

> Th' *extravagant and erring* spirit hies
> To his confine.
>
> (*Ham* I.i.155–6)

> Exchange me for a goat
> When I shall turn the business of my soul
> To such *exsufflicate and blown* surmises.
>
> (*Oth* III.iii.178–80)

> Be *aidant and remediate*
> In the good man's distress.
>
> (*KL* IV.iv.17–18)

Often they appear in groups of near-synonyms, 'copious' diction:

> Brutus is noble, wise, valiant, and honest;
> Caesar was mighty, bold, royal, and loving.
>
> (*JC* III.i.126–7)

> How weary, stale, flat, and unprofitable
> Seem to me all the uses of this world!
>
> (*Ham* I.ii.133–4)

> If I be not by her fair influence
> Fostered, illumined, cherished, kept alive.
>
> (*TGV* III.i.183–4)

> 'Romeo is banished' – to speak that word
> Is father, mother, Tybalt, Romeo, Juliet,

All slain, all dead. 'Romeo is banished' –
There is no end, no limit, measure, bound,
In that word's death.

(RJ III.ii.122–6)

Though sometimes it show greatness, courage, blood –
And that's the dearest grace it renders you –
Yet oftentimes it doth present harsh rage,
Defect of manners, want of government,
Pride, haughtiness, opinion, and disdain.

(1 Hen IV III.i.175–9)

Since his addiction was to courses vain,
His companies unlettered, rude, and shallow,
His hours filled up with riots, banquets, sports,
And never noted in him any study,
Any retirement, any sequestration,
From open haunts and popularity.

(Hen V I.i.54–9)

The bonds of heaven are slipped, dissolved, and loosed,
And with another knot, five-finger-tied,
The fractions of her faith, orts of her love,
The fragments, scraps, the bits, and greasy relics
Of her o'er-eaten faith, are given to Diomed.

(TC V.ii.153–7)

Not every member of such lexical 'sets' is a polysyllabic Latin borrowing, of course, although most groups contain one or more ("Fostered, *illumined*, cherished, kept alive", "Death, *desolation*, ruin, and decay"). Furthermore, these examples are almost all from 'serious' plays. Comedy rarely lends itself to such deliberate parallelisms of vocabulary, although parallel syntactic structures are another thing altogether.

Not everybody understood all of these borrowed words by any means, and, if dictionaries were in short supply until the later seventeenth century, doublets might still arise in the search for efficient communication. But clowns can always be sure of a laugh by misunderstanding hard words; it is good stage business. Both Armado and Berowne use Costard as a messenger-boy:

ARMADO   Bear this significant to the country maid Jaquenetta.
           There is remuneration; for the best ward of mine
           honour is rewarding my dependants . . .

COSTARD   Now will I look to his remuneration. Remuneration?
           O that's the Latin word for three farthings.

Berowne, the aristocrat, is, however, more generous:

BEROWNE   And Rosaline they call her. Ask for her,
            And to her white hand see thou do commend
            This sealed-up counsel. There's thy guerdon. Go.
COSTARD   Gardon, O sweet gardon! Better than remuneration –
            a 'leven-pence farthing better.

                                        (*LLL* III.i.131–8, 168–72)

The obvious examples are, I suppose, Dogberry and Verges in *Much Ado* whose inability to distinguish between *sensible* and *senseless*, *apprehend* and *comprehend*, *odious* and *odorous*, *auspicious* and *suspicious* or to grasp the meaning of *tolerable*, *tedious*, *malefactors* or *verify* is part of their general muddleheadedness. But Mistress Quickly and Elbow (another constable) in *Measure for Measure*, each of whom is capable of confusing *protest* and *detest*, are little better; nor indeed is Bottom ("we may rehearse most *obscenely* and courageously"; "I have an *exposition* of sleep come upon me"). Mistress Quickly (whose outstanding lexical confusion is perhaps *honeysuckle* and *homicidal*, *2 Henry IV*, II.i.48) later manages to combine her failure to understand Latin grammar with an indecent pun on *genitive case* (pudendum):

EVANS   What is your genitive case plural, William?
WILLIAM   Genitive case?
EVANS   Ay.
WILLIAM   Genitive – *horum, harum, horum*.
QUICKLY   Vengeance of Jenny's case! Fie on her! Never name
            her, child, if she be a whore.
EVANS   For shame, 'oman.
QUICKLY   You do ill to teach the child such words. He teaches
            him to hick and to hack, which they'll do fast enough
            of themselves, and to call "horum". Fie upon you!

                                        (*MWW* IV.i.55–65)

Elbow uses *respected* when he means *suspected*, Dogberry the other way round. Perhaps some of these pairs *were* confused, it is difficult to be sure, since malapropisms by clowns are rare before Shakespeare.

Somewhat higher up the social scale is Ancient Pistol, but with him Latinate diction is part of his bravado. Falstaff's heart is *fracted and corroborate* (*Hen V* II.i.119). *Fracted* is perhaps acceptable for 'broken', but *corroborate*, literally 'made strong', is clearly absurd as a doublet. Yet somehow this does not detract from the melancholy at the imminent death of Falstaff, any more than does Mistress Quickly's failure not long afterwards to understand women as *devils incarnate* ("A could never abide carnation, 'twas a colour he never liked". II.iii.30–1). Sir Andrew Aguecheek demonstrates a variant on the game of misapprehension: he is honest and simple enough to admit that he does not understand:

By my troth, I would not undertake her in this company. Is that the meaning of 'accost'?

(*TN* I.iii.55)

What is *pourquoi*? Do or not do?

(I.iii.88)

(a reminder that Latin was not the only source of linguistic difficulty)

SIR TOBY   Approach, Sir Andrew. Not to be abed after midnight, is to be up betimes, and *diluculo surgere*, thou knowest –

SIR ANDREW   Nay, by my troth, I know not; but I know to be up late is to be up late.

(II.iii.1–5)

Diluculo surgere, 'to rise at daybreak (is most healthy)', was a Latin phrase from an Elizabethan school-book which Sir Andrew had evidently never studied. But he stores up three fine-sounding words, perhaps in his commonplace book:

> *Odours, pregnant, and vouchsafed.* I'll get 'em all three all ready
> (III.i.87)[22]

Lorenzo, *Merchant of Venice* III.v.61, says of Lancelot Gobbo, "The fool has planted in his memory / An army of good words."

As late as *The Winter's Tale*, the Clown is sure that "Advocate's the court-word for a pheasant" (IV.iv.737). He probably confuses it with *avocet*, a bird of the snipe family. The first *OED* entry is 1674, but *advocate* was earlier spelt *avocat* before it became Latinised in spelling (a 'court word'?) during the Renaissance. By 1613, however, the Induction of *Bartholomew Fair* attacks the stage-practice of "mistaking words". Had it by that time become old-fashioned, or simply too unsophisticated for Ben Jonson? Whichever it was, Shakespeare had long since realised its appeal to an audience:

SPEED   How now, Signior Launce? What news with your mastership?

LAUNCE   With my master's ship? Why, it is at sea.

SPEED   Well, your old vice still: mistake the word.

(*TGV* III.i.276–9)

Old vice perhaps, but good for several more laughs yet.

CHANGES IN MEANING

Another aspect of Latin loan-words in the Renaissance is that the *form* of Shakespeare's word will often be easily recognisable to us but its *sense* may not correspond to our present-day meaning. Since the borrowings were often comparatively recent, the word's signification will still be close to that which it had in Latin. The problem of semantic change is not in fact quite so serious a problem as has sometimes been suggested. Any moderately attentive reader of Shakespeare will be aware when the modern meaning of a word will not fit the Elizabethan context. For instance, when Old Capulet says that Romeo "bears him like a *portly* gentleman" (I.v.66), the word seems inapplicable to a youth so agile in climbing up to Juliet's balcony. Even less likely is Marlowe's Zenocrate being described as *portly (1 Tamburlaine* I.ii.187). On the other hand, when Hector says that Achilles can be recognised by his *large and portly size* (*TC* IV.v.161), we do not feel the need for explanation because we have the gloss *large* to guide us: we expect the two words to be at least partly synonymous. Even so, the etymological meaning (from Latin *portare*) of 'dignified', one who *carries* himself well, may apply to Achilles almost as much as it obviously applies to Romeo and Zenocrate. Again, in *As You Like It*, the *humorous* Duke is the villainous one, anything but a comic character. When Hamlet welcomes the players, the *humorous* man (II.ii.322) is not the comedian but the character actor, especially the man who played unusual, 'fantastical' characters, like Jaques or Lucio in *Measure for Measure*. Here we need to know something about the medical idea of humours, which were originally thought of as fluids so that the *humorous* night (*RJ* II.i.31) simply means 'humid', 'damp'. In a complete, well-balanced man no one humour predominates, but in most of us one quality or another will be especially prominent and will largely determine our disposition. Jonson used this as a theory of comedy (*Every Man in His Humour*). For the Elizabethans, then, a man whose humours often changed was temperamental or capricious.

So there are several aids we can summon to our assistance. The etymological meaning will often help and this will be especially so with Latin borrowings. Hence *prevented* ('forestalled'), *admire* ('marvel at'), *secure* ('free from suspicion'), luxury ('lust'), *accident* ('something which happens', not necessarily unpleasant), *err* ('wander') and *extravagant* ('out of bounds') – the Ghost in *Hamlet* is *th'extravagant and erring spirit* – *honest* ('honourable' or, of women, 'chaste'), *pregnant* ('significant'), *modern* ('commonplace'), *vulgar* ('ordinary'), and several others. Secondly there is our general, 'background' knowledge of the age, such as the theory of humours or the acceptance that in both the English and the Roman histories *policy* (now a neutral word) and *politician* have a distinct flavour of underhand dealing. Thirdly, and most important, the context will frequently guide us to the Elizabethan meaning or at least put us on the alert to look for a meaning other than the twentieth-century one. If the word in question appears in the same phrase as another word, the same part of speech and apparently synonymous, we are doubly fortunate. Take the word *rank*. One of its Middle English meanings was 'luxuriant' (of growth): the late fourteenth-century romance *Sir Gawain and the Green Knight* speaks of *rawez* (hedgerows) *rych and ronk*. The sense of 'grossly rich', 'overblown', was, however, already possible in the fourteenth century, although the use suggesting an excessively strong *smell* did not apparently arise before the sixteenth century. In *Hamlet, rank* means 'gross': the world is an unweeded garden, "things *rank and gross* in nature/Possess it merely" (I.ii.136). Hamlet advises his mother "do not spread the compost on the weeds/ To make them *ranker*" (III.iv.152). Earlier, Claudius, trying in vain to pray, cries out "O, my offence is *rank*, It smells to heaven" (III.iii.36). But *rank and gross* or something rank which smells stands oddly against the Authorised Version (1611, and therefore later than *Hamlet*) where one lot of ears of corn in Pharaoh's dream (Genesis 41) were *rank and good*. The language of the Authorised Version is, however, conservative, like most religious register: it seldom reminds us of Shakespeare so much as of the English of half a century before. But here we can, exceptionally, catch a word in the course of change, so that the unpleasant connotation of *rank* is clearly now the usual one and the favourable sense will shortly disappear.[23]

Sometimes the difficulty is just a matter of interpreting the prefix or suffix: *questionable* means 'able to be questioned', *deceivable* 'deceitful', *comfortable*, 'comforting', *sensible* 'sensitive', *unexpressive* 'inexpressible', *unvalued* 'priceless' and *timorous* 'frightening', not 'frightened'. But the most difficult cases of semantic change are those where the modern meaning of the word might just fit the immediate Elizabethan context, although a wider context will often show it to be inappropriate. *Hamlet* will once more provide a useful example. In response to Ophelia's explanation to her father of Hamlet's abstracted behaviour towards her, Polonius asserts (II.i.102) "this is the very *ecstasy* of love". Similarly Hamlet, outraged that Gertrude should claim to love Claudius after that paragon, her first husband, blurts out:

> Nor sense to *ecstasy* was ne'er so thralled
> But it reserved some quantity of choice
> To serve in such a difference.

(III.iv.75–7)

Now we may quite naturally associate ecstasy with love, but I have not been quite fair here, because even a cursory reading of the surrounding lines of either quotation would suggest 'madness' (and a self-induced madness at that) as a better equivalent. This would be confirmed when, on another occasion (III.i.161), Ophelia speaks of Hamlet's mind as "blasted with ecstasy", and when Gertrude, who has not been able to see the Ghost which has been clearly visible to Hamlet, dismisses the whole episode:

> This is the very coinage of your brain.
> This bodiless creation ecstasy
> Is very cunning in.

(III.iv.138–40)

Ecstasy in *Hamlet*, then, clearly means madness, unreasonably extravagant behaviour.

In a similar way, careful reading *in context* will show that Shakespeare usually meant 'absolute', 'complete', by his use of *mere* (*Ham* I.ii.136, above) and 'wicked', 'malicious' by *shrewd* (from Old English *screawa*, 'shrewmouse', thought to have a poisonous bite) – Cassius (II.i.158) adjudges Antony a *shrewd contriver* and argues that he should be killed with Caesar. Cymbeline (V.v.47) calls the Queen most *delicate* fiend, that is, 'subtle'. *Advertisement* means 'information' at *1 Henry IV* III.ii.172 but 'exhortation' (closer to the modern sense) at IV.i.36. Edmund (*KL* II.i.72) speaks of "*suggestion*, plot and damned practice"; the other two terms imply a pejorative meaning for *suggestion* which it does not have now (although the adjective *suggestive* sometimes does). *Obsequious* (e.g. *3 Hen VI* II.v.118, *R III* I.ii.3, *Ham* I.ii.92) should be interpreted as 'dutiful', not 'sycophantic': all three contexts refer to mourning and our own use of *obsequies* should guide us here. *Ostentation* (*Cor* I.vi.86) has no sense of showing off, merely of show. Of the two instances of *sanctimonious* in Shakespeare, one (*MM* I.ii.7) has the present meaning, but the other (*Temp* IV.i.16) is simply equivalent to 'holy'. *Officious* usually carries the implication of interfering, but *tenderly officious* (*WT* II.iii.158) can hardly bear this interpretation. When her father calls Juliet a *peevish, self-willed harlotry* (IV.ii.14), it is our equivalent of 'silly, obstinate girl'. In these last few examples we have become involved with the tone of the word and the expected response to it, and such matters of semantic shading are difficult to establish exactly for earlier periods. Perhaps the best example is still the one F. P. Wilson quoted some years ago:[24]

> When you shall these unlucky deeds relate,
> Speak of me as I am: nothing extenuate,
> Nor set down aught in malice. Then must you speak
> Of one that loved not wisely, but too well;
> Of one, not easily jealous but, being wrought,

Perplexed in the extreme.

(*Oth* V.ii.337–42)

These lines, from Othello's dying speech, are not, as we might at first think, an example of understatement. *Unlucky* and *perplexed* were much stronger words then than now, and together with *wrought* ('overwrought') suggest Othello's unbearable mental agony.

COMPOUNDING AND ARCHAISMS

Loan-words are the easiest way of enriching the word-stock of a language, especially if circumstances bring that language into contact with one that is much more prestigious in particular fields (as Latin was in philosophy, science or medicine, for example). But alternatives do exist. Old English (c. 700–c. 1100) borrowed comparatively few words and those chiefly from Latin to express new concepts resulting from the coming of Christianity. Instead it employed its own resources to make compounds (where no part of the two words is lost in the process of joining them together and where they continue to exist individually, as in Modern English *gas-cooker, dark-blue, over-turn*) or to engage in *affixation* (the addition of a prefix or suffix to an existing word or root, as in Modern English *postgraduate, bitterness, motherhood*). The two processes are essentially the same and it does not seem worthwhile separating them in general discussion. Compounding and affixation can, of course, involve earlier loan-words which have become part of the English lexicon; in the examples above *gas* is borrowed from Dutch (perhaps based on Greek *chaos*) and *post-* from Latin. Equally the status of a word may change: Old English *had* meant 'rank', 'position', but it is now simply the suffix *-hood*, having passed from full lexical to grammatical status. Middle English (c.1100–c.1500), however, borrowed extensively from French, and the proportion of compounds therefore drops considerably. Renaissance theorists saw compounding specifically as the use of English compounds to provide, by analogy, alternatives to foreign words borrowed ready-made. Thus, as we have already seen, Cheke uses *biwordes*, not *parables* and *uprising*, not *resurrection*. Lever has *backset* for *predicate*, *saywhat* for *definition*, and *yeasay* instead of *affirmation*. Such native, self-explanatory compounds might well be more intelligible than several of the foreign-sounding loans, 'inkhorn' terms. Sir Philip Sidney believed English to be especially rich in compounds:

> But for the uttering sweetly and properly the conceits of the mind,
> which is the end of speech, that hath it [English] equally with any other
> tongue in the world; and is particularly happy in compositions of two
> or three words together, near the Greek, far beyond the Latin: which is
> one of the greatest beauties can be in a language.[25]

I shall, however, use 'compounding' in a wider sense than this, closer
to its modern meaning, since I wish to examine how Shakespeare uses
compounds of all kinds to achieve particular stylistic effects. Another
possibility was to venture outside standard English and to introduce
(especially into poetry) dialect words or words which had been used
by the great national writers of the fairly recent past. But this was not
so common, and certainly not as productive, as the increased use of
compounds.

The most important Elizabethan writer to examine these last two
possibilities of extending the lexicon is Spenser, and it is worth
delaying a moment to consider how successful he was. His poetic
and stylistic credo is best expressed in the Dedicatory Epistle (to
Gabriel Harvey) at the beginning of *The Shepherd's Calendar*, 1579.
This shows the work to be a conscious linguistic experiment within
the traditional poetic form of the pastoral which aims, as Puttenham
said, "under the veil of homely persons and in rude speeches, to
insinuate and glance at greater matters". Spenser's choice of diction
would commend itself to nationalistic critics of overmuch borrowing
such as Cheke, Ascham and Wilson, but his occasional defensive
attitude in the Epistle reminds us that he had his opponents too.
Sidney blamed him for "framing of his style to an old rustick
language" and Ben Jonson believed that Spenser, in affecting the
ancients, "writ no language". The Epistle is allegedly composed by
E. K. who points out the contribution made to Spenser's diction by
native English words:

> For in my opinion it is one special prayse, of many whych are dew
> to this Poete, that he hath laboured to restore, as to theyr rightfull
> heritage such good and naturall English words, as haue ben long time
> out of vse and almost cleane disherited. Which is the onely cause,
> that our Mother tonge, which truely of it self is both ful enough for
> prose and stately enough for verse, hath long time ben counted most
> bare and barrein of both. Which default when some endeuoured to
> salue and recure, they patched vp the holes with peces and rags of other
> languages, borrowing here of the french, there of the Italian, euery
> where of the Latine, not weighing how il those tongues accorde with
> themselues, but much worse with ours. So now they haue made our
> English tonge, a gallimaufray or hodgepodge of al other speches.
> Other some not so wel seene in the English tonge as perhaps in other
> languages, if them happen to here an olde word albeit very naturall

and significant, crye out streight way, that we speak no English, but gibbrish.[26]

This approach is in part carried over to *The Faerie Queene* (1590), although there are perhaps fewer archaisms and certainly more compounds than in *The Shepherd's Calendar*. It seems to have been these compounds that attracted later poets so that Spenser became 'the poet's poet'. Spenser's archaisms were chiefly from Chaucer but also from fifteenth-century writers such as Malory and Lydgate. Although *The Faerie Queene* is set in a remote and romantic past, there was for Spenser no necessary connection between archaism and artificiality. Some of the most common Spenserian archaisms are *algates* ('at least'), *dight, doom, eke, forthy* ('therefore'), *hent* ('carried off'), *hight* ('called'), *stour* ('time'), *vnnethes* ('scarcely'), *whylome* ('formerly') and *yore* ('long ago'). But possibly as important in determining the tone of Spenser's poetry are some of his grammatical forms. The endings *-est* and *-eth* were still living forms in the sixteenth century but became less common as the seventeenth century progressed, as did the use of *do* or *did* as empty tense markers. On the other hand, *gan* with following infinitive to represent a past tense (*gan call* = 'called') and the prefix *y-* on past participles were decidedly obsolescent, if not already obsolete; so was the *wh-* spelling (*whott* for *hot*), and *-ght* (*spight* for *spite*) occurred far less frequently than before. One or more of his variant forms – *before/afore/tofore; astonished/astonied; dreariness/drearihead/dreariment* – are usually also obsolete, although if the word were connected with another word in more general use (e.g. *embracement, avengement*) it would not give readers undue difficulty. Several of these practices, together with Spenser's frequent alliteration, are illustrated in these three typical stanzas:

> One day nigh wearie of the *yrkesome* way,
> From her *vnhastie* beast she *did alight*,
> And on the grasse her daintie limbes *did lay*
> In *secret shadow*, farre from all mens *sight*:
> From her *faire* head her *fillet* she *vndight*,
> And laid her stole aside. Her angels face
> As the great eye of heaven shyned bright,
> And made a *sunshine* in the *shadie* place;
> *Did* never mortall eye *behold* such heauenly grace.

> *It fortuned* out of the thickest wood
> A ramping Lyon rushed suddainly.
> Hunting full greedie after *saluage* blood;
> Soone as the royall virgin he *did spy*,
> With gaping mouth at her ran greedily,
> To have *attonce* deuour'd her tender corse:
> But to the pray *when as* he drew *more ny*,

His bloudie rage asswaged with remorse,
And with the sight amazd, *forgat* his *furious forse*.

In stead thereof he kist her wearie feet,
And *lickt* her *lilly* hands with fawning tong,
As he her wronged innocence *did weet*.
O how can beautie maister the most strong,
And simple truth subdue auenging wrong?
Whose yeelded pride and proud submission,
Still *dreading death*, when she had marked long,
Her hart *gan melt* in great compassion,
And drizling teares *did shed* for pure affection.

(*Faerie Queene*, Book I, canto 3, stanzas 4–6)

But by 1600 much of this must have seemed very old-fashioned indeed; to employ deliberate archaisms is to invite the law of diminishing returns. Shakespeare does not often use archaisms, but in the mechanicals' own play of Pyramus and Thisbe they clearly represent, together with the alliteration, the attempt by the uneducated to supply the appropriate poetic heightening:

For if you will know
By moonshine *did* these lovers *think* no scorn
To meet at Ninus' tomb, there, there to woo.
The grisly beast – which Lion *hight* by name –
The *trusty Thisbe*, coming first by night,
Did scare away, or rather *did affright*.
And as she fled, her mantle she *did fall*,
Which *Lion vile* with bloody mouth *did stain*.
Anon comes Pyramus – sweet youth, and tall –
And finds his *trusty Thisbe's* mantle slain.
Whereat with blade – with *bloody*, *blameful blade* –
He *bravely broached* his *boiling bloody breast*.

(*MND* V.i.135–46)

By the time of *Pericles* (? 1608), archaisms are the mark of the first three Gower choruses which are further set apart from the play proper by their octosyllabic couplets, the metre which Gower had himself used. Periphrastic *do* is not, of course, yet archaic, although it may have seemed old-fashioned or excessively formal. *Did provoke, did begin, did die, do testify* all occur in the first chorus; *iwis, speken, forthy* and *escapend* in the second; *yslacked* in the opening line of the third. This may be the language of 'ancient Gower' but hardly of modern Shakespeare. Compounds, however, are a different matter, and to these I shall return.

36

Notes and References

1. *English Works of Roger Ascham*, ed. W. A. Wright (1904), p. xiv.
2. Peroration to the *First Part of the Elementarie* (Scolar Press edition, Manston, 1970), pp. 254, 258.
3. Ascham, ibid., p. 215.
4. Quoted by Briggs (1983), p. 97.
5. T. Wilson, *Arte of Rhetorique*, ed. G. H. Mair (1909), pp. 164–5.
6. *The Complete Works of George Gascoigne*, ed. J. W. Cunliffe (1907), I, pp. 465–73.
7. In *1 Henry VI*, III.i.99, the Bishop of Winchester is called *an inkhorn mate*, i.e. a pedant.
8. Mulcaster spoke of the latest terms borrowed into English "either of pure necessitie in new matters, or of mere brauerie, to garnish it self withall" (quoted by Barber (1976), p. 81).
9. The fullest account of the fortunes of English in the Renaissance is Jones (1953) from which I take the quotations from Borde and Pettie. Rowlands is quoted from *The Knave of Clubbes* (1609), spelling modernised. See also Hall (1977).
10. *The Arte of English Poesie*, eds G. D. Willcock and A. Walker (1936), p. 147.
11. *Ecclesiastical Polity*, ed. E. Rhys (1907), p. 161
12. *Seventeenth Century Prose*, ed. B. Vickers (1969), pp. 102–3.
13. *The Macro Plays*, ed. M. Eccles, Early English Text Society (1969), p. 262, lines 122–4.
14. Quoted from N. F. Blake, *Caxton's Own Prose* (1973).
15. Pearsall (1970).
16. For early dictionaries see Starnes and Noyes (1946).
17. Garner (1982 and 1983), both reprinted in Salmon and Burness (1987), pp. 207–34. On word-formation in Shakespeare see also Salmon (1970), reprinted in Salmon and Burness (1987), pp. 193–206.
18. Salmon (1970) considers this in terms of surface structure and underlying deep structure.
19. Houston (1988) notes *crescive, defunction, rivage, flexure, englutted, congreeted*, all from *Henry V* (p. 74).
20. Compare *Duchess of Malfi* I.i.64 and III.ii.187.
21. Bullough (1966), ch. 6, p. 350.
22. Rather similar is Balurdo's repetition of fashionable words in Marston's *Antonio's Revenge*.
23. Outside Hamlet, in which *rank(er)* is used more often than in any other play, the word is applied to people five times, to animals twice, to weeds five times, and otherwise collocates with *offence, opinion, thought, speeches, jests, feud and riots.*
24. Wilson (1969), pp. 100–29.
25. *An Apology for Poetry*, ed. G. Shepherd (1965), p. 140. Shepherd's note, p. 232, gives examples of Sidney's compounds.
26. *The Shepherd's Calendar* is quoted from *The Yale Edition of the Shorter Poems of Edward Spenser*, ed. W. A. Oram et al. (1989) and *The Faerie Queene* from the edition by A. C. Hamilton (1977).

CHAPTER THREE
The uses of vocabulary

SHAKESPEARE'S CONTEMPORARIES

If we go searching for indications of how his immediate predecessors in the drama might have contributed to Shakespeare's growing ability to vary and exploit the lexical resources available to him, the results are meagre, just as the whole quest for influences is disappointing:

> He was not only the greatest of the Elizabethan dramatists, but he did far more than any other man to create the drama and establish it. This was possible because he had the most complete facility for assimilation and rejection. He learnt and built on the work of his predecessors, yet the influence is generally so indirectly perceptible that we cannot often say with confidence 'Here is a trace of Marlowe: here of Spenser: here of Kyd'. Just as it is very difficult to pin down any passage in Shakespeare to a particular source (apart from the obvious ones like Holinshed and North), so there is nothing of the notebook method in his attitude to other poets.[1]

If we consider the best-known of these plays, those most often anthologised (as in the Everyman collection by T. W. Craik), the language does not often remind us of Shakespeare. Norton and Sackville's *Gorboduc*, the first play to be written in blank verse, was performed in 1562: "A play in the quen hall at Westmynster by the gentyll-men of the Tempull", a learned audience of the sort Shakespeare was sometimes to cultivate later (in *Troilus and Cressida*, for example). It is uncompromisingly Senecan, with lengthy speeches full of impeccable advice to counsellors, as in I.ii or the final speeches of Arostus and Eubulus in V.ii. Each character holds the stage in turn, speaking not to one another but to the audience. Oratory is the order of the day, and it is easy to imagine that, after its first production, *Gorboduc* might well have been read more often than performed. The play contains several doublets, for the characters are, after all, courtiers and speak courtiers' language, but hardly any of them are remarkable. There are few compounds (did these come in later, with Spenser?) and virtually no Latinate vocabulary. But the syntax is often Latinate: perhaps another mark of courtliness, perhaps the result of regular reading of the classics. *Cambises*, by Thomas Preston and perhaps even earlier than *Gorboduc*, is more pronounced in its Latin diction, but, unattractive as this may be, it is almost always used in speeches by, to, or about, courtly characters:

> COUNSELLOR Behold, I see him now *aggress* and enter into place.
> SISAMNES O puissant prince and mighty king, the gods preserve your grace.
> Your grace's message came to me, your will *purporting* forth;
> With grateful mind I it receiv'd, according to mine oath,
> *Erecting* then myself with speed, before your grace's eyes,
> The tenor of your princely will from you for to *agnise*.
>
> (75–80)

The morality tradition, which sits somewhat uneasily side by side with the Senecan influences, is responsible for the colloquialisms and irregular short lines of the comic characters and one (too lengthy) attempt at stage Zummerset (754–826). With all its faults, the style is more varied than that of *Gorboduc*. The domestic tragedy *Arden of Feversham* (published 1592) is more promising material and carries further the variations in style evidently by this time becoming more common in Elizabethan drama. It contains several compounds and doublets (although of no great distinction) and its occasional Latinisms do not seem to be employed for any special reason. But the colloquialisms, the braggadocio that was later to become the fustian of Pistol, and an occasional venture into a deliberately high style for the 'Ovid-like' lovers, all suggest that the author was alert to the possibilities of varying his style with a change of character or of situation, even if he was as yet incapable of doing this very often.

No reader of *The Spanish Tragedy* can fail to see its effect on Shakespeare, especially in the feigned madness of Hamlet and the final holocaust where the stage is littered with corpses. But it is more difficult to pinpoint much linguistic influence. Doublets, compounds and Latinate diction are evidently by this time (1592) an accepted part of Elizabethan drama, especially in a play with strong Senecan pretensions. The drama of Marlowe is another thing altogether. There is, first of all, much more of it than of any one of his predecessors and a far greater range within the canon. Some two months older than Shakespeare, secret-service agent and freethinker, in 1593 Marlowe was stabbed to death in a tavern brawl, not yet thirty and at a time when, in all probability, Shakespeare had written little more than the *Henry VI* trilogy. Yet, apart from *The Spanish Tragedy*, his is the only work before 1600 fit to set beside Shakespeare's. The opening of *Tamburlaine* (published 1590 but possibly composed 1587) immediately announces Marlowe's dramatic and poetic credo:

> Threat'ning the world with *high astounding terms*,
> And scourging kingdoms with his conquering sword.
> (*1 Tam* Prol. 5–6)[2]

Tamburlaine is the self-made man, the Scythian shepherd who comes to rule half the world, whose own hand turns Fortune's wheel about. He is orator as well as conqueror, and since his conquests occur off-stage, the oratory is doubly important. "You see, my lord, what working words he hath" says his lieutenant Theridamas at II.iii.25, the same Theridamas who had been "won with thy words and conquered with thy looks" (I.ii.228). The pitiful Mycetes cannot compete:

> Brother Cosroe, I find myself aggriev'd,
> Yet insufficient to express the same,
> For it requires a great and thund'ring speech.
> (*1 Tam* I.i.1–3)

Perhaps Joseph Hall (*Virgidemiarum*, 1597) was thinking of Marlowe when he spoke of drama as containing "terms Italianate, Big-sounding sentences, and words of state". Ben Jonson was more outspoken still: "the Tamerlanes, and Tamer-Chams of the late Age, which had nothing in them but the scenicall strutting, and furious vociferation, to warrant them to the ignorant gapers".[3] The devices for making Elizabethan English sound impressive are certainly there in *Tamburlaine*: Latinate diction, doublets, compounds. Yet the Latinate diction compares poorly with Shakespeare's. In fact there is not so very much of it. Nor are the compounds as remarkable as might be expected. Doublets are rather more numerous yet not very suggestive, and copious language appears seldom. The continuation of *Tamburlaine* relies more on classical references and polysyllabic, exotic-sounding names; Marlowe had so far extended the bounds of Tamburlaine's conquests and his megalomania in Part I that only the death of Zenocrate and finally of Tamburlaine himself remained to make Part II really memorable. Shakespeare could, no doubt, appreciate all these features, although he would soon equal or surpass them. What was perhaps more impressive to him in *Tamburlaine* was the sheer amount of rhetoric, not simple verbal figures at line length but rhetoric on a grander scale, *amplificatio*. Tamburlaine *declaims* (Alleyn became famous in the part): he does not change his style throughout the two plays. D. Peet, in a discussion of the rhetoric of *Tamburlaine*,[4] aptly quotes Puttenham:

> and then we lay on such load and so go to it by heapes as if we would winne the game by multitude of words and speaches.
>
> (*Arte*, p.236)

We do not need to analyse these speeches in detail: the general effect is easily communicated.

After *Tamburlaine* the chronology of Marlowe's plays becomes uncertain. *The Jew of Malta* was performed in 1592 but may well have been composed about 1590; *Dr Faustus* and *Edward II* were both written about 1592. The syntax of these two plays shows a greater experimentation, but this does not seem to be true of the vocabulary. *Faustus* still exhibits something of Marlowe's fascination with man's superhuman aspirations, although our initial sympathy with the hero is lessened by his increasing arrogance and his refusal to heed one warning after another. Surprisingly, neither compounds nor doublets are very many or very remarkable. The speeches of Chorus might be expected to produce some Latinate diction and elaborate syntax, but although Chorus 2 contains words like *gratulate* and a pair like *admired and wondered*, the Epilogue (also spoken by Chorus) relies on the hackneyed metaphor of Apollo's laurel bough and the alliteration of *fiendful fortune*. I do not mean to detract from the magnificent feeling of mounting terror in the concluding scene if I say that the diction of *Faustus* is, finally, disappointing. In *The Jew of Malta*, and to some extent in *Edward II*, intrigue becomes all-important and the diction and syntax consequently plainer. There are rather more compounds and doublets in *Edward II*, but apart from one or two examples (*overwoo*, II.v.87, *counterbuff'd*, III.ii.19) they are mostly rather ordinary. There is not much obvious Latinate diction in either play: *refluence* (*Jew*, III.v.18) is the only really unusual word. The speech of the Herald (*Edward II*, III.iii.156–71) with its complex syntax, its Latinate terminology (*effusion, putrefying, empale, consecrate*) and its image of the vine is perhaps something of an exception, but it is really only a gesture showing Marlowe's ability to use the appropriate style for affairs of state.

Shakespeare, therefore, probably learned little about the vocabulary of drama from his fellow-playwrights, but when he began to write Spenser was the major narrative poet. As a supporter of those who advocated a greater use of the resources of native English, Spenser will not be expected to provide much by way of Latinate vocabulary. *Ingenerate* (*The Faerie Queene* III.vi.3), *degendered* (5.Prol.2), *arrogate* (*Mutability Cantos* 16) are examples, but one has to look quite hard in *The Faerie Queene* to find them. The doublets and triplets, such as *wearie and fordonne* ('tired out', I.x.47), *An vncouth, saluage and vnciuile wight/Of griesly hew, and fowle ill fauour'd sight* (II.vii.3), *Strife and debate, bloudshed, and bitternesse* (II.vii.12), *Immortall and vnchangeable* (*Mutability Cantos*, 54), *rule and raigne* (*Mutability Cantos*, 58) are neither especially distinguished nor especially Latinate. Compounds, however, are a different matter. *True-seeming* (lyes), *euer-drizling* (raine), *rosy-fingred* (Morning), *sun-bright* (armes), *foole-happie, bloudie-mouthed, fruitfull-headed* (beast), *deaw-burning* (blade), *raw-bone* (cheekes), *fire-mouthed* (Dragon), *newly-budded* (pineons), *fire-spitting* (forge), *eye-glutting* (gaine), *counterfeisance* ('deception'), *vp-standing* (heares), *wingyheeld, hartfretting* (payne), *Lion-like, sky-ruling* (Jove) form a fairly typical list which, even so, does not include any of the numerous examples of affixation. Almost all these compounds are, perhaps not surprisingly in such descriptive writing, adjectival, and their construction is frequently noun (or adjective) plus participle. The concentration of verbal energy into the participle is useful not only to the descriptive poet but also to the poetic dramatist, and it was a habit Shakespeare never lost.

Compounds come thickest and fastest in Shakespeare's early plays. In English, verb compounds are far less common than noun compounds, and in poetry I suspect that we notice noun compounds far less than adjectival ones. The kind of appositional compounds Shakespeare uses occasionally:

> You are too senseless-obstinate, my lord.
>
> (*R III* III.i.44)

> To undergo with me an enterprise
> Of honourable-dangerous consequence.
>
> (*JC* I.iii.124)

> Be not so holy-cruel. Love is holy.
>
> (*AW* IV.ii.32)

are, I imagine, not much to our taste now. Shakespeare's favourite type of compound seems to have been the adjective whose second element is a participle. In the early plays these tend to be rather self-consciously poetical and often too obviously transparent, perhaps still under the influence of Spenser whose narrative poetry gave him time for embellishment which the dramatist could not always spare. Take a relatively early play like *Romeo and Juliet* where almost two-thirds of the compounds are of this grammatical type:

> Gallop apace, you fiery-footed steeds.
>
> (III.ii.1)

(Spenser himself had used *fiery-footed team*.)

> Come, civil night,
> Thou sober-suited matron, all in black.
>
> (III.ii.10–11)

> Dove-feathered raven! Wolvish-ravening lamb!
>
> (III.ii.76)

and contrast it with a relatively late play like *Antony and Cleopatra*: (a handsome man) *loose-wived* I.ii.73; (these three) *world-sharers* II.vii.70; *high-battled* (Caesar) III.xiii.29. These do not merely luxuriate in description; they make us think. It is rare to find a line like "*New lighted* on a *heaven-kissing* hill" so late as *Hamlet* (III.iv.60). The line is part of a high-style speech meant to convey a general impression of the excellence of old Hamlet. It may be beautiful poetry, but in itself it has little or no particularising force. How, on the contrary, do you expand an encapsulated phrase like *summer-seeming lust* (*Macbeth* IV.iii.86)?

Romeo and Juliet, however, has a direct source which is a poem, Arthur Brooke's *The Tragicall Historye of Romeus and Juliet* (1562), in fourteen-syllable lines.[5] It is often poor stuff, perhaps because the very length of the lines invites expansion. It contains some alliteration but little or no Latinate language, and its compounds and doublets are distressingly obvious. At its worst it can descend to lines like this:

> On Wensday next, (quod Juliet) so doth my father say:
> I must give my consent, but (as I do remember)
> The solemne day of marriage is, the tenth day of September.
>
> (2070–2)

Our immediate reaction may be to marvel at what Shakespeare could make of such bare bones. Yet it may serve to remind us that Shakespeare was a narrative poet as well as a dramatist. *Venus and Adonis* and *The Rape of Lucrece* were almost certainly written during 1592–4 when the London companies were on tour because of a particularly bad outbreak of plague in the capital. They should be placed side by side, not only with Spenser but more particularly with poems like Lodge's *Scylla's Metamorphosis* (printed 1589 but possibly composed earlier), Marlowe's *Hero and Leander* (1598, completed by Chapman), and Drayton's *Endymion and Phoebe* (1595).[6] They are all in the mode of the then fashionable Ovidian erotic poetry, although it should be remembered that *Lucrece* is history and not myth. They include some doublets and copious language and Drayton has rather more by way of Latinate language (though the words are not really unusual). But they all contain several compounds and are essentially exercises in decorative and rhetorical embellishment. The opening stanza of *Venus and Adonis* contains four adjectival compounds, each with a past participle in second position:

> Even as the sun with purple-colour'd face
> Had ta'en his last leave of the weeping morn,
> Rose-cheek'd Adonis hied him to the chase;
> Hunting he loved, but love he laugh'd to scorn:
>   Sick-thoughted Venus makes amain unto him,
>   And like a bold-faced suitor 'gins to woo him.

The descriptions of the amorous and over-powering heroine and the somewhat petulant hero give scope for many more similar compounds such as *time-beguiling* (sport), *flint-hearted* (boy), *blue-veined* (violets), *strong-necked* (steed), *round-hoofed, short-jointed, deep-sweet* (music), *bate-breeding* (spy), *earth-delving* (conies), *life-poisoning* (pestilence), *cold-pale* (weakness), *deep-dark* (cabins), *green-dropping* (sap). These sometimes take their place as part of the copious language of description:

> Were I hard-favoured, foul, or wrinkled-old,
> Ill-nurtured, crooked, churlish, harsh in voice,
> O'erworn, despised, rheumatic and cold,
> Thick-sighted, barren, lean, and lacking juice,
>   Then mightst thou pause . . .

(133–37)

> But this foul, grim, and urchin-snouted boar.

(1105)

> Hard-favoured tyrant, ugly, meagre, lean.

(931)

The Rape of Lucrece is half as long again, and this is all the more remarkable in that Shakespeare does not describe Tarquin's first visit to Collatine's palace and merely mentions his eventual banishment.

Most readers nowadays feel that Lucrece is far too articulate and that the long stretches of monologue alienate rather than retain our sympathy, but the poem had nevertheless gone through nine editions by 1655. The declamatory, rhetorical style gives ample scope for embellishment by doublets, copious language, alliteration and above all, compounds, one to every nineteen or so lines. Most of the latter are of the now familiar adjectival kind, such as *lust-breathed* (Tarquin), *death-boding* (cries), *hot-burning* (will), *night-wandering* (weasels), *night-waking* (cat), *pity-pleading* (eyes), *surfeit-taking* (Tarquin), *all-hiding* (cloak), *fleet-winged* (duty), *salt-waved* (ocean), *cloud-kissing* (Ilion), *Tarquin-stained*. The copious lexis is fairly obviously decorative:

A dream, a breath, a froth of fleeting joy.

(212)

Be moved with my tears, my sighs, my groans.

(588)

For princes are the glass, the school, the book,
Where subjects' eyes do learn, do read, do look.

(615–16)

Her sacred temple spotted, spoiled, corrupted,
Grossly engirt with daring infamy.

(1172–3)

Another characteristic of Spenser's descriptive style is the generalised and sometimes generic adjective which was to pass via Milton into much eighteenth-century 'occasional' poetry. The pattern is frequently disyllabic adjective plus monosyllabic noun: *wandring sheepe, fertile land, grassie plaine, cloudie storme* and *bitter showre*. There are fewer examples in Shakespeare than in Spenser, but the trick does occur occasionally, as in *Venus and Adonis*:

He burns with *bashful shame*; she with her tears
Doth quench the *maiden burning* of his cheeks;
Then with her *windy sighs* and *golden hairs*
To fan and blow them dry again she seeks.

(49–52)

His *louring brows* o'erwhelming his fair sight,
Like *misty vapours* when they blot the sky.

(183–4)

All this has been a long prologue to the play, but it is important to realise that by the mid-1590s other writers besides Shakespeare were experimenting with Latinate diction, poetic compounds and copious lexis. It would, too, have been scarcely possible for Shakespeare, in *Love's Labour's Lost*, to satirise the prevailing attitudes towards language if these had not been sufficiently widespread. Instances of Latinate borrowing should by now be easy enough for the reader to discover in the group of Shakespeare's earliest plays to which I now turn. The exact order of the *Henry VI* trilogy, *Richard III* and *Titus Andronicus* may be uncertain, but it is likely that all five were composed between 1591 and 1594.

There are not too many Latin loans in *Titus Andronicus*, except in the long scene which takes up the whole of Act I and which deals with imperial affairs. There are more examples in the three parts of *Henry VI* in which Shakespeare, unhistorically, suggests that the Wars of the Roses began through a quarrel between young aristocrats in the Temple Garden: II.iv. of *1 Henry VI* consequently shows a good deal of legal terminology, such as *quillets, significants, subscribe, attached, attainted, apprehension, cognizance*. (Although some of these words had almost certainly entered English via French, they originated in Latin and may have been felt as Latinate in this context.) Not surprisingly, the three plays are frequently involved with questions of succession and justice; even the demagogue Jack Cade has heard of *jurisdiction regal*. Latinate adjective sometimes qualifies Latinate noun and the result becomes doubly impressive: *factious emulations* (*1 Hen VI* IV.i.113); *vehement instigation* (*Richard III* III.vii.138). Even better is the hypocritical reluctance of Richard III to accept the crown:

> But if black scandal or foul-faced reproach
> Attend the sequel of your imposition,
> Your mere enforcement shall acquittance me
> From all the impure blots and stains thereof.
>
> (III.vii.230–3)

Moral abstractions, carried over from the morality plays, can produce their own Latinate diction:

> Virtue is choked with foul ambition,
> And charity chased hence by rancour's hand;
> Foul subornation is predominant,
> And equity exiled your highness' land.
>
> (*2 Hen VI* III.i.143–6)

The adroit 'placing' of a word so as to secure maximum stress is already evident:

> Wounds will I lend the French instead of eyes,
> To weep their *intermissive* miseries.
>
> (*1 Hen VI* I.i.87–8)

> The presence of a king engenders love
> Amongst his subjects and his loyal friends,
> As it *disanimates* his enemies.
>
> (<i>1 Hen VI</i> III.i.183–5)

Two polysyllabic Latin words sometimes occur within the line (as at
2 Henry VI III.i.145 above) or an impressive-sounding line is achieved
by a Latin-derived word followed by a compound ("As cognizance of
my blood–drinking hate", *1 Hen VI* II.iv.108).

EXPLOITING THE RANGE

What is noteworthy in these plays, and especially in *1 Henry VI*, are
the uncommon Latinate words, as if Shakespeare, like some of his
contemporaries, was savouring the ability of Elizabethan English to
borrow such terms. *Attainture* first entered English in 1538 but was
always unusual and occurs only here in Shakespeare; the two instances
of *reguerdon*, rare both as noun and as verb although appearing in
Gower and in Chaucer's *Boethius*, are the only two in the canon.
Proditor, periapts (first recorded in 1584) and *immanity* (defined in
Cawdrey's 1604 dictionary as "beastlie crueltie or hugenesse and
greatnes" and glossed as 'bloody strife' in *1 Henry VI*) are similarly
unique within Shakespeare's plays. *Contusions* occurs from c. 1400 in
the medical sense but was apparently never frequent in general use.
Corrosive likewise had a medical and scientific sense from the late
fourteenth century, but the metaphorical use ('destructive', 'wasting')
was evidently becoming more common in the Elizabethan period;
the *OED* has examples from Elyot, Mulcaster, Hooker, Lyly and
Greene, but the word occurs only twice in Shakespeare, once at *1
Henry VI* III.iii.3 and once at *2 Henry VI* III.ii.403. Other forms,
rare in themselves, might be easily understood by reference to a
more common word with the same root: *embassade* occurs only at
3 Henry VI, IV.iii.3, but *embassador* was a common Tudor spelling;
extraught was perhaps a variant of *extracted* (cf. *distraught*); *neglection*
('neglect') and *guardant* ('guard') are other examples of unusual affixes.
The number of such words is greatest in *Henry VI* (especially in Part
1) but one might add *enacts* from *Titus Andronicus* IV.ii.118, the only
example of the noun from Shakespeare (although *Hamlet* III.ii.207 has
enactures). *Richard III*, too, contributes its quota of unusual Latinate
diction. *Inductions*, I.i.32, is the first *OED* entry for the sense 'initial
step' (cf. *1 Hen IV* III.i.2), but 'preface', 'preamble' (to a book)

dates from 1533 (More) and the dramatic sense ('opening scene') is found at IV.iv.5 *Recomforture*, IV.iv.425, is the only occurrence in Shakespeare and in the *OED*. *Diffused* ('shapeless', I.ii.78) and *expiate* ('fully come', III.iii.23 – changed to *expir'd* in Folios 2–4) are rare as past participles.

Doublets are fairly numerous in all five plays, but not all are Latinate by any means, and on the whole they are fairly straight-forward, suggesting that the reason for their use was not intelligibility but a desire to add weight to the line. Almost half of those in *Titus Andronicus* occur in Act V where the enormity of Titus's revenge becomes evident. 'Linked' doublets occasionally appear:

> Her valiant courage and undaunted spirit
>
> (*1 Hen VI* V.v.70)
>
> By false intelligence or wrong surmise
>
> (*R III* II.i.55)

Compounds, similarly, are numerous, but rarely innovatory or otherwise remarkable. *2 Henry VI* III.i.335 ("Let pale-faced fear keep with the mean-born man.") is fairly typical. *Church-like* humours (I.i.245), *silken-coated* slaves (IV.ii.120) and *chair-days* ('old age', V.ii.48), all from the same play, are more imaginative, but other passages show in their choice of compounds a sense of strain rare in Shakespeare but more common in some of his contemporaries:

> And for myself, foe as he was to me,
> Might liquid tears or heart-offending groans
> Or blood–consuming sighs recall his life,
> I would be blind with weeping, sick with groans,
> Look pale as primrose with blood–drinking sighs,
> And all to have the noble Duke alive.
>
> (*2 Hen VI*.ii.59–64)

Weeping-ripe (*3 Hen VI* I.iv.172) and *water-standing* eye (*3 Hen VI* V.vi.40) are little better. In this play *clear-shining* and *fair-shining* occur within a few lines of one another in II.i, and elsewhere *hard-hearted, gentle-hearted, soft-hearted, sad-hearted, proud-hearted* suggest that Shakespeare's imagination was scarcely at fever pitch. *Richard III* contains *key-cold, numb-cold* and *icy-cold. Titus Andronicus* is a play with comparatively few compounds, but it introduces the three-member type which Shakespeare used occasionally later: *worse-than-killing* lust (II.iii.175), *never-heard-of* torturing pain (II.iii.285). On the other hand, this play has several alliterative phrases – analagous to compounds – a device which Shakespeare came to associate with an outmoded style. *Ling'ring languishment* (II.i.110) and *dainty doe* (II.i.117, later on to become Bottom's "O dainty duck, O dear!") are satirical – they occur in the same speech of Aaron – but *the fields are fragrant* (II.ii.2) and *dawning day* (II.ii.10) are part of an early attempt, not wholly successful, at the high 'prologue' style. *Brinish bowels* (III.i.97), however it appeared to the Elizabethans, strikes us as simply unfortunate. In *Richard III* there is a high incidence of compounds. Few are arresting ("I will converse with iron-witted fools/And unrespective boys", IV.ii.28, and "impotent and snail-paced beggary", IV.iii.53, both link a compound with a Latinate term) but there are few tired examples either; most suggest careful, encapsulated thought. Richard is variously referred to as *hell-governed, elvish-marked, bunch-backed* (twice), *villain-slave, stone-hard, self-misused* and *hell-hound*.

Aaron in *Titus Andronicus* is perhaps the first major Shakespearean character to use deliberate colloquialisms. It is difficult to be completely sure of what was colloquial for the Elizabethan audience; all one can do is to check one's impression from the context against the *OED* and a Shakespeare concordance. *Brabble* (*Titus Andronicus* II.i.62) was not common, although it was increasing in frequency in the later sixteenth century; it seems to imply an undignified quarrel – Aaron's is a *petty brabble* and in *Twelfth Night* Antonio is "desperate of shame and state/In private brabble" (V.i.61). *Jet*, in the same speech, looks colloquial and was fairly common in the sixteenth century, but more often with the meaning 'strut', 'swagger' than 'encroach' which the context here seems to suggest. *Pack*, 'conspire' (IV.ii.156) is not very usual, although there are examples from the early sixteenth century. The sense of 'suffer for it' for *smoke* (IV.ii.111) seems clear, but whether there is any more direct reference to burning is not obvious. *Some certain snatch* (II.i.95) occurs in the middle of a passage of bawdy word-play and one meaning is pretty obviously sexual, but other instances outside Shakespeare suggest a quick movement (compare modern *snatch*). Aaron is fond of racy epithets, as when he describes Tamora's two sons who ravished Lavinia:

> That codding spirit had they from their mother,
> *As sure a card as ever won the set.*
> That bloody mind, I think, they learned of me,
> *As true a dog as ever fought at head.*

(TA V.i.98–101)

In one of the rhetorically-pointed laments of the noble women characters in *Richard III*, the Duchess of York asks

> Why should calamity be full of words?

Queen Elizabeth replies, in a style itself expansionist:

> Windy attorneys to their client's woes,
> Airy succeeders of intestate joys,
> Poor breathing orators of miseries,
> Let them have scope! Though what they will impart
> Help nothing else, yet they do ease the heart.

and the Duchess, evidently convinced, continues:

> If so, then be not tongue-tied: go with me
> And in the breath of bitter words let's smother
> My damned son that thy two sweet sons smothered.
> The trumpet sounds. Be copious in exclaims.
>
> (IV.iv.126–35)

"Be copious in exclaims": the play does exactly that. There are several examples of simple lexical parallelism:

> No doubt, no doubt. O, 'tis a parlous boy,
> Bold, quick, ingenious, forward, capable.
>
> (III.i.154–5)

> And yet within these five hours Hastings lived,
> Untainted, unexamined, free, at liberty.
>
> (III.vi.8–9)

and more extended instances at III.vii.116–21 and IV.iv.168–73 where it is noticeable that Shakespeare manages both variation in word-order and syntactical balance.

This, however, is only one of the styles of *Richard III*. The hero himself dominates the play, the longest of the histories, and his exuberance, vitality and individualism are characteristic of Marlovian heroes. The other characters are distanced from the audience by rhetorical speech-patterns, and Richard can employ these too, most obviously in the two extended examples of *stichomythia*, first with Anne (I.ii) and later with Elizabeth (IV.iv). In each of these he achieves the apparently impossible: to marry the woman whose husband and father-in-law he had killed, and to persuade a mother to give her daughter's hand to the man "who slew her brothers and her uncle". The extreme formal expression emphasizes the outrageous nature of his requests. But our feeling that Richard is simply 'more real' than the other characters is largely because of his ability to change style from rhetorical to colloquial. "I would I knew thy heart", says Anne; "Tis figured in my tongue", Richard replies. His language is indeed often *figured*, but in his deliberate use of colloquialisms to reveal to the audience his true feelings about both people and events he is a truer Machiavel than Aaron:

> Which done, God take King Edward to His mercy
> And leave the world for me to bustle in!
>
> (I.i.151–2)

The sanctimonious "take King Edward to His mercy" gives way to the *bustle* of further plotting (the word perhaps also refers to Richard's gait):

> Amen! And make me die a good old man!
> That is the *butt-end* of a mother's blessing;
> I marvel that her grace did leave it out.
>
> (II.ii.109–11)

> Marry, as for Clarence, he is well repaid;
> He is *franked up to fatting* for his pains –
> God pardon them that are the cause thereof!
>
> (I.iii.312–14)

The verb *bustle* is recorded once only in Middle English, but, although it is used reflexively in later sixteenth-century English, it apparently occurs first as a phrasal verb (*bustle in*) in North's *Plutarch*. *Butt-end*, the sole instance in Shakespeare, is also in North (was Shakespeare already reading for the later Roman plays?). This instance of *franked up*, and another in *Richard III* (IV.v.3), are the only two examples in the canon, although the noun *frank* occurs in *2 Henry IV* II.ii.140. *Cog* (I.iii.48) and *costard* (I.iv.156) are found rather more often. *Cog* seems to have developed from its original sense of 'cheat at dice' to 'cheat' (generally) and by the end of the century to 'wheedle' or 'flatter', as here. The other Shakespearean examples closest to *Richard III* are "I'll mountebank their loves / *Cog* their hearts from them and come home beloved" (*Cor* III.ii.132–3, where Coriolanus sarcastically chooses the terms *mountebank* and *cog* to describe his appeal to the plebs for their votes) and "Ay, and you hear him *cog*, see him dissemble" (*Timon of Athens* V.i.93). D. M. Burton[7] cites several examples, all from Act I, of Richard's plain diction. *Cog, meed, duck, plain, perch* are all monosyllables. *Wrens, Jacks, bachelor, stripling, grandam* are colloquialisms and *weeder-out, royalize, childish-foolish* are found only here. They reveal Richard's impatience with the empty gestures of feudalism; he is not a man for meaningless artifice. His final rallying-call to his army (V.iii) is also full of racy terminology, good stirring stuff: *babbly dreams; pell-mell; A scum of Britains and base lackey peasants; a paltry fellow; a milksop; whip; rags of France; poor rats; beaten, bobbed and thumped.*

SATIRISING LANGUAGE

Two plays, especially, Jonson's *Poetaster* (acted 1601) and Shakespeare's *Love's Labour's Lost* (1593–4) satirise the attitudes towards language which have been our concern in the previous chapter. Jonson was criticising not only inkhornism but also, in the character of Tucca the military parasite, the 'realistic' (but in its own way copious) language which we shall examine later in the *Henry IV* plays. But most of Jonson's ridicule is reserved for Crispinus the poetaster (hack-writer) who, in V.iii.,[8] is given by Horace an emetic which makes him vomit words such as *retrograde, reciprocal, incubus, glibbery, lubricall, defunct, magnificate, spurious, snotteries, chilbrained, clumsy* ('benumbed'), *barmy froth, puffy, inflate, turgidous, ventositous, oblatrant, furibund, fatuate, strenuous, conscious dampe, prorumped, clutcht, snarling gusts, quaking custard, obstupefact.* Caesar's comment on all this is "Here be words, Horace, able to bastinado a man's ears" (V.iii.390, just as the Bastard in *King John* complains that Hubert of Angers "gives the *bastinado* with his tongue"). Not all these words have been identified in the works of Marston whom Jonson (Horace) satirises under the name of Crispinus, nor are these the only inkhorn terms in the play: *gratulate, ornatures, extrude* and *acceptive* might also qualify. Furthermore, linguistic condemnation is (as elsewhere in Jonson) allied to condemnation of the moral laxity of some of the characters, whether from the Court or from the City. Renaissance educationalists like Elyot or Ascham saw appropriate language as one of the marks of a good man.

Love's Labour's Lost is much more comprehensive and subtle in its satire. It opens with the King of Navarre and his three attendant lords (chief of whom is Berowne) vowing to live apart from society for three years and to pass their time in study and contemplation:

> Our court shall be a little academe,
> Still and contemplative in living art.

> (I.i.13–14)

When, in Act II, this same court of Navarre is visited by the Princess of France and her three attendant ladies, the outcome would seem inevitable. The interest, then, is less in plot than in attitudes to life, and these will be mirrored in the language employed. There is a third set of characters: Armado, a fantastical Spaniard – the name, as well as in all probability his costume, would be a give-away; Holofernes, a schoolmaster; Nathaniel, a parish priest; Costard, the clown; and Dull, the parish constable. These are not quite a group since Holofernes and Nathaniel do not appear until Act IV, scene ii (to enliven a possibly flagging interest?) and Armado and Holofernes do not in fact meet until V.i., but they are developed from stock comic types with immediately recognisable linguistic attitudes (the Folio text calls Armado simply 'Braggart', Holofernes 'Pedant' and Nathaniel 'Curate').

We may begin with Armado since he appears first. The men from Navarre regard him as comic relaxation for their high-minded existence. He is prepared for before he actually appears:

> BEROWNE   But is there no quick recreation granted?
> KING   Ay, that there is. Our court, you know, is haunted
>   With a refined traveller of Spain,
>   A man in all the world's new fashion planted,
>   That hath a mint of phrases in his brain . . .
> BEROWNE   Armado is a most illustrious wight,
>   A man of fire-new words, fashion's own knight.
>   (I.i.159–63, 175–6)

and immediately the connection is made between *new fashion* and *fire-new words*, those Latinate terms which were still in process of acclimatisation.[9] Next, a letter from Armado is delivered to the King:

> So it is, besieged with sable-coloured melancholy, I did commend the black-oppressing humour to the most wholesome physic of thy health-giving air; and, as I am a gentleman, betook myself to walk. The time when? About the sixth hour; when beasts most graze, birds best peck, and men sit down to that nourishment which is called supper. So much for the time when. Now for the ground which? which, I mean, I walked upon. It is ycleped thy park. Then for the place where – where, I mean, I did encounter that obscene and most preposterous event, that draweth from my snow-white pen the ebon-coloured ink which here thou viewest, beholdest, surveyest or seest. But to the place where? It standeth north-north-east and by east from the west corner of thy curious-knotted garden.
>
>   (I.i.227–38)

There is some order and method about this (*when*? . . . *which*? . . . *where*?) and indeed balance: "beasts most graze, birds best peck, and men sit down to that nourishment which is called supper". But in these last words we see Armado addicted to the vices of rhetoric. First of all he offends against decorum, just as Berowne had previously forecast: "How low soever the matter, I hope in God for high words." He cannot simply say *supper* but *that nourishment which is called supper*. In the quotation as a whole, most of the nouns have their accompanying adjectives, either Latinate (*obscene and most preposterous*) or compound (*sable-coloured, black-oppressing, health-giving, snow-white, ebon-coloured, curious-knotted*). Not satisfied with a doublet, Armado produces no fewer than four synonyms (*viewest, beholdest, surveyest* or *seest*) and the last three add nothing further to the meaning. His method is simply to elaborate in language which *sounds* impressive, either etymologically or in sheer weight of words. He is "the *varnish* of a complete man", a variation on the more regular Elizabethan metaphor, *painted* (which is in fact used in the play at II.i.14, IV.i.16 and IV.iii.237); as we might say, he has a *veneer* of good manners.

And so he goes on. There is a second letter in IV.i. At III.i.122 he releases Costard from custody ("Thou wert immured, restrained, captivated, bound") and at V.i.82 he tells Holofernes:

> Sir, it is the king's most sweet pleasure and affection to congratulate the Princess at her pavilion in the posteriors of this day, which the rude multitude call the afternoon.

He even produces a neologism, a coinage of his own, but typically a Latin-sounding one, in *repasture* (IV.i.94) a blend of *repast* and *pasture*. On his first appearance in I.ii (by which time we have already been asking ourselves if the man can really be as ridiculous as has been alleged) he is provided with a diminutive page, Mote,[10] in the tradition of the boys in Lyly's plays. Mote's function is to prick the bubble of Armado's inflated language, and so of his own view of himself, sometimes by parody, sometimes by a deliberate monosyllabic reply:

ARMADO	How canst thou part sadness and melancholy, my tender juvenal?
MOTE	By a familiar demonstration of the working, my tough signor.
ARMADO	Why tough signor? Why tough signor?
MOTE	Why tender juvenal? Why tender juvenal?
ARMADO	I spoke it, tender juvenal, as a congruent epitheton appertaining to thy young days, which we may nominate tender.
MOTE	And I, tough signor, as an appertinent title to your old time, which we may name tough.

(I.ii.7–17)

Holofernes also uses an abundance of synonyms, and cannot, in the real world outside his classroom, forget his pedagogical methods. Like many Elizabethan schoolmasters, he teaches translation by trying out the various English equivalents of a Latin word:

HOLOFERNES	The deer was, as you know, in *sanguis*, blood; ripe as the pomewater, who now hangeth like a jewel in the ear of *caelum*, the sky, the welkin, the heaven; and anon falleth like a crab on the face of *terra*, the soil, the land, the earth.

NATHANIEL   Truly, Master Holofernes, the epithets are sweetly
                         varied, like a scholar at the least.

                                                            (IV.ii.3–9)

Nathaniel not only admires but echoes him:

NATHANIEL   I praise God for you sir. Your reasons at dinner have
                         been sharp and sententious, pleasant without scurrility,
                         witty without affection, audacious without impudency,
                         learned without opinion, and strange without heresy.
                         I did converse this *quondam* day with a companion
                         of the king's, who is entitled, nominated, or called, Don
                         Adriano de Armado.

HOLOFERNES   *Novi hominem tanquam te*. His humour is lofty,
                         his discourse peremptory, his tongue filed, his
                         eye ambitious, his gait majestical, and his general
                         behaviour vain, ridiculous, and thrasonical. He is
                         too picked, too spruce, too affected, too odd, as it
                         were, too peregrinate, as I may call it.

NATHANIEL   A most singular and choice epithet.

                                                            (V.i.2–14)

No doubt Nathaniel writes down the "most singular and choice
epithet" *peregrinate* for use on a future occasion, and this is surely
how many of these fashionable new words must have achieved some
currency. The rhetorician John Hoskins, writing in 1599, advises his
pupil to compile a list of synonyms but to use them selectively, not
like a *schoolmaster*. He says that *accumulation* (one of the sub-divisions
of Amplification)

> hath his due season after some argument of proof. Otherwise it is like
> a schoolmaster foaming out synonymies, or words of one meaning, and
> will sooner yield a conjecture of superfluity of words than of sufficiency
> of matter. . . . You will be well stored for this purpose when you have
> made up your *synonyma* book after my direction.[11]

The admiration for book-learning appears in Nathaniel's patronising
remark about the constable Dull (IV.ii.24): "Sir, he hath never fed of
the dainties that are bred in a *book*." But if this is Armado over again, it
is Armado with a difference. Armado doesn't get things wrong, only
far more complicated than necessary. Holofernes occasionally gets the
spellings fashionably wrong because he gets the etymology wrong:

> I abhor such fanatical phantasimes, such insociable and point-device
> companions; such rackers of orthography, as to speak 'dout' *sine* 'b'
> when he should say 'doubt', 'det' when he should pronounce 'debt' –
> d,e,b,t, not d,e,t. He clepeth a calf 'cauf', half 'hauf'; neighbour *vocatur*
> 'nebour', neigh abbreviated 'ne'. This is abhominable, which he would
> call 'abominable'.

                                                            (V.i.17–24)

Doubt and *debt* appear in Middle English as *doute* and *dette*, without the *b*, because they had been borrowed immediately from French and not from the original Latin *dubitum* and *debitum*. But such was their veneration for Latin that the Elizabethans restored the *b* (together with the *d* in *advantage* and *adventure*, the *l* in *false*, the *c* in *verdict* and the *p* in *receipt*). Purists expected pronunciation to follow the spelling. In medieval Latin and in earlier English, *abominable* was often wrongly etymologised as *ab* + *homo* ('away from man' and hence 'inhuman') instead of from Old French *abominable*, in turn from Latin *abominabilis*, and therefore 'deserving of imprecation' because it was an ill *omen*.

Dull is beyond the linguistic pale; like those later Shakespearean constables he misunderstands ("I myself *reprehend* his own person, for I am his grace's farborough."), but Costard is rather more complex. In part he is the simple peasant who cannot understand the newly fashionable words like *enfranchise, remuneration* and *guerdon*, and comically and stupidly mixes up letters from Armado to Jaquenetta (with whom he is himself in love) and from Berowne to Rosaline. Yet Armado calls him *rational hind*, 'intelligent yokel' (I.ii.113) and to Holofernes one of Costard's puns is "A good lustre of conceit in a turf of earth". He is therefore also semantic juggler, as he shows in puns with the King towards the end of I.i. and by taking his part with Boyet, Rosaline and Maria in a series of sexual innuendoes on archery and courtship in IV.i. which Maria ends by accusing him of talking *greasily*. Does Costard later in Shakespeare's career become two characters: on the one hand the country bumpkin and mistaker of words, on the other the clever clown – perhaps Touchstone (who after all loves Audrey, a country girl like Jaquenetta) rather than Feste? Launcelot Gobbo in *The Merchant of Venice* is another example of this early uncertainty in characterisation. Initially he is only marginally cleverer than his father and similarly addicted to malapropisms. When he returns in III.v. (he has been off stage since II.v.) he still confuses *agitation* and *cogitation* but is enough of a punster to deserve Lorenzo's retort "How every fool can play upon the word!" It is Costard, together with Mote, who makes what must surely be Shakespeare's own comment on the exaggerations of the whole trio, Armado, Holofernes and Nathaniel:

MOTE   They have been at a great feast of languages and
                      stol'n the scraps.
COSTARD   O, they have lived long on the alms-basket of words.
                                       (V.i.36–9)

Yet towards the end of the final and very long scene, the tone of *Love's Labour's Lost* suddenly changes. At V.ii.712 the messenger Marcade (Mar-Arcady, spoiling the pastoral existence)[12] brings news of the death of the King of France, and the ladies must return home. The speech of sympathy of the King of Navarre is made in the old style, now to be discredited, as the Princess replies "I understand you not." It is Berowne who perceives that

> Honest plain words best pierce the ear of grief

although it must be admitted that the rest of his speech (V.ii.748–71) is hardly so straightforward. Berowne had, from the beginning, been sceptical of the possiblility of living such an austere life and of renouncing women's company altogether. Yet he *will* couch almost every speech so as to reveal his brilliance and ingenuity. This linguistic irresponsibility is noticed by Rosaline, the very lady with whom he is in love:

> Oft have I heard of you, my Lord Berowne,
> Before I saw you, and the world's large tongue
> Proclaims you for a man replete with mocks,
> Full of comparisons and wounding flouts,
> Which you on all estates will execute
> That lie within the mercy of your wit.

> (V.ii.830–5)

The ladies are, quite simply, kinder than the men, although the play has constantly put the men on the defensive. They are high-spirited too, but they realise that life has a serious side. The reason for the Princess's visit to Navarre, we are told, was "serious business, craving quick dispatch" (II.i.31). When Holofernes, Armado, Nathaniel, Costard and Mote ("The pedant, the braggart, the hedge-priest, the fool, and the boy", as Berowne slightingly calls them) present their play of the Nine Worthies, it is the ladies who are encouraging and the men whose witty comments disconcert the actors (just as the courtiers in *A Midsummer Night's Dream* make fun of the mechanicals' play), so much so that Holofernes blurts out

> This is not generous, not gentle, not humble.

> (V.ii.626)

So it is appropriate that the play does not end with a multiple wedding. Jack hath not Jill – or, at least, not yet, for the men are put on probation for twelve months to prove their love by devoted service. As Jane Donawerth remarks,[13] hitherto love has appeared to be more of a social custom than a necessary need. Berowne's therapy, as prescribed by Rosaline, is the strictest:

> To weed this wormwood from your fruitful brain,
> And therewithal to win me, if you please,
> Without the which I am not to be won,
> You shall this twelvemonth term from day to day
> Visit the speechless sick, and still converse
> With groaning wretches; and your task shall be
> With all the fierce endeavour of your wit
> To enforce the pained impotent to smile.

(V.ii.836–43)

and it involves the direction of his linguistic ability towards a new and more serious purpose. There is, however, some hope for him, as revealed by a return, in the last scene, to the imagery of language and fashion which had begun the play. The four men plan to woo the ladies by an elaborate masquerade in which they disguise themselves as Russians. The ladies, privy to the plot, dress up as one another and make their partners' protestations of love ridiculous. Berowne is the first to realise that the men's elaborate style has been its own disguise:

> Taffeta phrases, silken terms precise,
> Three-piled hyperboles, spruce affection,
> Figures pedantical – these summer flies
> Have blown me full of maggot ostentation.
> I do forswear them; and I here protest
> By this white glove – how white the hand, God knows! –
> Henceforth my wooing mind shall be expressed
> In russet yeas and honest kersey noes.

(V.ii.406–13)

Taffeta was used for expensive lining; three-piled velvet was the best weight. But russet was the characteristic reddish-brown colour of lower-class clothing, and kersey was a plain wool cloth. The contrast between (French) three-piled velvet and English kersey is made over again in *Measure for Measure* (I.ii.32–5). It has been argued that to see this image in *Love's Labour's Lost* as a way of rejecting art for nature is far too simple. It really only changes one kind of affectation for another: the silk, taffeta and velvet of the high style for the kersey of an assumed low style.[14] There is some truth in this at the time Berowne makes the remark, but he is *beginning* the process of rejecting artificiality which is to be continued in his sojourn amongst the groaning wretches and painted impotents. The two songs which conclude the play are similarly contrasted in style. Spring is idealised and generalised; we hear of shepherds, ploughmen, married men and maidens. The harshness of winter is realistic and individualised; its inhabitants are Dick, Tom, Marian and greasy Joan. Each stanza is delineated by *When . . . then . . .*; the rhetoric both gives shape to the lyrics and helps to point the contrast.

The entrance of Marcade with his news of the King of France's death provides the catalyst which forces *Love's Labour's Lost* to come to terms with real life. This does not happen – or not nearly so demonstrably – in a play which might be thought to be somewhat similar, *The Two Gentlemen of Verona*. Already Launce is capable of criticising the fashionable Petrarchan attitude to love:

> Why, man, if the river were dry, I am able to fill it with my tears.
> If the wind were down, I could drive the boat with my sighs.
> (II.iii.49–51)

There is some realisation in *The Two Gentlemen of Verona* that "words may substitute for or falsify experience",[15] but the devices which might force a dramatic confrontation of viewpoints remain undeveloped. The lovers seldom meet, the outlaws and Eglamour are comic-opera figures, Launce and Speed disappear in Act IV, and Valentine is too readily satisfied with Proteus's repentance. *Love's Labour's Lost*, the most linguistically-pointed of Shakespeare's plays, testifies to the general interest the new usages had aroused, even if, as seems possible, the play was designed for the private theatre. Yet in its final refusal to divorce language from life, it cannot be just 'mere verbal promiscuity' or 'linguistically narcissistic'.[16] The extreme view of the uselessness of language – "Vows are but breath, and breath a vapour is" – comes some time before the end of the play. The play is, then, not a repudiation of language, even of elaborate language which will take its proper place in the development of Shakespeare's stylistic repertoire, but an early refusal to "draw out the thread of their verbosity finer than the staple of their argument".

CREATING A STYLE

In his middle and later plays, Shakespeare begins to *use* Latinisms, copious diction and even compounds as indicators of particular styles. This will be illustrated more fully in the later chapters of this book which attempt to characterise those styles. But meanwhile we can glance at some individual effects which do not seem to reverberate beyond their particular play. *All's Well* is a muted play linguistically. There are no set pieces in the manner of Claudio on death in the contemporary *Measure for Measure*. The King does not dominate sufficiently; Bertram is brave but hardly heroic; Parolles is fool and coward, not villain. It is Parolles (a man of words, as his name suggests) who comes closest to possessing a manner of his own, but even in his case what is notable is what is said about him rather than what he says himself. Bertram does not really see through Parolles until the business of the drum, when he is revealed as "your devoted friend, sir, the manifold linguist and the armipotent soldier" (IV.iii.230). Lafew does, and already at II.v.43 recognises that "The soul of this man is his clothes". Later he informs the Countess:

> No, no, no, your son was misled with a snipped-taffeta fellow there, whose villainous saffron would have made all the unbaked and doughy youth of a nation in his colour. Your daughter-in-law had been alive at this hour, and your son here at home, more advanced by the King than by that red-tailed humble-bee I speak of.[17]
>
> (IV.v.1–6)

Parolles himself says that the French lords "wear themselves in the *cap* of the time". If these metaphors of language and clothes visualise Parolles as something of a later Armado, he is certainly not caricatured to that extent.

For some reason, the prefix *un–* seems to have been a favourite of Shakespeare's and several of his examples are the earliest recorded in *OED*. *Hamlet* is full of instances: *unaneled, unbated, uncharge, uneffectual, unfellowed, unfortified, ungartered, unhand, unhouseled, unimproved, unknowing, unmastered, unnerved, unpeg, unpolluted, unprevailing, unproportioned, unreclaimed, unrighteous, unshaped, unsifted, unsinewed, unsmirched, unwrung* are all unique, whereas *unforced, ungalled, unkennel, unschooled* and *unyoke* occur on one other occasion only. *Un–* was, in any case, increasing in use in the Tudor period, often as a translation of *in–* in French or Italian loan-words. However, *un–* is seldom prefixed to nouns (*untruth, unrest*) or to adverbs (*unawares*). In an interesting examination of the use of *un–* in *King Lear*,[18] it emerges that Lear uses the prefix quite often up to the end of III.iv. He gives away his kingdom to his daughters "while we/*Unburdened* crawl toward death" (I.i.41). Cordelia is to him *untender* (I.i.106) and *unfriended* (I.i.203). He threatens Goneril with "Th'*untented* woundings of a father's curse", i.e. too deep to be probed. Not all *un–* words are Lear's – Gloucester and Kent provide other examples – although some are spoken of him: the Gentleman describes him as running *unbonneted* through the storm (III.i.14) and Kent says that "His wits begin t'*unsettle*" (III.iv.155). Clearly these unusual epithets are a reflection of Lear's distortion of reality. Later uses of *un–* are both fewer in number and their novelty now represents his increasing perception. *Accommodated* was evidently a new word which Bardolph only half understands and Shallow admires (*2 Hen IV* III.ii.65–80), but to Lear Poor Tom is *unaccommodated* man (III.iv.103). Cordelia finally refers to his *untuned* and jarring senses (IV, vii, 16).

The whole of *Troilus and Cressida* is permeated with Latinate diction and with compounds. In this play of the breakdown of love amidst the posturings of two war-weary armies, it is not surprising that many of the compounds (especially those of Thersites) are pejorative, even insulting. But the amount of obviously Latinate diction and the apparently unusual nature of much of it are strange in a play of this date (? 1601). *Corrivaled, attributive, appertainments, assubjugate, abruption, calumniate, commixtion, deceptious, constringed* (closer to the Latin than the French-derived *constrained*), *insisture, monstruosity, maculation, multipotent, mirable, protractive, primogenity, oppugnancy, propugnation, refractory, unplausive, uncomprehensive, subduements* are unique within the Shakespeare canon, and rare elsewhere according to *OED*. One or two other words, such as *deracinate, medicinable, unrespective, prenominate* and *recordation*, each occur only once more in Shakespeare, although it is fair to point out that in a few instances the existence of other words from the same root – *corrival, monstrous, transport* – might make recognition easier. Ulysses amongst the Greeks and Hector on the Trojan side seem especially prone to Latinisms, but Agamemnon and Nestor too have been accused of 'verbal flatulence'.[19] Ulysses' famous 'degree' speech in Act I, scene iii, is full of all the marks of the high style: lists at lines 86–8, 96–9, 103–7; the conversion *vizarded* (83); the images of the hive, the untuned instrument, the wolf and the fever. And yet the gist of the speech is easily understood. Ulysses often uses formal metaphorical language to clothe quite simple ideas. Hector, too, is not one to use a straightforward word where a more impressive one will suffice:

> The obligation of our blood forbids
> A gory emulation 'twixt us twain.
> Were thy commixtion Greek and Troyan . . .
>
> (IV.v.121–3)

The play seems full of "words, words, mere words, no matter from the heart" (V.iii.107) and the idiom of the characters is insufficiently distinctive.[20]

Perhaps part of the explanation of the unusual amount of Latinate diction in *Troilus and Cressida* lies in its curious textual history. Permission was granted to James Roberts to print the play in 1603 (when it had evidently been acted by the King's Men), but apparently it did not appear in print until the 1609 quarto, the new printers of

which claim that it was "neuer stal'd with the Stage, neuer clapper-
clawd with the palmes of the vulgar". One suggestion is that the play
was performed before a sophisticated and cynical audience at one of
the Inns of Court. That may have been so – such an audience might
certainly respond to the play's Latinate diction – but it is unlikely
that the play was *composed* with such an audience in mind. Perhaps
it had not been any too successful on the public stage. The epistle to
the 1609 quarto calls the play a comedy, but its title page calls it a
history and it appears in the section of the First Folio containing the
tragedies. Either the Elizabethan terminology for describing genres
was unbelievably lax (Polonius, at least, knew several sub-divisions)
or else, then as now, the play presented its problems.

After *Troilus and Cressida*, copious language, where it occurs at
all, is hardly ever for mere augmentation but usually for dramatic
contrast (as we shall see in *Lear* and *Othello*). It is rare indeed in
Shakespeare to find words like Tourneur's *insculption* ('inscription')
and *circumvolved* ('enveloped') occurring for no apparent reason. Even
in Tourneur, the Latinate diction is sometimes deliberate, part of the
verbose Puritan jargon of Languebeau Snuffe:

> Sir, I want words and protestation to insinuate into your credit,
> but in plainness and truth, I will qualify her grief with the spirit of
> consolation.
>
> (Atheist's Tragedy I.ii.143–5)

All's Well, for example, yields only *prejudicates*, *captious* and *intenable*,
facinerious and *consolate* by way of Latinisms, and the *-ate* suffix
probably appears more unusual to us than it did to the Elizabethans.
When uncommon words appear in the tragedies and after, the
play sometimes slows down to let us savour them, perceive their
significance in that particular context:

> And what was he?
> Forsooth, a great arithmetician.
>
> (Oth I.i.18–19)

where the preceding short line prepares us for *arithmetician* and Iago's
contempt for the theorist Cassio, or:

> If it were done when 'tis done, then 'twere well
> It were done quickly. If the assassination
> Could trammel up the consequence, and catch
> With his surcease, success . . .
>
> (Mac I.vii.1–4)

where *it* is revealed in all its enormity, *assassination*. Both *arithmetician*
and *assassination* occur only here in Shakespeare.

As the discussion of individual plays later in this book should make clear, Shakespeare's progress with vocabulary reflects an increasing discrimination: not to use Latinisms, doublets or poetic compounds simply because they were fashionable or expected of an Elizabethan dramatist, but, by letting them stand out from the surrounding words, to allow them to make their own point as determiners of an appropriate style.

Notes and References

1. Bradbrook (1951), p. 83.
2. Marlowe is quoted from *Complete Plays and Poems*, ed. E. D. Pendry (1976).
3. *Discoveries, Works*, eds C. H. Herford and P. and E. M. Simpson (1947), VIII, p. 587.
4. Peet (1959). Compare Middleton, *The Roaring Girl*, 1611, Introduction: "your huge bombasted plays quilted with mighty words to lean purpose". Quoted Jardine (1983), p. 159.
5. Text in Bullough (1957), I, pp. 284–363.
6. Marlowe's *Hero and Leander*, Lodge's *Scylla's Metamorphosis* and Drayton's *Endymion and Phoebe* are in *Elizabethan Verse Romances*, ed. M. M. Reese (1968). For the lexis and syntax of Shakespeare's poems, see Partridge (1971).
7. Burton (1981), p. 82.
8. For *Poetaster*, see *Works* IV and King (1941). Compare *Discoveries*: "Wheresoever, manners, and fashions are corrupted, Language is. It imitates the publicke riot. The excesse of Feasts and apparell, are the notes of a sick State, and the wantonness of language, of a sick mind.", *Works*, VIII, p. 593.
9. *Fire-new* is first recorded in *Richard III* and *Love's Labour's Lost*, i.e. in the early 1590s. Compare *Twelfth Night*, III.ii.20, "Some excellent jests, fire-new from the mint".
10. In the New Penguin edition (1982), Kerrigan spells the name *Mote*, meaning 'particle' (he *is* diminutive) and argues (pp. 160–1) that English *mote* and French *mot*, 'word' (he *does* answer his master back) may both have been pronounced *mott* in Elizabethan English. Wells and Taylor also write *Mote* in the Oxford Complete Shakespeare. Hibbard, in the single-volume Oxford edition (1990, pp. 245–6) is not so sure and sees the page as insect-like; he therefore returns to *Moth*.
11. *Directions for Speech and Style*, ed. H. H. Hudson (Princeton, 1935), pp. 24–5.
12. Kerrigan, New Penguin edition, note to V.ii.711
13. Donawerth (1984), p. 155. Compare Newman (1985), p. 87.
14. Carroll (1976), pp. 176–82. For remarks on the concluding lyrics I am indebted to Heniger (1974).
15. Ewbank (1972), p. 40.

16. Respectively Calderwood (1965) and Matthews (1964); it is fair to add that this is not the conclusion to Calderwood's article. See also Anderson (1971).
17. "Saffron was used as a starch at the time, hence the link with the clothes of Parolles; it was also used to colour pastry, hence the unbaked and doughy youth of line 3" (New Penguin edition (1970) p. 205).
18. Roberts (1978).
19. MacAlindon (1969) and Thomson (1976).
20. Greene (1981).

CHAPTER FOUR
The new syntax

RHETORIC

Hitherto I have concentrated on vocabulary which is the most obvious and most easily accessible of linguistic features. I have been especially concerned with the Elizabethan expansion of the lexicon by borrowings, chiefly from Latin; the recognition and use of some of the more recent of these borrowings, both singly and in groups; and the suggestion that excessive borrowing might be limited by the development of alternative lexical strategies such as word-formation and archaisms. It is time now to turn to wider matters of clause and sentence, to the Elizabethan achievement of a variety of syntactic styles in English, and to Shakespeare's selection from these for different artistic purposes. To appreciate this we must first turn aside to examine the function of rhetoric.[1]

In classical times, and up to the Renaissance and even later, the word *rhetoric* did not carry its modern, frequently pejorative sense of 'bombast', 'mere hollow words', but meant the art of persuasion. One of its most influential Roman exponents was Cicero, who was an advocate, a calling in which it is naturally important to persuade an audience of the justice of your case. But the argument should be not only convincing but attractive; formality and elegance invite the listener to accept what he is being told without submitting it to the more rigorous tests of logic and reason. Knowledge of the detail of rhetoric passed to the Middle Ages largely through Cicero and through a book wrongly attributed to him, *De Rhetorica ad Herennium* (c. 80 BC). By medieval times, rhetoric was found not only in courts but also in preaching and literature, two other fields in which eloquence was important, and it formed part of the introductory liberal arts course in medieval universities, the Trivium, which consisted of grammar, logic and rhetoric. Several textbooks (in Latin) illustrated the application of rhetoric to literature by numerous examples which were usually taken from classical writers but occasionally from medieval authors too. One such book, the *Nova Poetria* by Geoffrey de Vinsauf (c. 1200), Chaucer certainly knew of, since he mentions it in *The Nun's Priest's Tale*. And of course numerous examples of the figures of speech (*figurae* or *colores*) which were so important in literature could be found in medieval works also.

The practice of rhetoric, as medieval and renaissance writers conceived it, derived from the concept of *decorum*, that different styles are suitable for different subjects: "the word must be the cousin to the deed", as Chaucer expresses it. But not only was the kind of subject–matter important, so were the intended audience and the literary kind in which the author chose to write, such as tragedy, pastoral or sermon, since the genre chosen would bring its own expectations of the kind of language employed. This has been argued all over again in books on modern stylistics, although there the terminology is different. The middle ages often spoke of the 'high', 'middle' and 'low' styles; these are the most common terms, but the high style, for instance, may be called 'elevated', 'grand' or 'ornate', and the 'low' style is often spoken of as 'plain'. The full range of figures or colours was reserved for the high style of (say) epic or tragedy. Geoffrey de Vinsauf had already suggested that the three levels of style might be applied to the three classes of society: aristocratic, middle and plebeian respectively. Kings must talk like kings and peasants like peasants. Puttenham, in 1589, still defines the three levels partly by the kind of literature involved and partly by the sort of characters it deals with. This will often work: Chaucer's Troilus or Shakespeare's Henry V will use the high style for much of the time. But it is not invariable: Chaucer's Miller does not tell the whole of his tale in the low style which the description of him in the *General Prologue* might lead us to expect.

The rhetorical text-books, however, seldom discuss genres like epic or tragedy, nor do they greatly concern themselves with ideas like character or plot which interest modern critics. Typically they consider their subject under five headings:

1. *Inventio* (conception): finding what to say – material may have to be assembled from different sources – and consideration of the

subject under several headings (called 'topics' or 'places').

2. *Dispositio* (arrangement): the general planning and ordering of the material. Beginnings were thought to be especially important, and an idea of the whole plan is often given near the beginning of a medieval story or an Elizabethan sermon.

3. *Elocutio* (phrasing): often the longest section of the textbook. Here the ornaments of style are listed and illustrated (64 of them in the *Rhetorica ad Herennium*). Sometimes these figures or colours are said to be of two kinds. *Tropes* (literally 'turns') involve a change of meaning from that which the word usually has, as in metaphor, hyperbole, pun, irony or allegory (in the latter the word has an additional 'covered' or 'secret' meaning). *Schemes* organise the thought rather than the individual words, e.g. antithesis, or the periodic sentence in Elizabethan writers. The words are employed in their literal sense but are arranged in an unusual or artificial way.

4. *Memoria* (memorising): concerned with tricks to improve the memory.

5. *Pronunciatio* (delivery): such things as modulation of the voice, facial expression, gesture.

Of these, sections 4 and 5 were often brief, although they are important in such periods as the middle ages, where oral delivery was more common than silent reading, and as time went on rhetoric became more and more concerned with section 3, the ornaments of style. These devices are particularly used for elaboration and illustration, for amplification was much more attractive than contraction – another aspect of copiousness in Renaissance literature. Some of these ornaments are common enough today (metaphor, antithesis) or are obvious to us as we read earlier literature (*descriptio*, description of persons or places; *digressio*, deliberately introduced digression), but many need to be explained since they are much less familiar now. In the textbooks, most of them have Latin or Greek names reflecting their origin, although Puttenham gives alternative English nomenclature, sometimes rather amusing, as when he speaks of hyperbole as "the Ouer-reacher, otherwise called the loud lyer". Here is a list of the more common ones in Elizabethan literature which may not be immediately recognisable from their titles; alternative names are given in parentheses:

adnominatio (traductio, paronomasia): repetition of the same word in a different form, e.g. similar words formed from the same root or the same word used in different senses.

anaphora (repetitio): repetition of the same word(s) at the beginning of successive clauses or of lines of poetry.

apostrophe (exclamatio): highly-charged emotional comment, frequently shown in successive lines beginning with 'O' or 'Alas!'

epistrophe: the same word ending successive clauses (the opposite of anaphora).

gradatio (climax): the final word(s) of one clause repeated at the beginning of the following clause, thereby advancing the argument since the second use will usually add extra detail or qualification.

isocolon: balance of two clauses of equal length.

parison: balance of two clauses of corresponding syntactic structure (isocolon and parison are often found together).

paromoion: deliberate patterning of sounds within the clause.

ploce: repetition of the same word or phrase, sometimes after the intervention of one or two other words.

stichomythia: a form of dialogue in which single lines are uttered by alternate speakers.

zeugma: using the same verb with two very different objects (as Pope's society lady may "stain her honour or her new brocade").

I have omitted from this list those figures which we would easily recognise today, such as antithesis or periphrasis, nor have I thought it necessary to distinguish the various types of pun, for example. I have not included either figures such as *occupatio* (mentioning something or somebody under cover of a pretended omission: 'Time would fail to speak of A and B and C'), *effictio* (description of outward appearance as opposed to moral worth), or *litotes* (understatement, frequently by negatives, 'He's no fool'), which seem to be more germane to the appreciation of medieval than Elizabethan literature. What is important is that the rhetorical figures provided writers with a ready-made means of organising material, especially passages of some emotional heightening which needed, as Puttenham said, to be distinguished from our ordinary talk. Jonson takes the same view: ". . . talking and Eloquence are not the same: to speake and to speake well are two things".[2] Because these figures were widely recognised – had indeed often been learned at school in handbooks which combined definitions with some of the charm of an anthology – the audience was left free to concentrate on their use as a means of characterisation or of deliberate embellishment. Their very familiarity, far from restricting the author, enabled him to emphasise what he felt to be important.

I have already referred to some of the best-known Elizabethan works of rhetoric, such as those by Puttenham and Wilson. Wilson, incidentally, constantly envisages a court with judges who have to be persuaded of the truth of a particular case, and we are reminded of the rise of rhetoric in classical trials. Another and generally a more entertaining book of rhetoric is John Hoskins's *Directions for Speech and Style* (probably 1599).[3] Hoskins, both lawyer and man of letters, was a friend of Jonson (whose *Discoveries* incorporated passages from the *Directions*), Raleigh (for a time a fellow-prisoner in the Tower), Donne, Daniel and probably Sidney whose *Arcadia* he greatly admires and frequently quotes from. The book is addressed to a young man whose father was a friend of Hoskins, and its aim is to improve not only the pupil's writing but also his public speaking and conversation. Anaphora, for instance, "beats upon one thing to cause the quicker feeling in the audience, and to awake a sleepy or dull person". Hoskins, like other Elizabethan rhetoricians, lists and illustrates the figures of rhetoric and, like them, is in no doubt that "to amplify and illustrate are two the chieftest ornaments of eloquence". The Preface sees rhetoric as the hallmark not only of the speaker himself but even of his subject-matter:

> Careless speech doth not only discredit the personage of the speaker but it doth discredit the opinion of his reason and judgment, it discrediteth the truth, force, and uniformity of the matter and substance.

Each of the three kinds of style, high, middle and low, has its appropriate 'vice' or exaggeration which may produce verbal flatulence or slackness. It was just as possible for the Elizabethans as it is for us to distinguish between artifice and plain words. Cordelia says that she lacks "that glib and oily art/To speak and purpose not" by means of which Goneril and Regan have falsely professed their love for Lear. The historian Holinshed, seeking to write in the plain (or low) style suitable for conveying information, states that "My speech is plaine, without any rhetoricall show of eloquence, having rather a regard to simple truth than to decking words".[4] Herbert uses this same term, *decking*:

> When first my lines of heav'nly joyes made mention,
> Such was their lustre, they did so excell,
> That I sought out quaint words, and trim invention;
> My thoughts began to burnish, sprout, and swell,
> Curling with metaphors a plain intention,
> Decking the sense, as if it were to sell.
>
> (*Jordan* 2)

He also employs the technical word *invention* and naturally thinks of elaboration ("burnish, sprout, and swell") as the mark of an obviously rhetorical style. *Painted* is another word often used in the Renaissance to describe this false rhetoric. Harrison (1534–93) says that he has tried in his *Description of England* "truly and plainly to set forth such things as I minded to entreat of, rather than with vain affectation of eloquence to paint out a rotten sepulchre".[5] Compare Shakespeare's Sonnet 82:

> And do so, love; yet when they have devised
> What strained touches rhetoric can lend,
> Thou, truly fair, wert truly sympathized
> In *true plain words* by thy true-telling friend:
>> And their *gross painting* might be better used
>> Where cheeks need blood; in thee it is abused.

In an age far less hygienic than our own, women's faces were painted to hide dirt or disease as well as to emphasise beauty, "Fairing the foul with art's false borrowed face", as Sonnet 127 expresses it. Morally, painting may be equated with sin, as in revenge tragedy or in Harrison's "rotten sepulchre". When Bacon, in *The Advancement of Learning* (1605), seems to be advocating less rhetoric, his argument is that the figures of speech have too often submerged the subject-matter: the balance of decorum had been destroyed. Although by the mid-late seventeenth century fewer works are obviously and consistently rhetorical, we still employ rhetoric today ('You could have heard a pin drop.' 'She has hundreds of dresses.').

If rhetoric, even where correctly employed in earlier literature, seems to us to overvalue the synthetic as opposed to the creative talent, to imply that writers can be made rather than be born, and to presuppose a separation of form and content, we should remember that some intellectual pleasure was presumably derived from the mere recognition of the figures and that, when Shakespeare began to write, his audience was accustomed to narrative and dramatic verse which deliberately and ostentatiously employed rhetorical artifice. In his own early plays, Shakespeare can sometime disappoint because he does not seem to us to have achieved the correct balance between style and subject-matter. The surface brilliance seems to obtrude and to detract from, rather than to inform, the emotions the passage is trying to convey. But separation of language from content, which seems unnatural to us, was something the rhetorical textbooks must have encouraged. A familiar metaphor in the Renaissance is that of language as a garment which can be put on: different styles can be applied to the same material.

And Elizabethan theories of composition were not ours. The plain style was not then considered especially virtuous: it was simply one amongst several possible styles. And, to go further, prose was not thought of as inferior to poetry but simply different. The work of prose-writers like Sidney, Hooker or Raleigh could contain easily as much rhetoric as poetry. A considerable writer, whether in poetry or prose, will learn to use his rhetorical devices for deliberate effect and will not simply show them off. Consequently, more than one of the three styles will appear in the same work. The high style often generalises, with a pronounced tendency towards the abstract and the static: humanity rather than the individual is its main concern. The middle style (which often uses the first person) is more persuasive and analytical, but it is essentially a polite style in which a reader is expected to share the writer's ideas of what is socially or artistically important. The plain (or low) style explains or describes, sometimes denigrates, but with a simplicity of lexis and syntax suitable to its often pragmatic approach.[6] Shakespeare will often write impressive rhetorical passages either because the subject under discussion at that moment demands them (e.g. the heightened language used for affairs of state) or as an indication of how we are to react to a particular character (an obvious instance would be the ridiculously inflated style of Osric which Hamlet parodies). Or there may be a deliberate breach of decorum where the style is clearly inappropriate to the subject, often to make a criticism of social behaviour.

Of those writers before Shakespeare who had been most notable for the balance and refinement of their style, the two most important are probably Lyly and Sidney. Lyly's *Euphues* (1578) is a tale of a student who leaves learning for the more attractive and glittering life of Naples. The hero (whose name means 'gentleman') acquires a close friend whom he betrays when he falls in love with the friend's intended wife; the girl, however, jilts Euphues who repents of his frivolous life and vows to return to study. The plot – if one can call it that – is, though, simply a peg upon which to hang a series of set speeches full of rhetorical embellishment, examples from natural history and knowledge culled from classical writers. There are few obvious Latin loans and the fewer doublets used are unremarkable, but the decoration and balance of the style can be illustrated from almost any page:

Too much studie doth intoxicate their braynes, for (saye they) althoughe yron, the more it is vsed the brighter it is, yet siluer with much wearing doth wast to nothing, though the Cammocke, the more it is bowed the better it serueth, yet the bow, the more it is bent & occupied the weaker it waxeth, though the Camomill, the more it is trodden and pressed downe, the more it spreadeth, yet the violet the oftner it is handled and touched, the sooner it withereth and decayeth. Besides thys, a fine wytte, a sharp sence, a quicke vnderstanding, is able to atteine to more in a moment or a very little space, then a dull and blockish heade in a month; the sithe cutteth farre better and smoother then the sawe, the waxe yeeldeth better and sooner to the seale, than the steele to the stampe or hammer, the smooth & plaine Beeche is easier to be carued and occupyed then the knotty Boxe. For neyther is ther any thing, but yt hath his contraries: Such is the Nature of these nouises that thincke to have learning without labour, and treasure without trauayle, eyther not vnderstanding or els not remembring, that the finest edge is made with the blunt whetstone, and the fairest Iewell fashioned with the harde hammer.

For as the Bee that gathereth Honny out of the weede, when she espyeth the faire flower flyeth to the sweetest: or as the kynde spanyell though he hunt after Byrdes, yet forsakes them to retryue the Partridge: or as we commonly feede on beefe hungerly at the first, yet seing the Quayle more dayntie, chaunge our dyet: So I, although I loued *Philautus* for his good properties, yet seing *Euphues* to excell him, I ought by Nature to lyke him better: By so muche the more therefore my change is to be excused, by how much the more my choyce is excellent: and by so much the lesse I am to be condemned, by how much the more *Euphues* is to be commended. Is not the Dyamonde of more valewe than the Rubie, because he is of more vertue? Is not the Emeraulde preferred before the Saphyre for his wonderfull propertie? Is not *Euphues* more prayse worthy than *Philautus* being more wittie?[7]

It must be one of the easiest styles to parody, as Falstaff does in a well-known passage from *1 Henry IV*, adapting an illustration from the first of our two extracts:

> For though the camomile, the more it is trodden on the faster it grows, yet youth, the more it is wasted the sooner it wears.
>
> (II.iv.393–5)

Earlier he uses the same style, although he concludes his intricately-balanced sentence with two puns of his own (*countenance*: 'face' and 'protection' and *steal*: 'move silently' and 'rob'):

> Marry then, sweet wag, when thou art King let not us that are squires of the night's body be called thieves of the day's beauty. Let us be Diana's foresters, gentlemen of the shade, minions of the moon. And let men say we be men of good government, being governed as the sea is, by our noble and chaste mistress the moon, under whose countenance we steal.
>
> (*1 Hen IV* I.ii.23–9)

Shakespeare's debt to Lyly, however, lay far less in parody than in the realisation that balance and precision (especially in prose) can be made a staple of comic wit and intrigue. For Lyly also wrote plays (in the second quotation Falstaff intends his audience to recall *Endimion*) and whilst his drama still has occasional comparisons from natural history, they are not nearly so numerous or so obvious as in *Euphues*, so that the attention is directed even more towards the construction of the speeches:

> A heate full of coldnesse, a sweet full of bitternesse, a paine full of pleasantnesse; which maketh thoughts haue eyes and harts eares; bred by desire, nursed by delight, weaned by ielousie, kild by dissembling, buried by ingratitude; and this is loue! Fayre Lady, wil you any?
>
> (Gallathea I.ii.16–20)

> Who would haue thought that *Tellus*, being so fayre by nature, so honourable by byrth, so wise by education, would haue entered into a mischiefe to the Gods so odious, to men so detestable, and to her freend so malicious?
>
> (Endimion V.iii.1–3)

Lyly's plays also included a number of clever, prattling boys, not surprisingly since they were chiefly acted by the children's companies. Their speech, too, is pointed and balanced, but it is wit rather than humour. It is influenced by the tradition of the clever servant, frequently a slave, in classical comedy, and it shows itself in the patter of Mote in *Love's Labour's Lost* or the Dromios in *The Comedy of Errors*.

SHAKESPEARE AND RHETORIC

As we might expect, it is in his comedies that Shakespeare most realises the advantages of the kind of mannered rhetoric Lyly had practised. *Love's Labour's Lost* has already been discussed in terms of his perception of the significant features of the expanding vocabulary. Its syntax is almost equally dependent on contemporary fashions. The delight in punning and in elaborately patterned language generally is the hallmark of the opposing quartets, the men from Navarre and the ladies from France. Shakespeare improves on Lyly's elegance, but the subject of comedy is still courtship. Although there is occasional copious lexis:

> About surrender up of Aquitaine
> To her decrepit, sick, and bed-rid father.
>
> (I.i.136–7)

> He made her melancholy, sad, and heavy;
> And so she died. Had she been light, like you,
> Of such a merry, nimble, stirring spirit,
> She might ha' been a grandam ere she died.
>
> (V.ii.14–17)

the complexity in this play is as much a matter of syntax, as perhaps seeming more appropriate for aristocrats: every fool can play upon the *word*. Their intricate style is often very like that of contemporary sonnets, and Shakespeare was almost certainly writing his own sonnets at this time:

> Why, all his behaviours did make their retire
> To the court of his eye, peeping through desire.
> His heart, like an agate with your print impressed,
> Proud with his form, in his eye pride expressed.
> His tongue, all impatient to speak and not see,
> Did stumble with haste in his eyesight to be;
> All senses to that sense did make their repair,
> To feel only looking on fairest of fair.
> Methought all his senses were locked in his eye,
> As jewels in crystal for some prince to buy;
> Who, tend'ring their own worth from where they were glassed,
> Did point you to buy them, along as you passed.
> His face's own margent did quote such amazes
> That all eyes saw his eyes enchanted with gazes.

> (II.i.234–47)

The positioning of *behaviours, court of his eye, heart, tongue, All senses, His face*, all near the beginning of the line, assists us to make our way through this elaborate speech by Boyet, the attendant lord on the Princess and her ladies – only a moment before he had spoken of *the heart's still rhetoric* – but the amount of the imagery and the subordination in the syntax make it rather difficult going. In an earlier speech by Berowne, one pun leads to another:

> Why, all delights are vain, but that most vain
> Which, with pain purchased, doth inherit pain:
> As, painfully to pore upon a book,
> To seek the light of truth, while truth the while
> Doth falsely blind the eyesight of his look.
> Light seeking light doth light of light beguile;
> So, ere you find where light in darkness lies,
> Your light grows dark by losing of your eyes.
> Study me how to please the eye indeed
> By fixing it upon a fairer eye,
> Who dazzling so, that eye shall be his heed
> And give him light that it was blinded by.

> (I.i.72–83)

Pain is both agony and difficulty; *light* both illumination (truth) and brightness; the verb *blind*, similarly, is literally to deprive of eyesight and metaphorically to conceal the truth. After she has listened to a later exchange of this kind between two of her own ladies, Rosaline and Katharine, the comment of the Princess is:

Well bandied both! A set of wit well played.

(V.ii.29)

Tennis, we recall, was a favourite Elizabethan game, and in *Henry V* the Dauphin sends Henry a set of tennis balls. A similar comment by Silvia (*Two Gentlemen of Verona* II.iv.32): "A fine volley of words, gentlemen, and quickly shot off," and Portia's reply to Nerissa: "Good sentences, and well pronounced" (*Merchant of Venice* I.ii.10) indicate by their mocking tone that already Shakespeare was using this elaborately-patterned syntax for deliberate exaggeration.

The style of *As You Like It*, a play with several resemblances to *Love's Labour's Lost*, such as its multiple wooings and a preference for conversation over action, has less of such polished symmetry than one might expect from its source, the euphuistic prose romance, Lodge's *Rosalynde*. But Shakespeare's Arden is more of a real forest than the usual pastoral idyll of euphuism. Perhaps Orlando comes closest to the euphuistic vogue:

> I beseech you, punish me not with your hard thoughts, wherein I
> confess me much guilty to deny so fair and excellent ladies anything.
> But let your fair eyes and gentle wishes go with me to my trial:
> wherein if I be foiled, there is but one shamed that was never gracious;
> if killed, but one dead that is willing to be so. I shall do my friends
> no wrong, for I have none to lament me; the world no injury, for in it
> I have nothing: only in the world I fill up a place which may be better
> supplied when I have made it empty.

(I.ii.171–80)

Even so, Orlando talks less than the heroes of Shakespeare's other comedies. Brilliance of language is becoming less important for its own sake and more important as an indication of character.[8]

In *Much Ado About Nothing*, on the other hand, as C. A. Owen says, "Beatrice and Benedick pursue a journey into self-knowledge without the help of supernatural agents, of a Forest of Arden, or of sexual disguise."[9] Benedick, though, becomes a changed man following his gulling by Don Pedro and the others. In his first soliloquy he is "full of confidence in his ability to keep the world at a proper distance for witty observation"; one hundred lines later "love has released him from the tyranny of elaborate syntax", although he salves his conscience with a neat double antithesis ("When I said I would die a bachelor, I did not think I should live till I were married"). By this stage of his career Shakespeare is using euphuism as one possible dramatic style which can be rejected when the plot demands it. This, then, is the early Benedick:

> May I be so converted and see with these eyes? I cannot tell; I think

not. I will not be sworn but love may transform me to an oyster; but
I'll take my oath on it, till he have made an oyster of me, he shall never
make me such a fool. One woman is fair, yet I am well: another is
wise, yet I am well; another virtuous, yet I am well; but till all graces
be in one woman, one woman shall not come in my grace. Rich she
shall be, that's certain; wise, or I'll none; virtuous, or I'll never cheapen
her; fair, or I'll never look on her; mild, or come not near me; noble,
or not I for an angel; of good discourse, an excellent musician, and her
hair shall be of what colour it please God.

(II.iii.21–33)

The balance ("One woman . . . my grace"), the punning (*noble/angel*),
the final throwaway phrase which nevertheless, since it is a little
longer than its predecessors, elegantly rounds off the speech – all
these imply a cleverness and self-satisfaction which is asking to be
given a cold douche of reality. Beatrice's early style is less obviously
symmetrical than Benedick's, for the lady is usually allowed to be less
dogmatic and inflexible so that she may eventually yield gracefully.
Her advice to Hero is, at first sight, euphuistic:

For hear me, Hero: wooing, wedding, and repenting, is as a Scotch jig,
a measure, and a cinquepace: the first suit is hot and hasty, like a Scotch
jig, and full as fantastical; the wedding, mannerly-modest, as a measure,
full of state and ancientry; and then comes repentance and, with his
bad legs, falls into the cinquepace faster and faster, till he sink into his
grave.

Yet *the first suit . . . the wedding . . . repentance* do not form the exact
parallel (*first . . . second . . . third*) that the schematic rhetoric of true
euphuism might have produced.

Euphuism has been aptly characterised as 'verbal pirouetting'.
Certainly it often has an air of artificiality, if not of superficiality,
and in the later 1580s it lost favour to Sidney's Arcadianism. *Arcadia*
was published in 1590 although composed some time before; a fuller
version was printed in 1593. It is a prose romance, and the complexity
of its adventures is matched by an equally complex style: its prose
requires time for proper appreciation. In his dedication Sidney calls
it an "idle work" and "a trifle, triflingly handled", although clearly
he hoped for the admiration of his audience. Lyly's prose elaborates,
frequently by describing the same subject in different parallel phrases;
Sidney's is much more varied because it almost always contains more
subordination. It is still, however, subject to rigorous control. His
model is Cicero, but Elizabethan English simply did not contain the
number of grammatical devices by which Latin signifies agreement.
Sidney therefore needs a good deal of linguistic signposting, and it is
a tribute to him that we (and his contemporaries) can find our way

through a long and complex sentence – in which the main verb, in true Ciceronian fashion, is often held back to the end – without losing the thread of his argument. Consider this passage from *Arcadia*:

> And therefore, *where* most princes, seduced by flattery to build upon false grounds of government, make themselves, as it were, another thing from the people, and so count it gain what they can get from them and, as if it were two counter-balances, that their estate goes highest when the people goes lowest, by a fallacy of argument thinking themselves most kings when the subject is most basely subjected; *he, contrariwise,* virtuously and wisely acknowledging that he with his people made all but one politic body whereof himself was the head, even so cared for them as he would for his own limbs; never restraining their liberty without it stretched to licentiousness nor pulling from them their goods which they found were not employed to the purchase of a greater good; but, in all his actions showing a delight in their welfare, brought that to pass that, while by force he took nothing, by their love he had all.[10]

It is one long sentence which pivots on the *where* and the *he contrariwise* which I have italicised (*they* did this, but *he*, contrariwise, did that). Within each half of the balance, however, there are degrees of subordination, incorporating rhetorical devices like parison and paromoion ("their estate goes highest when the people goes lowest") or, in a Chinese-box manner characteristic of Sidney, containing further pairs of pivoting correlatives (*never . . . nor . . . but*) within the larger structure. There is, in fact, a good deal of conversation in *Arcadia*, as in *Euphues*, but the speeches in both are excessively long and excessively formal, so that they seldom seem natural. A second passage from Sidney shows his achievement of variety within the same long sentence: it is this, above all, which makes him far more readable than Lyly. The extract is from the *Apology for Poetry*, 1595 (i.e. a defence, not of poetry against prose but of fiction against fact, especially against the allegedly superior claims of history and philosophy):

> The historian scarcely giveth leisure to the moralist to say so much, but that he, loaden with old mouse-eaten records, authorising himself (for the most part) upon other histories, whose greatest authorities are built upon the notable foundation of hearsay; having much ado to accord differing writers and to pick truth out of partiality; better acquainted with a thousand years ago than with the present age, and yet better knowing how this world goeth than how his own wit runneth; curious for antiquities and inquisitive of novelties; a wonder to young folks and a tyrant in table talk, denieth, in a great chafe, that any man for teaching of virtue, and virtuous actions is comparable to him.[11]

Again, this is most carefully structured. The main clause, *The historian*

. . . (he) . . . denieth . . . that any man . . . is comparable to him, spans
the sentence and is not complete until its end. Subordination begins
by participles (which in Latin would of course agree with their
antecedents but in English have to be emphasised by positioning each
at the beginning of its clause): *loaden . . . authorising . . . having . . .
acquainted . . . knowing*; but when this pattern has been established it
is varied, but not lost, by the use first of an adjective (*curious*) and then
of a noun in apposition (*a wonder*) in the same initial position in the
subordinate clause. The minor clauses themselves once more contain
lower levels of subordination ("histories, whose greatest authorities
are built upon the notable foundation of hearsay") and have their
own balance (the antithesis of "curious for antiquities and inquisitive
of novelties", with its additional invitation to speculate on the possible
difference in tone between *curious* and *inquisitive*).

With Sidney's rhetorical style in romance we might compare
Hooker's as he discusses the nature of the heavenly host. We have
considered the passage on pages 18–20 from the point of view of
lexis: its syntax is equally complex, equally copious. Similarly the
Donne passage below it, while not truly Ciceronian in style, for
Donne prefers to elaborate the same idea at paragraph length rather
than to refine and concentrate, is planned on a large scale. The first
of its two long sentences proceeds via the repeated *Let me . . . let
me . . .* to pivot on *yet if . . . if . . .* The following sentence, even
longer, with its crescendo of seven *when's*, rises to the twice-repeated
the *Almighty God himself*, the second occurrence of which introduces
the counter-balance, the *pondus gloriae*, without which *we are weighed
down* (fortissimo) *irreparably, irrevocably, irrecoverably, irremediably*.
And this was, of course, preached, in the majesty of St Paul's.
Within this single extract the rhetorical devices of subordination,
such as anaphora, antithesis, isocolon and parison, are evident, yet
the structure is looser than Sidney's and, being a sermon, contains
more redundancy. The complication arises less from Sidney's type
of complex subordination than from parallelism and repetition. For
Donne, who was painted in his funeral shroud and who preached
his last sermon on the subject of "Death's Duel", is nothing if not
dramatic and expansive.

It was easy, therefore, for Shakespeare to find examples of rhetoric
in the prose – and verse – of his contemporaries; he would have been
hard put to it to avoid them. The benefits of rhetorical structuring are,
however, more evident from early comedy than from early tragedy.
Too often the set speech of Senecan tragedy is isolated from its
surroundings. In static drama like this we miss any interaction of the

characters, and the formal parallelism of much of the style in a play like *Gorboduc* serves little purpose beyond repetition of ideas simple enough in the first place. The Epilogue of *Arden of Feversham* (a much better play) speaks of "this naked tragedy / Wherein no filed points are foisted in", as if rhetoric were a kind of top dressing. Kyd's *Spanish Tragedy* is better than this. Although dialogue is often set out in the formal, line-by-line exchange, *stichomythia*, and although rhetorical set speeches (which stylised, declamatory Elizabethan acting encouraged) are still frequent, there is a greater variation of tempo than hitherto.[12] Nevertheless, the rhetoric is easy to see:

> His men are slain, a weakening to his realm,
> His colours seiz'd, a blot unto his name,
> His son distress'd, a corsive to his heart.
>
> (I.ii.141–3)

> KING   Say, worthy prince, to whether dids't thou yield?
> BALTHAZAR   To him in courtesy, to this perforce:
>   He spake me fair, this other gave me strokes;
>   He promis'd life, this other threaten'd death;
>   He won my love, this other conquer'd me;
>   And, truth to say, I yield myself to both.
>
> (I.ii.160–5)[13]

Both passages are spoken by Balthazar who also shares with Bel-Imperia and her brother Lorenzo an example of *stichomythia* at I.iv.77–89. Lorenzo begins the exchange reasonably and plainly enough and concludes it with a plea to cease "these ambages" and use plain terms. Lorenzo's style is much more direct than Balthazar's rhetoric, and his sheer delight in villainy and the complexity of its execution are a foretaste of Iago. Yet too little of Kyd's writing strikes us as natural speech and the rhetoric obtrudes all too often.

Characters in these early plays, in fact, talk *at* one another; they seldom listen or respond, nor is there sufficient change of pace or tone. Too many moments are made into theatrical 'occasions' and conversation is infrequent. The *Henry VI* trilogy largely conforms to this pattern, although Shakespeare, by an indirect stage direction such as "Observe" or an invitation to the actor to supply his own gestures, does make some attempts to involve other characters who would otherwise be standing idle on stage. Usually, however, a character is first *described* and the general category into which he is then seen to fit is illustrated by almost all of his actions: Talbot's bravery and patriotism, Buckingham's ambition. This is still the morality tradition in which characters seldom need to reveal their nature in action. One would like to believe, with Clemen,[14] that the mention of the "silly stately style" (*1 Hen VI* IV.vii.72) is Shakespeare's recognition of such shortcomings; in fact, Joan of Arc's remark is more likely to refer to the dead Talbot's list of imposing titles.

There is a straightforward passage of *stichomythia* in *1 Henry VI* (IV.v.34–47) between Talbot who tries to persuade young John Talbot to leave the battle and his son who is determined to stay and fight, and another in *3 Henry VI* (III.ii.32–75) as Lady Grey misunderstands Edward's offer of love. In a similar but longer passage, *Richard III* I.ii.68–224, the antiphonal effect of the single-line responses is varied by two, three or four-line passages and the exchanges are occasionally even broken up into half lines. In this scene the formality of the rhetoric accentuates the outrageous nature of Richard's request to Anne that she marry him. *Stichomythia*, however, can occur in comedy as well as in tragedy. In *Love's Labour's Lost* it is more in the nature of banter, as is the repartee between Juliet and Paris (*RJ* IV.i.18–26). The first of two passages in Act I of *A Midsummer Night's Dream*, I.i.136–40, reveals the shared affection of Lysander and Hermia whose responses echo each other's love, despite parental opposition. In the second, 194–201, the figure points the contrast between the speakers, as it generally does: Helena yearns for Demetrius's love which Hermia would willingly repudiate.[15]

RHETORIC AND POETRY

Rhetoric works best when it is contained within a clearly-perceived framework such as the paragraph (in prose), the set speech or the short poem. Take Sonnet 73:

> That time of year thou mayst in me behold
> When yellow leaves, or none, or few, do hang
> Upon those boughs which shake against the cold,
> Bare ruined choirs where late the sweet birds sang.
> In me thou seest the twilight of such day
> As after sunset fadeth in the west,
> Which by and by black night doth take away,
> Death's second self, that seals up all in rest.
> In me thou seest the glowing of such fire
> That on the ashes of his youth doth lie,
> As the deathbed whereon it must expire,
> Consumed with that which it was nourished by.
>   This thou perceiv'st, which makes thy love more strong,
>   To love that well which thou must leave ere long.

The first line of each quatrain and of the concluding couplet has a similar syntactic structure (*thou mayst in me behold; In me thou seest* (twice); *This thou perceiv'st*). *What* is seen achieves a similar grammatical cohesion by the repetition of noun + of + noun (*That time of year; the twilight of such day; the glowing of such fire*). Lexical cohesion is managed by grouping words from nature in the first two quatrains (*yellow leaves, boughs, cold, birds sang, twilight, sunset, night*). In the third quatrain the prevailing metaphor of day ending is changed to that of fire consuming, and a different lexical set is therefore necessary: *glowing, fire, ashes, expire, consumed*. Kerrigan (New Penguin edition, pp. 265–6) suggests possible punning, another cohesive device. The *choirs* of line 4 are both church choirs and the *quires* (as the Quarto spells it) of books, which would go back to the *leaves* of line 2: the poet's earlier writings now seem to him barren and empty like the churches. As Death "seals up all in rest" (line 8), so the falconer *seels* or stitches up the eye of his hawk, an image that Shakespeare was to use again in *Macbeth* III.ii.46–7, "Come, seeling night / Scarf up the tender eye of pitiful day."[16]

It is most unlikely that the Sonnets, as we have them in the 1609 quarto, are in chronological order or otherwise specially arranged.[17] There is some general evidence of grouping: numbers 1–17 argue that the young man should marry and perpetuate his own virtues in his children; 1–126 seem to be addressed to this young man, 127–154 to a dark-haired woman; sonnets 40, 42 and 144 perhaps suggest an affair between the young man and the woman. But the publication of the sonnets was most probably not authorised by Shakespeare, and hence they may not have been revised for publication. Francis Meres speaks of Shakespeare's "sugared sonnets among his private friends" (*Palladis Tamia*, 1598). Many shorter Elizabethan poems are private in the sense that they were coterie poetry, meant to be shared by a small circle of friends. This may explain their frequent compactness and difficulty: their more abstruse poetic effects could be savoured at leisure and they were often not published immediately. We have to quote Donne's sonnets, both divine and secular, from the edition of 1633 (he died in 1631). Shakespeare's sonnets, although evidently written at different times, are likely to be early. Sonnet writing was a literary fashion in the 1590s and it had passed its peak by 1600. The sonnets of the 1590s, though, are frequently different in tone from Shakespeare's, "always sweet, always lachrymose, always unreal" in Patrick Crutwell's words,[18] mellifluous, but, if one reads many at a stretch, monotonous too. Their conventional diction is satirised by Shakespeare in Sonnet 130 ("My mistress' eyes are nothing like the sun").

There are indications that the sonnet form was early seen by Shakespeare as potentially leading to artificiality. The occasional sonnets in *Love's Labour's Lost* have already been mentioned. Lady Capulet describes Paris (a cardboard lover if ever there was one) in terms of a book (I.iii.82–95) and the description takes the form of a sonnet. The book image is also a *conceit*. By the later sixteenth century *conceit*, originally meaning simply 'thought', 'concept', signified a witty thought. The wit lay in the comparison of two objects which appeared to be completely unlike; by bringing together characteristics of each, the conceit uses the one to explain and analyse the other. In Lady Capulet's conceit "This precious book of love, this unbound lover" conceals his love just as a volume conceals its contents. The comparison is made continuous through the number of shared lexical items: *volume, writ, pen, content, margent* (what we would call footnotes were often written in the margin in Elizabethan books), *unbound, cover, clasps, story*. An extended comparison of this sort often involves puns. Here, for instance, *content* is both the content(s) of the book and also satisfaction: Paris is *unbound* (like the book) but also not yet bound by marriage ties. Sonnet 122 makes a somewhat similar comparison:

> Thy gift, thy tables, are within my brain
> Full charactered with lasting memory,
> Which shall above that idle rank remain
> Beyond all date, even to eternity —
> Or, at the least, so long as brain and heart
> Have faculty by nature to subsist;
> Till each to rased oblivion yield his part
> Of thee, thy record never can be missed.
> That poor retention could not so much hold,
> Nor need I tallies thy dear love to score;
> Therefore to give them from me was I bold,
> To trust those tables that receive thee more.
> > To keep an adjunct to remember thee
> > Were to import forgetfulness in me.

Tables are memorandum books (compare Hamlet and his tables) which are naturally *charactered* (written); *rank* could possibly mean 'leaves' (of a book); *rased* is our "erased"; *record, retention, tallies* prolong the image which closes with a return to the *tables* of the opening line. The concluding couplet reveals the point of the conceit: the poet needs no memento (*adjunct*) since he could never forget his beloved, and if the young man had given him the *tables* as a gift he was right to have given them away. Sonnet 80 employs the rather conventional conceit of the storm-tossed lover, as does the second quatrain of 116. Sonnet 133 achieves lexical cohesion by images of slavery, imprisonment and torture.

Berowne, we may remember, was *conceit's expositor* (*Love's Labour's Lost* II.i.72) and Boyet describes the ladies' witty repartees as *conceits*:

> The tongues of mocking wenches are as keen
> As is the razor's edge invisible,
> Cutting a smaller hair than may be seen;
> Above the sense of sense, so sensible
> Seemeth their conference. Their conceits have wings
> Fleeter than arrows, bullets, wind, thought, swifter things.
>
> (V.ii.256–61)

But a poem's success depends not only on the freshness (even the novelty) of the comparison but on whether the conceit appears merely cerebral or else emotional with the speaker passionately involved with his subject. The flaccid comparisons of Tudor poetry are often contrasted with the more complex and intense conceits of Donne who, as well as the celebrated compasses and absent lovers (*A Valediction: Forbidding Mourning*) sees souls in terms of gold leaf (the same poem), tears in terms of coins, globes and floods (*A Valediction: Of Weeping*), and lovers in terms of angler and fish (*The Bait*). The occasional unpoetical and rather bizarre images should not come as a surprise to us either. Many Elizabethan writers were not only men of letters but made a career in politics, diplomacy or the church (as eventually with Donne). Science, philosophy, religion, as well as literature, were all of interest to the cultivated society within London and outside it (in the country houses that increasingly reflected wealth and status) for which these poems were originally designed. Such poems made demands on the reader and were expected to be read more than once before they yielded up their secrets. It is no accident that the 1920s, with their credo that poetry *must* be difficult if it is to reflect the variety and complexity of modern civilisation, saw a revival of interest in metaphysical poetry.

About the turn of the century there seems to have been a vogue for unusual and witty comparisons. It can be seen in some of the essays of Bacon in the first (1597) edition: "Men fear death as children fear to go into the dark"; "Fortune is like the market, where, many times, if you can stay a little, the price will fall"; "Wives are young men's mistresses, companions for middle age, and old men's nurses". Several of the character-writers round off their essays by a paradoxical or punning sentence:

> . . . when the time, or term, of his life is going out, for Doomsday
> he is secure; for he hopes he has a trick to reverse judgement.
>
> (Earle, *An Attorney*)

The rhetorician Hoskins suggests that the comparison of "things
seeming unequal" is especially "forcible":

> But this is not so forcible an amplification . . . as when things seeming
> unequal are compared, and that in similitudes as well as examples; as
> in my speech of a widow compared to a ship, *both ask much tackling and
> sometimes rigging*. And you shall most of all profit by inventing matter
> of agreement in things most unlike, as London and a tennis court: for *in
> both all the gain goes to the hazard*.
>
> (p. 18)

Bacon himself, despite his stress on scientific observation as opposed
to received authority, can be surprisingly 'conceitful', even in his
more philosophical prose. He argued that his illustrations transformed
"conceits intellectual to images sensible", and will occasionally include
several in the same paragraph:

> For men have entered into a desire of learning and knowledge, some-
> times upon a natural curiosity and inquisitive appetite; sometimes to
> entertain their minds with variety and delight; sometimes for ornament
> and reputation; and sometimes to enable them to victory of wit and
> contradiction; and most times for lucre and profession; and seldom
> sincerely to give a true account of their gift of reason, to the benefit and
> use of men: as if there were sought in knowledge a couch whereupon
> to rest a searching and restless spirit; or a terrace for a wandering and
> variable mind to walk up and down with a fair prospect; or a tower of
> state for a proud mind to raise itself upon; or a fort or commanding
> ground for strife and contention; or a shop for profit or sale; and not
> a rich storehouse for the glory of the Creator and the relief of man's
> estate.[19]

In passages of this kind, Bacon would have considered that he
was using metaphor to illustrate and to demonstrate, and so to
comprehend – not in the least as mere decoration or elaboration.

Sometimes poets – or poetically-inclined characters in drama –
pretend to be worried at their inability to produce the expected
illustrations in sufficient number and unlikeliness for a conceit.
George Herbert spoke of his early determined search for witty
comparisons:

> When first my lines of heav'nly joyes made mention,
> Such was their lustre, they did so excell,
> That I sought out quaint words, and trim invention;
> My thoughts began to burnish, sprout and swell,
> Curling with metaphors a plain intention,

Decking the sense as if it were to sell.

(Jordan 2)

Richard II passes some of his imprisonment in devising unusual poetic correspondences:

> I have been studying how I may compare
> This prison where I live unto the world;
> And for because the world is populous,
> And here is not a creature but myself,
> I cannot do it. *Yet I'll hammer it out.*
> My brain I'll prove the female to my soul,
> My soul the father, and these two beget
> A generation of still-breeding thoughts,
> And these same thoughts people this little world,
> In humours like the people of this world.
> For no thought is contented.

(V.v.1–11)

One of the best-known sonnets (18) begins conventionally "Shall I compare thee to a summer's day?" But the next line immediately denies the validity of the comparison: "Thou art more lovely and more temperate", and the poem proceeds to explain why the conceit would be inappropriate. Most interesting of all, Shakespeare's Sonnet 76 seems to express some early dissatisfaction with his own poetry:

> Why is my verse so barren of new pride,
> So far from variation or quick change?
> Why with the time do I not glance aside
> To new-found methods and to compounds strange?
> Why write I still all one, ever the same,
> And keep invention in a noted weed,
> That every word doth almost tell my name,
> Showing their birth and where they did proceed?
> O, know, sweet love, I always write of you,
> And you and love are still my argument.
> So all my best is dressing old words new,
> Spending again what is already spent:
>   For as the sun is daily new and old,
>   So is my love still telling what is told.

Again, the puns on dress (*quick change, weed(s), dressing*) help to bind the sonnet together. Why does the poet *keep invention in a noted weed* ('go on writing in the same old style') and spend his time *dressing old words new* instead of following contemporary fashion with its *new pride* (decoration), *variation, quick change* or *compounds strange* ('compound words' or 'compound drugs', the opposite of simples, or perhaps both)? In terms of the sonnet's argument, the reason is the continually renewed freshness and satisfaction of his love, but the poem may have as much to tell us about Shakespeare's developing poetic skills. Certainly he is not above a 'metaphysical' conceit when occasion serves, as in Othello's final words:

> I kissed thee, ere I killed thee; no way but this,
> Killing myself, to die upon a kiss.

> (V.ii.354–5)

but one's impression is that occasion did not serve any too often.

What sonnet writing perhaps taught Shakespeare most was the art of cohesion within a clearly defined (fourteen line) passage. This cohesion is frequently lexical, as has been shown, but may be simply a matter of repetition of a phrase in the same metrical position, just as each quatrain of Sonnet 49 begins "Against that time . . ." or Sonnet 64 "When I have seen . . .". Sonnet 4 is rather more complex:

> Unthrifty loveliness, why dost thou spend
> Upon thyself thy beauty's legacy?
> Nature's bequest gives nothing, but doth lend,
> And being frank she lends to those are free.
> Then, beauteous niggard, why dost thou abuse
> The bounteous largess given thee to give?
> Profitless usurer, why dost thou use
> So great a sum of sums yet canst not live?
> For having traffic with thyself alone
> Thou of thyself thy sweet self does deceive;
> Then how when Nature calls thee to be gone,
> What acceptable audit canst thou leave?
> > Thy unused beauty must be tombed with thee,
> > Which, used, lives th'executor to be.

Unthrifty, spend, legacy, bequest, lend, frank . . . free (both 'generous'), *niggard, largess, usurer, sums, traffic, audit, use* ('invest' or 'use up'), *executor* form a remarkable lexical set, but there are syntactical parallels too: *why dost thou spend, why dost thou abuse, why dost thou use,* and *unthrifty loveliness, beauteous niggard, profitless usurer,* all terms of address, all adjective plus noun, all near-paradoxical. The vocabulary of the sonnets is in itself not very remarkable. There are not very many obvious loans, a few – mostly adjectival – compounds, such as *world-without-end* hour (57) and *proud-pied* April (98). Little reminds us of the idioms of speech: "My love is as fair/ *As any mother's child*"(21); "In sleep a king, but waking *no such matter*"(87); "And Death once dead, *there's no more dying then*" (146). The 'speaking voice' occurs now and then in the sonnets by Shakespeare's contemporaries, although usually in those of a later date, for example in Drayton, writing in 1619:

Since, ther's no helpe, come let us kisse and part,
Nay, I have done: You get no more of me.[20]

The formality of Shakespeare's diction in the sonnets contrasts with the colloquial opening of several Donne poems ("Here, take my picture"; "For God's sake hold your tongue and let me love") with the aggression of their imperatives ("*Go* and *catch* a falling star . . .", followed by *Get, Tell, Teach, Find*). Donne's is a world where the man, usually the speaker, calls the tune, and it is a young man's world where stability in relationships is at a low premium. The imperatives suggest the challenge. When Donne's ideas or conceits seem to defy the laws of probability, they sometimes do so in a deliberately distorted syntax. The deceptively easy beginning of *Love's Growth* is followed by some much more difficult lines:

> But if this medicine, love, which cures all sorrow
> With more, not only be no quintessence,
> But mix'd of all stuffs, paining soul, or sense,
> And of the Sun his working vigour borrow,
> Love's not so pure, and abstract, as they use
> To say, which have no mistress but their muse,
> But as all else, being elemented too,
> Love sometimes would contemplate, sometimes do.[21]

In Shakespeare's sonnets, line ends and syntactical units usually coincide; in Donne's poems far less often. The ratiocination of this poem (as of several other Donne poems) is preserved by the simple connectives (*Because . . . But if . . . But . . . And yet . . . As . . . If . . . For . . . And though . . .*) all placed at the beginning of the line. But Shakespeare seems to make more use than Donne of deliberate parallelisms of syntax, and his language in the sonnets is both less intemperate and less colloquial.

THE VALUE OF RHETORIC

In commenting on *The Shepherd's Calendar*, E. K. had been content to point out the rhetorical figures: "a pretty Epanorthosis . . . and withall a Paronomasia", but in these early poems of Shakespeare (not only the *Sonnets* but also *Venus and Adonis* and *The Rape of Lucrece*) the more positive benefits of rhetorical structuring are beginning to emerge. By its need to adopt varying viewpoints in a debate, and to imagine the situations in which different types of speech or different emotional states could occur, rhetoric provided a training in characterisation through language. R. A. Lanham notes the changing attitudes of Venus: sexual temptress, energetic virago, anxious mother to a childlike Adonis, disappointed suitor. Each attitude has its appropriate style.²² Tarquin tries to control his desire for Lucrece in terms of a set debate ("madly tossed between desire and dread"). Lucrece's monologues on Night, Honour, Opportunity and Time (764–1036) foreshadow later set pieces, not always wholly serious, such as Fauconbridge on Commodity and Falstaff on Honour. And the picture of the Trojan War would have delighted the rhetoricians, not merely as embellishment but as a functional device.

Within the plays everyone will have his own remembered selection of set speeches. These are usually very tightly structured. The second half of Henry V's long speech on 'ceremony' in IV.i. – twenty-four lines from "No, thou proud dream . . ." to ". . . vantage of a king" – can scarcely be more than two sentences, the second beginning only three lines from the end ("And but for ceremony . . .") and is perhaps best seen as one single sentence. Punctuation is, of course, that of the modern editor; Elizabethan dramatic punctuation is both less full and more rhetorical – as a guide to speaking aloud – than is its present counterpart. Again, in *Coriolanus*, Aufidius reveals his own feelings about the hero (IV.vii.28–57), a puzzled mixture of admiration and envy. At the centre of the speech is an eleven-line sentence punctuated by the correlatives *Whether . . . whether . . . or whether . . . but one of those*. More surprising, perhaps, is the cohesion of a speech by Iago:

> Virtue? A fig! 'Tis in ourselves that we are thus, or thus. Our bodies
> are our gardens, to the which our wills are gardeners. So that if we
> will plant nettles or sow lettuce, set hyssop and weed up thyme, supply
> it with one gender of herbs or distract it with many, either to have
> it sterile with idleness or manured with industry, why the power and
> corrigible authority of this lies in our wills. If the beam of our lives
> had not one scale of reason to poise another of sensuality, the blood
> and baseness of our natures would conduct us to most preposterous
> conclusions. But we have reason to cool our raging motions, our carnal
> stings, our unbitted lusts: wherof I take this, that you call love, to be a
> sect or scion.

(I.iii.316–29)

This begins with allegory ("Our bodies are our gardens"), continues with parison ("plant nettles or sow lettuce, set hyssop or weed up thyme") and antithesis ("either to have it sterile with idleness or manured with industry", and *reason* versus *sensuality*). Some of the words are Latinate (*corrigible, preposterous*) and the same ideas are repeated in different words but in the same grammatical relationship ("our raging motions, our carnal stings, our unbitted lusts"). The garden imagery runs throughout the passage and binds it together.

Drama, however, does not consist solely of set speeches. Some early Tudor drama, including some plays of Shakespeare, had tried to make too many scenes into theatrical spectacles. Rhetoric is often eloquent, but unfortunately static too. Brian Vickers sums it up admirably:

> Rhetoric books are admirable guides to compositional techniques, but they are based on the model of a single speaker, or writer, addressing an audience directly. They did not attempt to cope with drama, which has a multitude of speakers, a plural vision, and may not represent the dramatist's personal opinions anywhere.[23]

The practice of rhetoric contributed a welcome tautness to formal exchanges, of whatever kind, but even in comedy, where devices such as parison, antithesis and punning accentuate the wit of the clever characters, Shakespeare early realised that this was only part of the play. In *Love's Labour's Lost* the rhetorical structures helped to characterise the formal, articulate – but also pompous – behaviour of the aristocrats which was finally shown to need correction. In *As You Like It* and *Much Ado*, the rhetoric is far less schematic. In the histories and the tragedies, especially, men need to talk naturally, even inconsequentially, whilst the more deliberate, formal syntax can take its place, together with the copious lexis, as markers of the special occasion.

Notes and References

1. A good short introduction is Nash (1989). See also Dixon (1971) and Vickers (1971).
2. "Figuratiue speech is a noueltie of language euidently (and yet not absurdly) estranged from the ordinarie habite and manner of our dayly talke and writing", *The Arte of English Poesie*, eds G. D. Willcock and A. Walker, (1936), p. 159; Jonson, *Discoveries, Works*, eds C. H. Herford and P. and E. M. Simpson (1947), VIII, p. 620.
3. *Directions for Speech and Style*, ed. H. H. Hudson, Princeton University Press, Princeton (1935).
4. Quoted Bullough (1960), III, p. 15.
5. Dedicatory letter to *The Description of England*, ed. G. Edelen (Ithaca, 1968), p. 6. The sentence is also in Holinshed's dedication.
6. See in detail Gilbert (1979a).
7. Quotations from *The Complete Works of John Lyly*, ed. R. W. Bond (1902).
8. Hunter (1962), p. 345.
9. Owen (1961) and Barish (1974); Beatrice's speech is analysed by Barish.
10. *Selections from Sidney's Arcadia*, ed. R. Syfret (1966), p. 116.
11. *An Apology for Poetry*, ed. G. Shepherd (1965), p. 105.
12. Barish (1966), Palmer (1966), Clemen (1961).

13. Further examples are (reference Craik): I.iv.14–15, I.v.6–9, II.i.19–28, II.i.113–21 (*gradatio*), III.iv.40–5, IV.iv.90–5. A longer example of *stichomythia* occurs at II.iv.24–49.
14. Clemen (1980). See also Burckhardt (1968), 47–67 and Turner (1964).
15. For rhetorical patterning in *MND* and other plays of the mid 1590s, see Brooks (Arden edition, 1979), pp. xlv–liii.
16. Sonnet 73 is also discussed by Fowler (1975), pp. 79–122 and by Nowottny (1962), pp. 76–82.
17. I am indebted to Booth (1969) and to Crutwell (1954). A general book is Muir (1979). For comment on individual sonnets, see Kerrigan (New Penguin edition, 1982, and Booth (1977) and for an examination of registerial variation, Gilbert (1979b).
18. Crutwell (1954), p. 16.
19. *The Advancement of Learning*, ed. A. Johnston (1974), p. 36.
20. *Poems of Michael Drayton*, ed. J. Buxton (1953), I, p. 17.
21. *The Songs and Sonnets of John Donne*, ed. T. Redpath (1956), p. 50.
22. Lanham (1976), ch. 4.
23. *Times Literary Supplement*, 8 October 1982.

CHAPTER FIVE

Loosening the structures

ELABORATING A STYLE

How do we assimilate information? When we listen to speech (as in a theatre) we are helped by the degree of stress, intonation, gesture. Even so, the important statements need to stand out, and this may be partly achieved by rhetorical parallelism. The opening of Act III of *Measure for Measure* is the challenge to the imprisoned Claudio by the disguised Duke: "Be absolute for death . . ." After the opening half-line, all the arguments are in fact concentrated in the second half-lines: "Reason thus with life . . . a breath thou art . . . thou art death's fool . . . Thou art not noble . . . Thou'rt by no means valiant . . . The best of rest is sleep . . . Thou art not thyself . . . Happy thou art not . . . Thou art not certain . . . If thou art rich, thou'rt poor . . . Friend hast thou none . . . Thou hast nor youth nor age." The majority of these clauses begin *Thou art* or *Thou hast*, but there is just sufficient variation of word-order ("Happy thou art not", "Friend hast thou none") to avoid monotony. The concluding remark, "What's yet in this . . . ?" also occupies a second half-line. The justification for the Duke's arguments (all the clauses beginning with *for*) and the illustrative imagery come in the intervening lines.

This, however, is a set speech. Earlier in the same play Claudio needs to explain to Lucio – and so to us – why what has hitherto passed in Vienna as a misdemeanour only now apparently results in imprisonment. The parallelism of this speech is not nearly so marked (I.ii.155–70), but the repetition, both of subject and predicate, conveys the sense: "The *new* deputy . . . *newly* in the seat . . . this *new* governor . . ." (does what?) "lets it *straight* feel the spur . . . Awakes me all the enrolled penalties . . . puts the drowsy and neglected act / *Freshly* on me . . ." (and why?) "for a *name* . . .'Tis surely for a *name*". Apart from the *new(ly)*, *straight* and *freshly*, which are repeated because it is the arbitrary nature of the decision which infuriates Claudio, and the word *name*, which is used twice because he believes the introduction of the new regime is simply to advance Angelo's reputation, the variation of title (*deputy, governor*) and the different images in the predicate prevent the speech from becoming repetitious. Furthermore, this is a single, fifteen-line sentence where, despite the parentheses, we do not lose the thread.

The same multiplicity of parts within a single whole is characteristic of Marlowe's syntax. His sentences are apt to be quite long, but the main clause can almost always be perceived without difficulty. What Shakespeare may have been taught by Marlowe (although this would reinforce a lesson learnt from writing narrative poetry) was the ability to elaborate by way of relative, participial and adverbial clause:

> *The warlike soldiers and the gentlemen*
> That heretofore have fill'd Persepolis
> With Afric captains taken in the field,
> Whose ransom made them march in coats of gold,
> With costly jewels hanging at their ears,
> And shining stones upon their lofty crests,
> Now living idle in the walled towns,
> Wanting both pay and martial discipline,
> *Begin in troops to threaten civil war,*
> *And openly exclaim against the king.*

> (*1 Tam* I.i.140–9)

> And if we should with common rites of arms
> Offer our safeties to his clemency,
> *I fear the custom proper to his sword,*
> Which he observes as parcel of his fame,
> Intending so to terrify the world,
> By any innovation or remorse,
> *Will never be dispens'd with till our deaths.*

> (*1 Tam.* V.i.11–17)

> By Cairo runs to Alexandria bay
> Darote's steam, wherein *at anchor lies*
> *A Turkish galley* of my royal fleet,
> Waiting my coming to the river side,
> Hoping by some means I shall be releas'd;
> *Which*, when I come aboard, *will hoist up sail*
> *And* soon put forth into the Terrene Sea,
> Where 'twixt the isles of Cyprus and of Crete,
> *We quickly may in Turkish seas arrive.*

> (*2 Tam* I.ii. 19–27)

Then in my coach, like Saturn's royal son
Mounted his shining chariot gilt with fire,
And drawn with princely eagles through the path
Pav'd with bright crystal and enchas'd with stars
When all the gods stand gazing at his pomp,
So *will I ride through Samarcanda streets,*
Until my soul, dissevered from this flesh,
Shall mount the milk-white way, and meet him there.

                     (*2 Tam* IV.iii.125–32)[1]

It is the sheer flow of the verse – even though the lines are end-stopped more often than not – which as much as any other single feature contributes to the grandeur of *Tamburlaine*. This is what amplification (beloved of the rhetoricians) really meant for Marlowe. Side by side with these passages from Marlowe, we may place Portia's reply to Bassanio who has just correctly chosen the lead casket. The passage (*Merchant of Venice* III.ii.150–65) is rather too long to quote in its entirety, but it is almost certainly intended to be a single sentence. What is noticeable, however, is the variety of construction which avoids monotony: *Though . . . yet . . .* (correlatives), *a thousand times . . . ten thousand times . . .* (lexically and syntactically parallel), *that* ('so that') . . . *but* (coordination) . . . *which* (subordination) . . . *Happy . . . happier . . . Happiest . . .* (parallel clauses introduced by the same adjective). Not all the examples need come from drama. The opening seventeen-line stanza of Spenser's *Prothalamion* coils around a main clause, "Calme was the day . . . When I . . . Walkt forth", with a wreath of secondary clauses at various levels of subordination:

Calme was the day, and through the trembling ayre,
Sweete breathing Zephyrus did softly play
A gentle spirit, that lightly did delay
Hot Titans beames, which then did glyster fayre:
When I whom sullein care,
Through discontent of my long fruitlesse stay
In Princes Court, and expectation vayne
Of idle hopes, which still doe fly away,
Like empty shaddowes, did aflict my brayne,
Walkt forth to ease my payne
Along the shoare of siluer streaming Themmes,
Whose rutty Bancke, the which his Riuer hemmes,
Was paynted all with variable flowers,
And all the meades adornd with daintie gemmes,
Fit to decke maydens bowres,
And crowne their Paramours,
Against the Brydale day, which is not long:
     Sweete Themmes runne softly, till I end my Song.

The syntax reflects the slow, therapeutic stroll along the river bank which helps to relieve the poet's discontent.

Copiousness, then, is not merely a matter of vocabulary. The elaboration may be by relative, infinitive or adverbials, as in *Richard III* I.ii.230–6:

> What? I that killed her husband and his father
> To take her in her heart's extremest hate,
> With curses in her mouth, tears in her eyes,
> The bleeding witness of my hatred by,
> Having God, her conscience, and these bars against me,
> And I no friends to back my suit at all
> But the plain devil and dissembling looks?

where the infinitive in fact acts as the main verb in colloquial usage: 'I actually managed to take her . . .'. Or the noun itself may be extended, not simply by adding further nouns but by noun phrases in apposition:

> Macbeth does murder sleep – the innocent sleep,
> Sleep that knits up the ravelled sleave of care,
> The death of each day's life, sore labour's bath,
> Balm of hurt minds, great nature's second course,
> Chief nourisher in life's feast.

> *(Mac II.ii.36–40)*

The simple, additive, colloquial structure allows us to concentrate on the imagery. (Another good example is Berowne's speech of self-disgust, *Love's Labour's Lost*, III.i.)

In her book *Shakespeare's Grammatical Style*, Dolores M. Burton makes a very detailed and technical stylistic comparison of two plays, *Richard II* and *Antony and Cleopatra*. She finds the style of *Antony and Cleopatra* typically periodic: "sentences with a structure rather like an onion, whose minor syntactic elements surrounded the main clause that lies at the centre".[2] As a variant of this, the main clause may be interrupted by an elaborating subordinate clause (or clauses). The object of the resumed main clause can equally well be modified, but it is important that the main clause itself remains simple, and usually in as normal a word-order as possible, so that it is easily assimilated in the theatre:

> *Our slippery people,*
> Whose love is never linked to the deserver
> Till his deserts are past, *begin to throw*
> *Pompey the Great and all his dignities*
> *Upon his son*; who, high in name and power,
> Higher than both in blood and life, stands up
> For the main soldier; whose quality, going on,

The sides o' th' world may danger.

(I.ii.186–93)

This is not a particularly remarkable passage, but it has its own balance. It is looser than the Ciceronian style of Sidney or Hooker, and it is more natural in that the main verb occurs quite early in the sentence instead of being delayed until near the end. It is therefore more suitable for drama. The sense of roundness and smoothness is characteristic of much of Shakespeare's later syntax.

It is perhaps too much to expect Shakespeare to have achieved such smoothness all at once. Three early cases of copious style show him trying – but perhaps not quite achieving – both lexical expansion and syntactical parallelism. The first example is from *2 Henry VI*:

> See how the blood is settled in his face.
> Oft have I seen a timely-parted ghost
> Of ashy semblance, meagre, pale and bloodless,
> Being all descended to the labouring heart,
> Who, in the conflict that it holds with death,
> Attracts the same for aidance 'gainst the enemy;
> Which with the heart there cools, and ne'er returneth
> To blush and beautify the cheek again.

(III.ii.160–7)

Here the five epithets applied to *ghost* (one pre-modifier and four post-modifiers) run smoothly, but *Being* apparently refers to blood *Who* to heart and *Which* once again to blood. *3 Henry VI* I.iv.141–2 is better (and shorter):

> Women are soft, mild, pitiful, and flexible;
> Thou stern, obdurate, flinty, rough, remorseless.

but the four adjectives of the first line are not quite matched by the five of the second. Similarly, *Titus Andronicus* V.iii.43–4

> A reason mighty, strong, and effectual,
> A pattern, precedent, and lively warrant,

leads us to expect three matching adjectives to follow *pattern*; instead we get noun plus adjective plus noun.

Some further examples, from *Richard III*, are more promising. I.ii.21–25 is more grammatically varied, with adjectives, relative clause and pronoun, but the referent (*child*) is clear, as was not the case in the example from *2 Henry VI* above:

> If ever he have child, abortive be it,
> Prodigious, and untimely brought to light,
> Whose ugly and unnatural aspect
> May fright the hopeful mother at the view,
> And that be heir to his unhappiness!

At I.ii.242–5 the expansion is embedded within the opening and closing lines which together constitute the main clause:

> A sweeter and a lovelier gentleman
> Framed in the prodigality of nature,
> Young, valiant, wise, and, no doubt, right royal,
> The spacious world cannot again afford.

In this, as in much else, *Richard III* shows a more assured writer at work.

Once the norm of a subordinate, easy-flowing syntax has been established, Shakespeare can exaggerate its characteristics (as he does, elsewhere with copious lexis) to achieve a special effect. Claudius is a ruler who has learned all about *policy* and *commodity* (in the Elizabethan senses). On stage he must show some presence. He is apparently an efficient ruler of Denmark; Hamlet's quarrel with him is almost wholly personal, and no one else appears to protest. He has obviously impressed Gertrude, shallow and unthinking as she may be. His strength and decisiveness are seen in the firm syntax of his contemptuous dismissal of the idea that Hamlet has been driven mad by love for Ophelia and his *quick determination* to remove from the court of Denmark the cause of potential trouble:

> Love? His affections do not that way tend;
> Nor what he spake, though it lacked form a little,
> Was not like madness. There's something in his soul
> O'er which his melancholy sits on brood,
> And I do doubt the hatch and the disclose
> Will be some danger; which for to prevent,
> I have in quick determination
> Thus set it down: he shall with speed to England
> For the demand of our neglected tribute.
>
> (III.i.163–71)

Nor has he lost his touch towards the close of the play in his masterly handling of Laertes' rebellion. He agrees that Laertes has a strong case against Hamlet, indeed some case against himself, but he persuades him to handle it his (Claudius's) way.

Yet, as his opening speech, with the subordination and parentheses of its syntax, reveals, he is a master of circumlocution too:

> Therefore *our sometime sister*, now our Queen,
> Th'imperial jointress to this warlike state,
> *Have we*, as 'twere with a defeated joy,
> With an auspicious and a dropping eye,
> With mirth in funeral and with dirge in marriage,
> In equal scale weighing delight and dole,
> *Taken to wife*.
>
> (I.ii.8–14)

Therefore suggests a logical progression, but, if we stop to think about it (which Claudius is sure we won't) there is no logic in the argument that because he and the court have duly mourned old Hamlet, *therefore* he has now married old Hamlet's queen. The troublesome business of a possible attack on Denmark by young Fortinbras is then disposed of in the same circumlocutory style and a suggested uncle-to-uncle agreement. Nevertheless, Claudius keeps the argument moving and demonstrates his control by occasional simpler and much more colloquial half-lines: *For all, our thanks; so much for him; Thus much the business is.* Once all that has been dealt with, he proceeds to the next item on the agenda: "And now, Laertes, what's the news with you?" His second long speech, to Hamlet this time, maintains its suavity by a lavish use of Latinate adjective with Latinate noun:

> But you must know your father lost a father;
> That father lost, lost his; and the survivor bound
> In filial obligation for some term
> To do obsequious sorrow. But to persever
> In obstinate condolement is a course
> Of impious stubbornness.

(I.ii.89–94)

At one and the same time Claudius manages to appear sympathetic and to suggest that, whilst *filial obligation* and *obsequious sorrow* may be natural, to prolong these into *obstinate condolement* and *impious stubbornness* is wholly unreasonable, "a fault to heaven / A fault against the dead", and (of course) a fault against himself. He later speaks diplomatically to Rosencrantz and Guildenstern about Hamlet's *transformation* (II.ii.5).

The first of these two quotations (I.ii.8–14) also illustrates a syntactical device which J. P. Houston finds especially characteristic of *Hamlet*,[3] holding back the verb, or sometimes a significant adverbial phrase, to the end of the sentence where it occurs in the first half-line which is followed by a heavy mid-line pause:

> But virtue, as it never will be moved,
> Though lewdness court it in a shape of heaven,
> So lust, though to a radiant angel linked,
> Will sate itself in a celestial bed
> And prey on garbage.

(I.v.54–9)

> Witness this army of such mass and charge,
> Led by a delicate and tender prince,
> Whose spirit, with divine ambition puffed,
> Makes mouths at the invisible event,

> Exposing what is mortal and unsure
> To all that fortune, death, and danger dare,
> Even for an eggshell.

> (IV.iv.47–53)

> Let my disclaiming from a purposed evil
> Free me so far in your most generous thoughts
> That I have shot my arrow o'er the house
> And hurt my brother.

> (V.ii.235–8)

The sentence, which has seemed to be meandering, comes to an abrupt and startling conclusion.

At the other extreme, colloquial syntax is harder to identify and to describe. The usages we can recognise are often not so much Elizabethan as perennial. Pause-fillers, an essential part of the communicative process, are not neglected. "Why, now", "faith", "Sir", or "I warrant you" give the illusion of colloquial speech, like our own "I mean", "actually", "Well, then" or "you know". Another simple trick is to begin a scene – or indeed a whole play – apparently in the middle of a conversation; a character denies what we have never heard uttered in so many words:

> Nay, but this dotage of our general's
> O'erflows the measure . . .

> (*AC* I.i.1–2)

> No, holy father, throw away that thought . . .

> (*MM* I.iii.1)

> No, faith, I'll not stay a jot longer.

> (*TN* III.ii.1)

Repetition may indicate self-pity, as it does with Gloucester's "O madam, my old heart is cracked; it's cracked" and "I know not, madam. 'Tis too bad, too bad!" (*King Lear* II.i.89, 95), or senility and purposelessness, as with Shallow:

> FALSTAFF   You must excuse me, Master Robert Shallow.
> SHALLOW   I will not excuse you; you shall not be excused;
> excuses shall not be admitted; there is no excuse
> shall serve; you shall not be excused.
> (*2 Hen IV* V.i.3–6)

> He hath wronged me; indeed, he hath. At a word, he hath, believe
> me. Robert Shallow, Esquire, saith he is wronged.
> (*MWW* I.i.103–5)

Lawrence Danson[4] suggests that Shylock, at his first meeting with Bassanio and Antonio, deliberately appears as an absent-minded;

doddering, but pedantic old man (a kind of Venetian Shallow) who
can barely bring his mind back to Bassanio's bequest:

SHYLOCK	Three thousand ducats, well.
BASSANIO	Ay, sir, for three months.
SHYLOCK	For three months, well.
BASSANIO	For the which, as I told you, Antonio shall be bound.
SHYLOCK	Antonio shall become bound, well.
BASSANIO	May you stead me? Will you pleasure me? Shall I know your answer?
SHYLOCK	Three thousand ducats for three months, and Antonio bound.

(*MV* I.iii.1–10)

I had forgot – three months, you told me so.

(I.iii.64)

who explains his poor puns ("land rats and water rats, water thieves
and land thieves, I mean pirates") and who is apparently unable to
work out the current rate of interest in his head:

Three thousand ducats, 'tis a good round sum.
Three months from twelve, then let me see, the rate . . .

(I.iii.100–1)

That this is a pose, meant to gratify Shylock's desire to see the Christians
squirm, is clear when he rounds on Antonio like the *stranger cur* the latter
has called him. Shakespeare apparently realised, early in his career, the
dramatic possibilities of deliberate, repetitive speech.[5]

The Nurse in *Romeo and Juliet* and Mistress Quickly in *Henry IV* find
it above all difficult to say things simply and without an over-abundance
of confirmatory evidence. The Nurse's rambling attempt to establish
Juliet's age (I.iii) is good, but Quickly's lengthy prose speeches are
perhaps better. She vainly attempts before the Lord Chief Justice to
tie down Falstaff to his earlier promises of marriage and repayment
of debts (*2 Hen IV* II.i.83–101), but the mere mention of Pistol and
his *swaggering* – something of a new word[6] – is enough to set her off:

HOSTESS	If he swagger, let him not come here. No, by my faith! I must live among my neighbours; I'll no swaggerers. I am in good name and fame with the very best. Shut the door. There comes no swaggerers here. I have not lived all this while to have swaggering now. Shut the door, I pray you.
FALSTAFF	Dost thou hear, hostess?
HOSTESS	Pray ye, pacify yourself, Sir John; there comes no swaggerers here.
FALSTAFF	Dost thou hear? It is mine ancient.

HOSTESS Tilly-fally, Sir John, ne'er tell me; an your ancient
swagger, 'a comes not in my doors. I was before
Master Tisick the debuty t'other day, and, as he
said to me – 'twas no longer ago than Wednesday
last, i'good faith – 'Neighbour Quickly,' says he –
Master Dumb our minister was by then – 'Neighbour
Quickly,' says he, 'receive those that are civil, for,'
said he, 'you are in an ill name' – now 'a said so
I can tell whereupon. 'For,' says he, 'you are an
honest woman, and well thought on; therefore take
heed what guests you receive; receive,' says he, 'no
swaggering companions.' There comes none here.
You would bless you to hear what he said. No, I'll no
swaggerers.

                (*2 Hen IV* II.iv.71–93)

The repetition of *swaggerers*; the rhyming *name and fame*; the
corruption of *deputy*; the colloquial *'a, by my faith, Tilly-fally,
well thought on, You would bless you*, but the fine, legal-sounding
whereupon; and, above all, the parentheses with their circumstantial
detail (*Wednesday last; Master Dumb our minister was by then*) and the
constant interjection of *says he* (because direct speech is somehow
more 'real') – all these establish her as a muddled, sentimental but
attractive character, addicted to pause-fillers (*by my troth; look you,
I warrant you*), indulged by Falstaff and Doll:

HOSTESS Cheater, call you him? I will bar no honest man my
house, nor no cheater, but I do not love swaggering;
by my troth, I am the worse when one says 'swagger'.
Feel, masters, how I shake, look you, I warrant you.
DOLL   So you do, hostess.

Another occasional feature of Shakespeare's syntax which can easily
be paralleled from present-day English is the use, for emphasis, of
both a noun and a pronoun. We pick out one feature for particular
attention and put it at the head of the sentence ('*That dress*, where
did you get *it*?') or we wish to emphasise a noun or even a noun
clause ('*It's* rather good *coffee, this*', '*It* does surprise me, *what he sees in
her.*'). Because this distorts normal word-order, we feel the necessity
to make doubly sure by the inclusion of a pronoun. Similarly, in
Measure for Measure, the excitable, interfering Lucio blurts out:

But yesternight, my lord, *she and that friar*,
I saw *them* at the prison. A saucy friar,
A very scurvy fellow.

                (V.i.134–6)

A further example of the same construction occurs in *Cymbeline* when
Cloten is trying to force his attentions upon Imogen:

> *The contract you pretend with that base wretch,*
> One bred of alms and fostered with cold dishes,
> With scraps o' th' court, *it is no contract, none.*
>
> (II.iii.115–17)

Jonson's comic style is usually less balanced than Shakespeare's and often nearer to the language of ordinary speech, but one kind of balance found quite often in his verse is a parallelism of strongly-stressed verbs at the head of short clauses:

> Here I *wear* your keys,
> *See* all your coffers and your caskets locked,
> *Keep* the poor inventory of your jewels,
> Your plate, and moneys; *am* your steward, sir,
> *Husband* your goods here.
>
> (*Volpone* I.iii.40–4)

> I, that have *preached* these things so oft unto you,
> *Read* you the principles, *argued* all the grounds,
> *Disputed* every fitness, every grace,
> *Called* you to counsel of so frequent dressings . . .
>
> (*Volpone* III.iv.23–6)

> I *ga'* you count'nance, credit for your coals,
> Your stills, your glasses, your materials;
> *Built* you a furnace, *drew* you customers,
> *Advanced* all your black arts; *lent* you, beside,
> A house to practise in.
>
> (*Alchemist* I.i.43–7)

This, too, is a feature of some speech styles. The very few purple passages in Jonson stand out against his realistic norm: Mammon's fantasies of using his newly-acquired riches to lead an aristocratic life with Dol (in reality a prostitute); the delights Volpone offers to Celia; or, rather differently imagined, the prose monologues of Justice Overdo. In these his syntax is much more subordinate than usual. Marston's preface 'To the Reader' states that *The Malcontent* is written "more honestly than eloquently" and in the play verse turns into prose or prose into verse within the same speech (the effect is less troublesome in the theatre than on the printed page).

SHAKESPEARE'S DEVELOPMENT OF STYLE

Editors comment on the 'low-keyed formality' and the self-defeating complexity of the syntax of *All's Well That Ends Well*,[7] as if Shakespeare was working towards, but had not yet achieved, the looser style of the final plays. It seems to me that the syntax of this play, like the characters, is a melange of styles which have not been properly integrated. Bertram who has, at best, proved weak and gullible, finally accepts Helena ungraciously. Helena appears to act out of character in herself suggesting the bed-trick (it is put *to* Isabella) and the introduction of the talisman – the ring placed on Bertram's finger in bed – is similarly artificial. Likewise the syntax: several passages are cast as couplets, especially the lengthy exchanges between Helena and the King (II.i.130–210) and the King's attempt to persuade Bertram to accept her (II.iii.124–43; here the switch from blank verse occurs in the middle of the speech). These may be intended to suggest an incantatory, aphoristic style, just as the formal sonnet form of Helena's letter in III.iv. conveys the *opposite* of her true feelings for Bertram. Act I, scene i had promised better. Helena's first verse speech establishes her as a straightforward, likeable girl, with its colloquialisms, one or two metaphors, and her ability to recognise Parolles for what he is (as Bertram cannot). Later oxymoron (168–70) and her witty replies to Parolles (187–202) show that she is intelligent too, in the manner of earlier comic heroines. Unfortunately all this does not last.

Timon of Athens, perhaps to be dated 1604 but not printed until the First Folio, possibly worked on spasmodically and, as some critics believe, in collaboration with Middleton, contains some passages whose syntax seems unnecessarily difficult. When Apemantus visits Timon in the woods, his speech begins with the rhythm which we shall see to be characteristic of *Macbeth: if this*, then *that; the one . . . the other*. But by trying to repeat as an aphorism what the earlier lines have stated more forcibly by means of antithesis (*courtier/beggar, misery/pomp*); the concluding three lines become almost impossibly concentrated:

> If thou didst put this sour cold habit on
> To castigate thy pride, 'twere well; but thou
> Dost it enforcedly. Thou'dst courtier be again
> Wert thou not beggar. Willing misery
> Outlives incertain pomp, is crowned before.
> The one is filling still, never complete,
> The other at high wish. Best state, contentless,
> Hath a distracted and most wretched being,
> Worse than the worst, content.

(IV.iii.240–9)

Not much of *Timon* is, however, of this kind. Timon's soliloquy in IV.i., his prayer to the gods as he looks back on the Athens he has left and heaps curses on the city, is as carefully balanced as almost anything in Shakespeare. Lines 1, 4, 6, 8, 10, 12, 13, 15, 21, 23, 25, 28, 30 and 32 all have a heavy caesura, but the second half-lines show different grammatical patterns (sometimes paired nouns – *Slaves and fools; Piety and fear* – sometimes noun followed by imperative – *Bankrupts, hold fast; Bound servants, steal*) and also some variation in metrical structure (*O thou wall* versus *Plagues incident to men*), so providing variety. The sentences are of roughly equal length, thus intensifying the hammer-blows of the curses, except for lines 15–19 where the list of features of an *ordered* society, observing 'degree' (religion, peace, justice, truth and the rest) make clear what it is that is to be overthrown and replaced by confusion. Line 32 marks the change of subject from the state of Athens to the feelings of the exiled Timon by a departure from this careful parallelism, and the speech concludes in a much looser syntax.

Other speeches in the play demonstrate a less insistent parallelism: the imperatives of IV.iii.111, 113, 115, 119, 123 all begin strongly-marked second half-lines, yet the opening of the speech is scarcely blank verse at all:

> That by killing of villains
> Thou wast born to conquer my country.
> Put up thy gold. Go on. Here's gold. Go on.
>
> (IV.iii.106–8)

The final plays seem to be characterised by a looser, almost experimental syntax. Perhaps 'experimental' is the wrong word, for it may be that Shakespeare had become so accustomed to writing blank verse that he was less conscious than we are of the variations in rhythm and syntax within the established pattern. But I prefer to think that the syntax of several of the later speeches marks a development beyond the syntax of the earlier tragic soliloquies (which demands separate treatment), that Shakespeare, while retaining the overall structure of a speech, was now able to convey the impression of a character thinking as he spoke, often under pressure. Most of us do not think in a particularly logical fashion; it is only when we rearrange or write up our thoughts that firm order and coherence creep in. In thinking aloud we make qualifications and objections, go off at a tangent and partially obscure straightforward communication of ideas. In Shakespeare's final plays, the increase in parentheses attempts to indicate something of this turmoil.

Since parentheses may be a matter of modern editorial punctuation, I will try to limit myself to obvious examples, and it may broaden the discussion a little if I begin with an example outside Shakespeare, from Beaumont and Fletcher's *Philaster*:

Then thus I turne
My language to you Prince, you forraigne man!:
Ne're stare, nor put on wonder, for you must
Indure me, and you shall. This earth you tread upon
(A dowry as you hope with this fair Princesse),
By my dead father (Oh, I had a father
Whose memory I bow to) was not left
To your inheritance, and I up, and living,
Having my selfe about me, and my sword,
The soules of all my name, and memories,
These armes, and some few friends, besides the gods,
To part so calmely with it, and sit still,
And say I might have beene. I tell thee *Pharamond*,
When thou art King, looke I be dead and rotten,
And my name ashes, as I: For heare me, *Pharamond*:
This very ground thou goest on, this fat earth,
My fathers friends made fertile with their faiths,
Before that day of shame, shall gape and swallow
Thee and thy nation, like a hungry grave,
Into her hidden bowells: Prince, it shall;
By the just gods it shall.

(I.i.173–93)[8]

The sentence "This earth . . . by my dead father . . . was not left to your inheritance" has been interrupted by two parentheses, and it is continued in irregular grammar by "and I up, and living". This in turn produces its own subordination ("Having . . . the gods") before concluding "To part so calmely with it". Elsewhere the emphasis of speech is indicated by *and you shall* (176), *as I* (187) and *By the just gods it shall* (193). The status of *made* (189) is at first uncertain: for a moment it appears to be a main verb, but *shall gape and swallow* (190) leads us to understand that line 189 is a relative clause without its pronoun. Of course all this analysis would not be necessary for an audience; the general tone is clear and the actor's voice can supply the necessary emphasis. My point is simply that this is the absolute opposite of 'literary' drama, for the style indicates to the actor how he is to play the scene.

Cymbeline, probably written in 1610, about the same time as *Philaster*, is full of parentheses. A very early example shows the parenthesis as part of a conversational style:

He that hath missed the Princess is a thing
Too bad for bad report, and he that hath her –
I mean, that married her, alack good man,
And therefore banished – is a creature such
As, to seek through the regions of the earth
For one his like, there would be something failing
In him that should compare. I do not think

So fair an outward and such stuff within
Endows a man but he.

(I.i.16–24)

Lines 21–22, following the strong pause after *his like*, seem to mean:
'Well, even if you found someone to compare with Posthumus, he
wouldn't be his equal', but they are elliptical in the manner of some
conversation. This play also has its share of difficult syntax:

You do seem to know
Something of me or what concerns me. Pray you,
Since doubting things go ill often hurts more
Than to be sure they do – for certainties
Either are past remedies, or, timely knowing,
The remedy then born – discover to me
What both you spur and stop.

(I.vi.93–9)

Yet the short syntactic units of the Queen's speech at III.v.56 or
Imogen's soliloquy in III.vi or Posthumus's in V.iv are at least as
characteristic of *Cymbeline* as the more difficult passages.

Pericles, on the other hand, has very few parentheses. The story,
however, requires Pericles to be a curiously passive figure. His
misfortunes do not result from guilt (as do Leontes's) or neglect
(like Prospero's).[9] The Epilogue speaks of "Virtue preserved from
fell destruction's blast", and a plot like this is less likely to produce
difficulties of syntax. Textually *Pericles* is a mess. It is almost certainly
a collaborative play and was not included in the First Folio, but it
might be worth considering why we can be reasonably sure that this
passage is by Shakespeare:

A terrible childbed hast thou had, my dear;
No light, no fire; th'unfriendly elements
Forgot thee utterly. Nor have I time
To give thee hallowed to thy grave, but straight
Must cast thee, scarcely coffined, in the ooze,
Where, for a monument upon thy bones,
And e'er-remaining lamps, the belching whale
And humming water must o'erwhelm thy corpse,
Lying with simple shells. O Lychorida,
Bid Nestor bring me spices, ink and paper,
My casket and my jewels. And bid Nicander
Bring me the satin coffer. Lay the babe
Upon the pillow. Hie thee, whiles I say
A priestly farewell to her. Suddenly, woman.

(III.i.56–69)

The simplicity and colloquialism of lines 56–8 give way to a more subordinate structure allowing time for a compound, *e'er-remaining*, and the striking adjectives *belching* and *humming*. This is followed in turn by the short, matter-of-fact phrases indicating the actions of 65–9 and incorporating their own stage directions. The air of confidence in the writing, the ability to vary pace and style within a short passage, demonstrate the ability of the experienced dramatist.

As Prospero, in Act I, scene ii of *The Tempest* (1611, and possibly Shakespeare's last play) explains to Miranda (and to us, the audience) how they arrived on the island, he appears torn between a natural desire for revenge on his enemies and the realisation that he can now, if he wishes, finally forgive them. Yet we do not see this indecision in soliloquy, and although he relives the experiences as he recounts them to Miranda, there is not the same sense of pressure as in some of the great tragedies or the slightly earlier *Winter's Tale*. Nor is there tension in the plot, for Prospero holds all the cards. There are several parentheses, but they are not as numerous as in *The Winter's Tale* and almost always much shorter. Although subordinate clauses occasionally occur out of their normal position in the sentence, the style is rarely exceptionally puzzling:

> Some food we had, and some fresh water, that
> A noble Neapolitan, Gonzalo,
> *Out of his charity, who being then appointed*
> *Master of this design*, did give us, with
> Rich garments, linens, stuffs, and necessaries
> Which since have steaded much. So, *of his gentleness*,
> *Knowing I loved my books*, he furnished me
> From mine own library with volumes that
> I prize above my dukedom.
>
> (I.ii.160–8)

A later example of distorted syntax:

> You are three men of sin, whom destiny –
> That hath to instrument this lower world
> And what is in't – the never-surfeited sea
> Hath caused to belch up you, and on this island
> Where man doth not inhabit, you 'mongst men
> Being most unfit to live. I have made you mad;
> And even with such like valour men hang and drown
> Their proper selves.
>
> (III.iii.54–61)

may owe its difficulty to the unnecessary addition of *you* (57) after the preceding *whom*, and the addition of "and on this island . . ." in a manner characteristic of speech idiom. The concluding lines (76–83) of this same speech by Ariel may be deliberately prophetic and puzzling. The well-known speech in which Prospero finally announces that he will abjure his magic powers seems to change construction in midstream and a new sentence to begin at V.i.44 without a finite verb having occurred in the previous sentence. But these are relatively isolated instances, from which *The Tempest* has sometimes acquired a false reputation as a 'difficult' play.

STYLE AND IMAGERY

The kind of imagery a writer chooses has clear implications for his syntax. Here, however, Shakespeare's development was from a looser to a more concentrated style. In discussing imagery, I am not concerned with the content of the images or indeed their thematic value in the play: for example, the imagery of light and darkness in *Romeo and Juliet* or that of Macbeth, the man in purloined clothes which are too big for him. Instead I shall consider expanded or concentrated images, since this aspect has clear implications for the form of expression. One would automatically associate the expanded image with the greater leisure for development provided by narrative poetry, and there are several examples in *Venus and Adonis* and *The Rape of Lucrece*. In these two poems there are also stanzas where image is added to image, intensifying the idea but achieving no deeper penetration of the subject:

> Unruly blasts wait on the tender spring;
> Unwholesome weeds take root with precious flowers;
> The adder hisses where the sweet birds sing;
> What virtue breeds iniquity devours.
>
> (*RL* 869–72)

King John (1596) IV.ii.9–16 will serve as an example from the early plays:

> Therefore, to be possessed with double pomp,
> To guard a title that was rich before,
> To gild refined gold, to paint the lily,
> To throw a perfume on the violet,
> To smooth the ice, or add another hue
> Unto the rainbow, or with taper-light
> To seek the beauteous eye of heaven to garnish,
> Is wasteful and ridiculous excess.

All the rhetoricians consider amplification at length; this is copiousness for its own sake, and the result is an additive syntax where the subject or complement comprises a series of short clauses each of which usually occupies a single line. It sometimes occurs in the Sonnets too, for example the beginning of Sonnet 35:

> No more be grieved at that which thou hast done:
> Roses have thorns, and silver fountains mud,
> Clouds and eclipses stain both moon and sun,
> And loathsome canker lives in sweetest bud.

But this is a prelude to the admission that the lover deliberately, if reluctantly, accepts his friend's faults: the diffuse opening is only the first stage in a developing argument, and some bounds to undue expansion are set by the tight metrical form of a short poem. A series of images on the same subject in *Richard III*:

> When clouds are seen, wise men put on their cloaks;
> When great leaves fall, then winter is at hand;
> When the sun sets, who doth not look for night?
> Untimely storms makes men expect a dearth.
>
> (II.iii.32–5)

is perhaps excusable since it is spoken by one of a group of citizens who take up the whole of this short scene and who clearly have a choric function. In another quotation from the same play the figure is close to a conceit, yet the lexical cohesion (*images, mirrors, cracked, glass*) just saves it from banality, and, more important, simile has given way to the concentration of metaphor:

> I have bewept a worthy husband's death,
> And lived with looking on his images;
> But now two mirrors of his princely semblance
> Are cracked in pieces by malignant death,
> And I for comfort have but one false glass
> That grieves me when I see my shame in him.
>
> (II.ii.49–54)

The characteristic image of the early plays is, however, that which demonstrates its correspondence point by point. In this it has something in common with the metaphysical conceit, but it is seldom consciously witty or especially unusual in its choice of comparison. It has clarity, certainly, but lacks dramatic vigour. *3 Henry VI* seems especially prone to this kind of image:

> This battle fares like to the morning's war,
> When dying clouds contend with growing light,
> What time the shepherd, blowing of his nails,
> Can neither call it perfect day nor night.

Now sways it this way, like a mighty sea
Forced by the tide to combat with the wind;
Now sways it that way, like the self-same sea
Forced to retire by fury of the wind.
Sometime the flood prevails, and then the wind;
Now one the better, then another best;
Both tugging to be victors, breast to breast,
Yet neither conqueror nor conquered;
So is the equal poise of this fell war.

(II.v.1–13)[10]

Lines 1 and 13 largely repeat one another and 9–12 are similarly otiose. The passage might be excused as being a rhetorical opening to the scene, and it is perhaps true that the reflective nature of the soliloquy encouraged the use of formal imagery. But when all is said, the passage is simply diffuse and if it were presented unseen perhaps not many critics would unhesitatingly attribute it to Shakespeare. Less protracted but little better are II.i.11–19 (again the concluding lines make everything doubly clear); III.ii.134–3 ("So do I wish the crown . . ."): III.ii.174–81 ("And from that torment I will free myself . . ."); and finally V.iv.1–38 which is a notable extended exercise in nautical imagery.

Richard II is another case in point. One of its best-known images is at IV.i.180 where Richard surrenders the crown to Bolingbroke:

Give me the crown.
Here, cousin – seize the crown. Here, cousin –
On this side, my hand; and on that side, thine.
Now is this golden crown like a deep well
That owes two buckets, filling one another,
The emptier ever dancing in the air,
The other down, unseen, and full of water.
That bucket down and full of tears am I,
Drinking my griefs whilst you mount up on high.

Again, this is explanatory: *full of water* is paralleled by *full of tears* in the following line.[11] Later, when Bolingbroke's triumphant entry into London in the company of the deposed Richard is narrated by York to his wife, there is no continual contrast: Bolingbroke is described first and then Richard.[12] The comparison of Richard to the actor who has the misfortune to follow the star player on stage is clinched by the final two lines:

As in a theatre the eyes of men,
After a well graced actor leaves the stage,
Are idly bent on him that enters next,
Thinking his prattle to be tedious:
Even so, or with much more contempt, men's eyes

Did scowl on gentle Richard.

(V.ii.23–8)

Later still, Richard, musing on the passing of time, indulges in a metaphysical conceit: "For now hath time made me his numbering clock." (V.v.50). But the 'proof' ("So sighs, and tears, and groans / Show minutes, times, and hours") is not usually supplied so directly in metaphysical poems.

Madeline Doran believes that the change from a predominantly explicit imagery, where the points of comparison are explored singly, to a rapid succession of images, often suggested rather than elaborated, takes place between *Richard II* and *Henry IV*.[13] In general terms this is, I think, correct. Yet one cannot be too precise. The imagery of *Richard III* (? 1592–3, but definitely preceding *Richard II*) is certainly more taut than that of most of the early plays:

> Who builds his hope in air of your good looks
> Lives like a drunken sailor on a mast,
> Ready with every nod to tumble down
> Into the fatal bowels of the deep.
>
> (III.iv.98–101)

> Richard yet lives, hell's black intelligencer,
> Only reserved their factor to buy souls
> And send them thither.
>
> (IV.iv.71–3)

> The wretched, bloody, and usurping boar,
> That spoiled your summer fields and fruitful vines,
> Swills your warm blood like wash, and makes his trough
> In your embowelled bosoms – this foul swine
> Is now even in the centre of this isle.
>
> (V.ii.7–11)

The play is a storehouse of rhetorical devices, but the formal and often repetitive expression does not extend to the imagery. This may be because so much of the play is either spoken by or about Richard himself. The sardonic self-awareness (so far beyond Marlowe's villains) would go ill with flaccid expansion and embellishment in the imagery. Equally, 2 *Henry IV* contains at least one extended and over-explicit image of the old kind:

> When we mean to build,
> We first survey the plot, then draw the model,
> And when we see the figure of the house,
> Then must we rate the cost of the erection,
> Which if we find outweighs ability,
> What do we then but draw anew the model
> In fewer offices, or at least desist

To build at all? Much more, in this great work –
Which is almost to pluck a kingdom down
And set another up – should we survey
The plot of situation and the model,
Consent upon a sure foundation,
Question surveyors, know our own estate,
How able such a work to undergo
To weigh against his opposite; or else
We fortify in paper and in figures,
Using the names of men instead of men,
Like one that draws the model of an house
Beyond his power to build it, who, half-through,
Gives o'er and leaves his part-created cost
A naked subject to the weeping clouds,
And waste for churlish winter's tyranny.

(I.iii.41–62)

However, Professor Doran is certainly correct in pointing out the much more concentrated images of *Henry IV* where double meanings are frequently left implicit:

. . . two-and-twenty knights
Balked in their own blood, did Sir Walter see.

(*1 Hen IV* I.i.68–9)

Balked is, as in Middle English, 'piled up (in ridges)', but equally there is a strong implication of 'thwarted'. It would be easy to multiply examples from the rush of images in the middle and later plays (the pace seems to slacken a little in the final plays). Such images are frequently linked:

Have you not set mine honour at the *stake*,
And *baited* it with all th' *unmuzzled* thoughts
That tyrannous heart can think?

(*TN* III.i.115–17)

And Pity, like a naked new-born babe
Striding the blast, or heaven's cherubin, *horsed*
Upon the sightless curriers of the air,
Shall blow the horrid deed in every eye,
That tears shall drown the wind. I have no *spur*
To *prick* the sides of my intent but only
Vaulting ambition which *o'erleaps* itself
And *falls* on the other.

(*Mac* I.vii.21–8)

The "naked new-born babe / Striding the blast" is one of Shakespeare's mixed metaphors, like Lady Macbeth's question shortly afterwards: "Was the hope drunk / Wherein you dressed yourself?" (I.vii.35) or Macbeth's "Put rancours in the vessel of my peace" (III.i.66); *Macbeth* seems a play especially prone to such conceits. Antony's "O thou day o' th' world / Chain mine armed neck" (IV.viii.13) or Hamlet taking arms against a sea of troubles (III.i.59) are similarly unanalysable in sensuous terms. They may be explained – or explained away – as symbolic, but perhaps Dr Johnson came nearer to the truth:

> . . . that fulness of idea, which might sometimes load his words with more sentiment than they could conveniently convey, and that rapidity of imagination which might hurry him to a second thought before he had fully explained the first.[14]

One can, in fact, discover the same image handled much more succinctly later:

> I see thy glory like a shooting star
> Fall to the base earth from the firmament.
> Thy sun sets weeping in the lowly west,
> Witnessing storms to come, woe, and unrest.
>
> (*R II* II.iv.19–22)

> Finish, good lady; the bright day is done,
> And we are for the dark.
>
> (*AC* V.ii.193–4)

In the later image, as Miss Holmes (whose example it is) comments "There is no lingering twilight, brightness and dark are tropical."[15] Simile has become metaphor. Where the image is striking, and perhaps unusual in its context, Shakespeare does sometimes explain, but the explanation is not so protracted or so obvious as in the earlier plays:

> And the ebbed man, ne'er loved till ne'er worth love,
> Comes deared by being lacked. This common body,
> Like to a vagabond flag upon the stream,
> Goes to and back, lackeying the varying tide,
> To rot itself with motion.
>
> (*AC* I.iv.43–7)

The initial difficulty, the *ebbed* man who is finally welcomed to power only when he is no longer available, is made more intelligible by the continuation of the same image in *flag* ('reed') and *stream*. (*Lacked* also perhaps gave rise to the following metaphor, *lackeying*.) Other more directly explanatory instances are:

> The hearts
> That spanieled me at heels, to whom I gave
> Their wishes, do *discandy, melt their sweets*
> On blossoming Caesar.
>
> (*AC* IV.xii.20–3)

His delights
Were *dolphin-like; they showed his back above*
The element they lived in.

(*AC* V.ii.88–90)

ULYSSES   We saw him at the opening of his tent. He is not
              sick.
AJAX   Yes, *lion-sick, sick of proud heart.*

(*TC* II.iii.86–8)

          neither allied
To eminent assistants, but *spider-like*
Out of his self-drawing web, 'a gives us note,
The force of his own merit makes his way.

(*Hen VIII* I.i.61–4)

Let music sound while he doth make his choice,
Then if he lose, he makes a *swanlike end,*
Fading in music. That the comparison
May stand more proper, my eye shall be the stream
And watery deathbed for him.

(*MV* III.ii.43–7)

The initial effect of the last image (as with most of the others, the
simile is stressed: *dolphin-like, spider-like, swan-like*) is unfortunately
spoiled by its prolongation ("That the comparison / May stand more
proper . . ."). But *The Merchant of Venice* is an early play.

At their best, the later images both work by suggestion and
are given support by their context. In considering Shakespeare's
development as a dramatist between 2 *Henry VI* and *Macbeth*,
G. R. Hibbard discusses *Macbeth* III.ii.46–50:

          Come, seeling night,
Scarf up the tender eye of pitiful day,
And with thy bloody and invisible hand
Cancel and tear to pieces that great bond
Which keeps me pale.

and remarks:

Night as the falconer, and day as the suffering falcon, have taken
on the attributes of living things through a kind of verbal shorthand
that concentrates on action, as distinct from pictorial description. The
nouns "falcon" and "falconer" are not used at all, but we see why
night's hand is "bloody and invisible".[16]

The lexical set is in fact continued in *tear to pieces,* and Hibbard
may well be correct in suggesting that the implicit pun *seeling /
sealing* led to the new image of *that great bond.* In another example of
concentrated metaphor, Cornwall and Regan explain their late visit
to Gloucester's house:

CORNWALL   You know not why we came to visit you –
REGAN   Thus out of season, threading dark-eyed night.
(KL II.i.118–19)

The needle is not mentioned directly, but *threading* and *eyed* imply it, and *dark-eyed* (unique in Shakespeare and otherwise not especially meaningful) suggests the difficulty of threading a needle in the dark. *Out of season* may again refer to night, or may mean that it is winter, no good time for a journey.[17] All this Shakespeare achieved in a single line.

Jonson's images are compellingly visual and frequently morally reductive; their realism is often a welcome counterbalance to the artificiality of humour in comedy:

> Would you would once close
> Those filthy eyes of yours that flow with slime
> Like two frog-pits, and those same hanging cheeks,
> Covered with hide instead of skin (Nay, help, sir)
> That look like frozen dish-clouts set on end.
(Volpone I.v.56–60)

> He vomits crooked pins! His eyes are set
> Like a dead hare's hung in a poulter's shop!
(Volpone V.xii.25–6)

> . . . you did walk
> Piteously costive, with your pinched-horn-nose,
> And your complexion of the Roman wash,
> Stuck full of black and melancholic worms,
> Like powder-corns shot at th' artillery-yard.
(Alchemist I.i.27–31)[18]

They are, too, almost all similes where the more leisurely syntax (as opposed to that of the metaphor) allows us to assimilate the unusual comparison. There are fewer such images in Shakespeare before the last plays, although Falstaff ("My skin hangs about me like an old lady's loose gown. I am withered like an old apple-john", *1 Hen IV*. III.iii.2, and "you shall see him laugh till his face be like a wet cloak ill laid up", *2 Hen IV*, V.i.77) has the same manner but a very different tone.

Webster's style, on the other hand, is complex, nervous, staccato, and his images sometimes seem deliberately far-fetched, unpoetic in a 'metaphysical' manner, although they are usually briefer than Donne's:

> As men to try the precious unicorn's horn
> Make of the powder a preservative circle

And in it put a spider, so these arms
Shall charm his poison, force it to obeying
And keep him chaste from an infected straying,

(*White Devil* II.i.14–18)

He and his brother are like plum-trees, that grow crooked over standing
pools, they are rich, and o'erladen with fruit, but none but crows, pies,
and caterpillars feed on them. Could I be one of their flatt'ring panders,
I would hang on their ears like a horse-leech, till I were full, and then
drop off.

(*Malfi* I.i.49–54)

FERDINAND	. . . This will gain
	Access to private lodgings, where yourself
	May, like a politic dormouse –
BOSOLA	As I have seen some
	Feed in a lord's dish, half asleep, not seeming
	To listen to any talk: and yet these rogues
	Have cut his throat in a dream.

(*Malfi* I.ii.204–10)

Some of them seem, at first sight, to resemble Jonson's images in
their 'realism':

There was a lady in France, that having had the smallpox, flayed the
skin off her face to make it more level; and whereas before she look'd
like a nutmeg grater, after she resembled an abortive hedgehog.

(*Malfi* II.i.29–32)

A politician is the devil's quilted anvil,
He fashions all sins on him, and the blows
Are never heard.

(*Malfi* III.ii.321–3)

. . . How tedious is a guilty conscience!
When I look into the fishponds in my garden,
Methinks I see a thing, arm'd with a rake
That seems to strike at me.

(*Malfi* V.v.4–7)[19]

But not quite – an *abortive* hedgehog, a *quilted* anvil, a rake in a
fishpond? There is, in each case, one disturbing feature. A few of them
are so clotted that the interpretation, and therefore any real assessment
of their effectiveness, is difficult, especially in the theatre:

We see that trees bear no such pleasant fruit
There where they grew first, as where they are now set.
Perfumes the more they are chaf'd the more they render
Their pleasing scents, and so affliction
Expresseth virtue, fully, whether true,
Or else adulterate.

(*White Devil* I.i.45–50)

where *perfumes* is a noun, not the verb it might first seem, and we have to decide whether *affliction* or *virtue* can be true or else adulterate. Or this, which simply has too many images all at once:

> Thou art a box of worm seed, at best, but a salvatory of green
> mummy: what's this flesh? a little crudded milk, fantastical
> puff-
> paste: our bodies are weaker than those paper prisons boys
> use to keep flies in: more contemptible; since ours is to preserve
> earth-
> worms: didst thou ever see a lark in a cage? such is the soul in
> the body: this world is like her little tuft of grass, and the heaven
> o'er our heads, like her looking-glass, only gives us a miserable
> knowledge of the small compass of our prison.

> (*Malfi* IV.ii.124–32)

More memorable are the single dramatic images, although once again the choice of objects for comparison is unusual: "I am i' th' way to study a long silence"; "I have caught / An everlasting cold. I have lost my voice / Most irrecoverably"; "We are merely the stars' tennis-balls".

Whether the imagery and its syntax are meant to indicate the turbulence and the bizarre nature of Italian society (it is noticeable that the Duchess of Malfi herself, uncontaminated by the corruption all around her, speaks much more simply) or whether they merely reflect Webster's notebook manner of composition,[20] his is a distinctive style, at the linguistic limits of Jacobean tragedy. Shakespeare's later images sometimes have the striking realism of Jonson's and something of the unusual nature of Webster's. Their increasingly concentrated expression achieved much greater dramatic import than the expanded images of the early plays, although they hardly ever became as impenetrable as some of Webster's. In his syntax generally, Shakespeare learned to reserve pronounced rhetorical expression for set speeches or special effects of characterisation. Most of his characters appear, for most of the time, to be 'talking naturally', although, once again, typical features of colloquial language may be exploited to show comedy on the one hand or extreme perturbation on the other.

Notes and References

1. Marlowe is quoted from *Complete Poems and Plays*, ed. E. D. Pendry (1976).
2. Burton (1968), pp. 52–3.
3. Houston (1988), especially pp. 80–1. Other examples are I.ii.202–11, I.iii.46–51, III.iii.89–95, III.iv.64–8, IV.iii.42–5.
4. Danson (1978), pp. 139–57.

5. A later example of pretended muddleheadedness is Pompey's attempt to obfuscate the case tried before Angelo and Escalus, *MM* II.i.117–24.

6. Chapman (writing in 1598) speaks of *swaggering* as a new word and it seems to appear first in the 1590s (*OED*). Shakespeare would then be amongst its earliest recorded users, and this, as well as her garrulity, may account for Quickly's repetition of a word she does not understand. Most of Shakespeare's uses are by soldiers or else by lower-class characters.

7. Everett (New Penguin edition, 1970), p. 13; Hunter (Arden edition, 1959), p. lvii.

8. *Philaster*, Beaumont and Fletcher, *Dramatic Works*, ed. F. Bowers (1966), I.

9. Wall (1971), pp. 263–4.

10. Cf. *3 Hen VI*: I.iv.40–3, II.i. 129–31, II.ii.11–18. For some similar remarks, including a good example from *Titus Andronicus*, see Hibbard (1981). Two examples of the extended image in *The Spanish Tragedy* are II.i.3–7 and II.ii.7–17.

11. Cf. *2 Hen VI*: II.iv.53–7, III.i.31–3, III.ii.254–69 and *MV* II.vi.14–19 (with its repetition of both *How like the prodigal* and *the strumpet wind*).

12. Burton (1968) p. 206.

13. Doran (1976), pp. 221–33.

14. *The Yale Edition of The Works of Samuel Johnson*, ed. A. Sherbo (1968), VIII, p. 54.

15. Holmes (1929), p. 38.

16. Hibbard (1981), p. 29.

17. Watkins (1950), p. 279. Two further examples are *AC* I.v.10–12 (thoughts as seeds carried by the wind) and III.xiii.65 (rats leaving a sinking ship).

18. Jonson's three chief comedies are conveniently available in the Penguin edition by M. Jamieson (1966), from which I quote.

19. Webster is quoted from *John Webster, Three Plays*, ed. D. C. Gunby, Penguin edition (1972).

20. Brown (1960), p. xlviii; Mulryne (1960); Kernan (1975), p. 395. Further examples are *White Devil* III.ii.5–7, V.i.159–61; *Malfi* III.iii.58–9.

CHAPTER SIX
Some uses of grammar

UNDERSTANDING SHAKESPEARE'S GRAMMAR

We can read Shakespeare much more easily than Chaucer. For that obvious reason I need spend comparatively little time on grammatical matters. However, despite the great simplification in morphology (the shapes of words, including inflexions) between Chaucer and Shakespeare, Shakespeare's grammar and syntax are not yet completely our own. Anyone who wishes to investigate the less important differences – of importance, that is, to the philologist but less so to the literary critic – may find them illustrated in three books whose approach is usually very different from mine: G. L. Brook, *The Language of Shakespeare* (1976), C. Barber, *Early Modern English* (1976), and E. A. Abbott, *A Shakespearean Grammar* (published in 1870 and still useful). Nor shall I delay over certain differences which I suspect afford little difficulty to the reader and even less to the theatre-goer. We no longer, with the eighteenth century, wish to correct Shakespeare, and so his double comparisons, double superlatives and multiple negatives[1] do not bother us:

> Nor that I am *more better*
> Than Prospero, master of a full poor cell.
>
> > (*Temp* I.ii.19–20)

> This was the *most unkindest* cut of all.
>
> > (*JC* III.ii.184)

Nor I know *not*
Where I did lodge last night.

(*KL* IV.vii.67–8)

Nor, really, do the occasional strange-looking forms of the past tense or past participle of strong verbs (those verbs which indicate the change from present to past by a change in the stem vowel, e.g. *sing/sang, drive/drove*). Present–day English has one vowel only throughout the past tense of these verbs and usually (though not always) another vowel for the past participle (*drove/driven, drank/drunk*). Old English mostly alternated two vowels within the past tense and had a third for the past participle. Things had begun to settle down in Middle English, but even in Shakespeare's time the forms were not always those we have today:

I *drave* my suitor from his mad humour of love.

(*AYLI* III.ii.399)

Even now he *sung*.

(*KJ* V.vii.12)

Thou hast perpendicularly *fell*.

(*KL* IV.vi.54)

It is fair to add that some of these are alternatives to the 'modern' form. Even as late as the eighteenth century, the original title of Gray's poem was "Elegy *Wrote* in a Country Churchyard".

Two other points of grammar are also unlikely to make us pause for long. By Shakespeare's time *who, which* and *that* were all in use as relative pronouns (Chaucer uses *whose* and *whom* as relatives, but not *who*). However, all three could still be used with personal antecedents:

I am married to a wife
Which is as dear to me as life itself.

(*MV* IV.i.279–80)

Nor do I think the man of safe discretion
That does affect it.

(*MM* I.i.71–2)

Most older and middle-aged people still pray "Our father *which* art in heaven" in the form of the 1662 Book of Common Prayer. Barber (1976: 218–19) suggests that *who* and *which* became more characteristic of a formal style and *that* of colloquial, informal contexts. In Elizabethan English *which* can also have a resumptive function when it begins a phrase or clause and refers back to all the items of a preceding catalogue:

For there, they say, he daily doth frequent
With unrestrained loose companions,
Even such, they say, as stand in narrow lanes

> And beat our watch, and rob our passengers,
> *Which* he – young wanton, and effeminate boy –
> Takes on the point of honour to support
> So dissolute a crew.
>
> (*R II* V.iii.6–12)

The possessive *its* was a late arrival in English. It is first recorded in 1598, but it does not appear in the quartos of Shakespeare's plays. There are some ten instances in the 1623 First Folio, interestingly – though perhaps coincidentally – usually in the later plays. In Old English *his* was the neuter genitive ('of it') just as much as the masculine genitive, and this can still be found in Shakespeare:

> How far that little candle throws *his* beams!
>
> (*MV* V.i.90)

> When yond same star that's westward from the pole
> Had made *his* course t'illume that part of heaven.
>
> (*Ham* I.i.36–7)

Shakespeare also uses *it* as a genitive form:

> It [the Ghost] lifted up *it* head and did address
> Itself to motion like as it would speak.
>
> (*Ham* I.ii.216–17)

> That nature which contemns *it* origin.
>
> (*KL* IV.ii.32)

But since editors often normalise to *its*, most modern readers never become aware of the variation. There are, incidentally, no examples of *its* in the Authorised Version of 1611 and only three in Milton. The Authorised Version, too, will sometimes use *his* ("If the salt have lost his savour", "Every creature after his kind") but more often will employ an alternative word ("The earth is the Lord's and the fulness *thereof*", "four cubits the breadth *thereof* and three cubits the height *of it*"). By the time of Dryden, towards the end of the seventeenth century, *its* had become usual, although until c. 1800 it is frequently found with an apostrophe, *it's*.

But these usages give rise to little difficulty in practice. One or two others, however, are worth considering more carefully, since they may either give a mistaken impression of deliberately old-fashioned language or today's reader may miss a real grammatical distinction in Shakespeare simply because it is not one we have retained. The first might be the case with the Elizabethan use of *do* and the alternative forms – *eth* and – *s*. The second might apply to the difference in usage between *thou* and *you*.

Do has had a chequered history. From early times it has had the possible meaning of 'perform' ('We must *do* something about that.')

or could be used as a substitute verb ('We ought to grow vegetables, like the neighbours *do* (grow vegetables).'). Shakespeare has examples of each of these. But the uses of *do* as an auxiliary verb have changed over the centuries. Nowadays we use the auxiliary *do* to ask questions or for emphasis ('*Do* you have a class at ten on Mondays?' 'Yes, I *do* have a Shakespeare class then.') or in negative constructions if no other auxiliary is present (compare 'I *did* not drive' and 'I *could* not drive'). Elizabethan English could use all these three, although they were not inevitable, as will be seen below. It had lost another, earlier, use of *do*, the Middle English causative, corresponding to *have* or *get* in present English ('I had my house painted', 'I got my car repaired').

In Elizabethan English, questions could be asked in two ways: by using *do*, as with most verbs in present-day English, or, a much older way, by simply inverting subject and verb:

> Where *sups he*? *Doth* the old boar *feed* in the old frank?
> *(2 Hen IV* II.ii.139)

> Why *look you* so pale?
> Who *sent you* hither? Wherefore *do you come*?
> *(R III* I.iv.173–4)

> What *did he* when thou sawest him? What *said he*? How *looked he*?
> Wherein *went he*? What *makes he* here? *Did he ask* for me?
> *(AYLI* III.ii.213–15)

Inversion is usual when the sentences begin with an interrogative (Rosalind's *What? How? Wherein?*), and of course this type of question is still used with a few modal verbs ('Why should he go?', 'When can he come?'). The eventual spread of *do* in questions was perhaps helped by its preservation of the usual word-order – subject, verb, object/complement – of English declarative sentences. "Did he ask for me?" simply precedes this by an auxiliary verb: aux SVO/C. Negatives without *do* are similarly common in Shakespeare:

> Indeed I think the young King loves you not.
> *(2 Hen IV* V.ii.9)

but almost half of his negative sentences were already using *do* with a word-order exactly that of present-day English:

> I know your lady does not love her husband.
> *(KL* IV.v.23)

But Shakespeare had one further use for *do* which we have since lost. *Do* (present) and *did* (past) were employed as 'dummy' auxiliaries, semantically empty, merely signalling tense but not altering the meaning of the main verb. 'I do love him' means the

121

same with or without the *do*; 'I did love him' equals 'I loved him', and any extra emphasis is simply because the main verb may be postponed a little. For example:

> Which of you shall we say *doth love* us most,
> That we our largest bounty may extend
> Where nature *doth* with merit *challenge*.
>
> (KL I.i.51–3)

> in which our valiant Hamlet –
> For so this side of our known world esteemed him –
> *Did slay* this Fortinbras; who, by a sealed compact
> Well ratified by law and heraldry,
> *Did forfeit*, with his life, all those his lands.
>
> (Ham I.i.84–8)

This usage seems to have arisen in the later Middle English period, and at first it is found especially in poetry (where it has the advantage of providing an extra syllable if needed) although by Shakespeare's time it was fully accepted in prose as well. It seems to have been losing ground by the mid seventeenth century, and at that stage the emphatic *do* begins to appear more often, as does the negative use. There seems to have been a limit on the number of uses of *do* at any one time, and the limit is obviously imposed by ambiguity. The 'dummy' *do*, however, brought occasional extra benefits. It could act as an additional tense marker in long and complex Elizabethan sentences.[2] It could assist the assimilation into English of new Latin borrowings; *illuminateth*, for instance, would sound clumsy. It could remedy ambiguities: *eat* and *ate* could sound alike in sixteenth-century pronunciation, so the Authorised Version uses *did eat*, not *ate* (at least in the gospels).

In the years just before Shakespeare, *-eth* and *-s*, as endings for the third person singular of the present indicative, were apparently genuine alternatives. So they often are for Shakespeare himself:

> Raz*eth* your cities, and subvert*s* your towns
>
> (1 Hen VI II.iii.64)

or the well-known lines from *The Merchant of Venice*:

> The quality of mercy is not strained,
> It dropp*eth* as the gentle rain from heaven
> Upon the place beneath. It is twice blest,
> It bless*eth* him that give*s* and him that take*s*.
>
> (IV.i.181–4)

As with the *do*-periphrasis, prosody may have played its part: *subverts* has two syllables, *subverteth* three. In Middle English, *-s* had been a feature of Northern, or at least North Midland, dialect; Chaucer, writing in London, had used *-eth*. But *-s* was spreading south in the later fifteenth century, and by the sixteenth century is part of London English; at first it may have been regarded as colloquial and informal. *-s* is more common in prose than in verse, and its eventual predominance in prose may have had the effect of making *-eth* sound formal and even a little old-fashioned. Yet the latter continued as a possible form, especially when there was nothing to be gained metrically by using *-s* (*useth, teacheth, judgeth*, but *loves* rather than *loveth*). It has been calculated that, in F1, there are almost four times as many *-eth* as *-es* endings in plays composed before 1600: afterwards *-es* outnumbers *-eth* by about six to one.[3] *Hath* and *doth*, though, are always much more common than *has* and *does*, and in these cases there may have been very little difference in pronunciation.

In the case of the 'dummy' *do* and the *-eth* inflexion, it would appear that both were possible forms for Shakespeare but that they may have suggested a rather dignified, slightly old-fashioned use.[4] It is difficult to be sure of shifts of tone within the small change of language and over a comparatively short period, but it seems permissible to use these two forms as corroborative evidence when I later try to distinguish certain formal styles.

We might well miss subtleties in Shakespeare's use of the second person unless alerted to the possibilities. If we go right back to the early Middle English period, there are four unambiguous forms: *thou* (nominative singular), *thee* (accusative singular), *ye* (nominative plural) and *you* (accusative plural). Nowadays, if we exclude religious language as a special register, we have only the single form *you*. Two factors have combined to produce this state of affairs, one grammatical and one social. The social one seems to have become operative first. From about the mid thirteenth century, and perhaps (like much else in Middle English) influenced by French practice, *ye* and *you*, as well as continuing for the plural, began to be used as a mark of respect in the *singular* when addressing a person regarded as one's superior. As this use of the 'polite' singular *ye/you* spread to include equals as well as superiors, so, by contrast, *thou* and *thee* were increasingly employed to inferiors – a master talking to his apprentice, say, or an older man to a very much younger one. It could also be deliberately insulting; Sir Toby teaches Sir Andrew how to pick a quarrel:

> Taunt him with the licence of ink. If thou 'thou' -est him some thrice it shall not be amiss.
>
> (*TN* III.ii.42–3)

123

Thou/thee could also indicate familiarity, from parent to child or between close friends. If it is asked how two almost opposite attitudes – insult and affection – could co-exist, the answer would seem to be that they would never occur within the same context. More and more, *thou* or *thee* was becoming a marked (unexpected) form, used in implied contrast to an unmarked (usual, expected) form, *ye* or *you*.

This, remember, was a social phenomenon. The original grammatical distinction between subject and objective forms continued longer, although increasingly *you* was used 'wrongly' for the subject. The Authorised Version, with its conservative, religious language, continues to distinguish them ("*Ye* have not chosen me but I have chosen *you*."; "*Ye* in me and I in *you*.") but Shakespeare is not so precise. Take Prospero's 'farewell' speech in *The Tempest* (V.i). It begins grammatically enough: "*Ye* elves of hills . . .", but within four lines we have "*you* demi-puppets . . . and *you* whose pastime is . . ." In fact, during the seventeenth century, *you* became the regular form for both nominative and accusative and both singular and plural, although *you was* (singular) and *you were* (plural) are sometimes found as late as the eighteenth century.

So, for our study of Shakespeare's style, the social distinction between *thou* and *you* is the more important. An amusing example from Deloney's *Jack of Newbury* (? 1597) shows the same usage in another writer. The hero is married twice; wife A has formerly been his employer and wife B his servant. After marriage he keeps on using *you* to A, but with B he uses both *thou* and *you*. Old habits died hard. It is easy enough to find examples from Shakespeare. In *1 Henry IV* III.ii, King Henry upbraids Hal for his wild life. He speaks more in sorrow than in anger, and so uses *thou* to his son; the Prince calls his father *you*. The same happens in the long conversation between them in *2 Henry IV* IV.v, where the dying king believes Hal cannot wait to get his hands upon the crown. Here Hal's *you* is not only respectful but a sign of remorse at having offended his dying father. When Hotspur is about to ride off to the wars (*1 Hen IV*, II. iii), his wife Kate enters:

> HOTSPUR   How now Kate? I must leave *you* within these two hours.
> KATE   O my good lord, why are *you* thus alone?

But after the opening unmarked *you* (aristocrats, anyway, normally use *you*), Kate switches to *thou* for the rest of the speech:

> Tell me, sweet lord, what is it that takes from *thee*
> *Thy* stomach, pleasure, and *thy* golden sleep?

(42–3)

But when Hotspur seems unappreciative of this wifely concern, and, worse, appears not to be listening, she switches back to *you* (76).

Hotspur responds with an affectionate *thou* or two, but Kate is not convinced:

> Do *you* not love me? Do *you* not indeed?
>
> (99)

Hotspur continues to tease her, but when war threatens wives must be kept in their place:

> Come, wilt *thou* see me ride?
> And when I am a-horseback, I will swear
> I love *thee* infinitely. But hark *you*, Kate
> I must not have *you* henceforth question me
> Whither I go, nor reason whereabout.
>
> (103–7)

A single switch of pronoun can indicate social class:

> FALSTAFF   Dost *thou* hear, hostess?
> HOSTESS   Pray *ye*, pacify yourself, Sir John.
>
> (*2 Hen IV* II.iv.77–8)

Disreputable he may be, but he is still a knight. Or a change from *you* to *thou* may show affection. Madeleine Doran notes that Antony uses *thou* of Caesar for the first time in his funeral oration.[5] Claudius calls Hamlet *you*, except for the one occasion when he is despatching him to England – he can afford to be expansive then. Hamlet calls Claudius *you* also, not only as subject to monarch but because there is so little love lost between them. He calls Horatio *thou* (his only friend in Denmark?) but Horatio uses *you* to his prince. The Ghost and Hamlet *thou* each other – perhaps to emphasise the affection between father and son as distinct from the cold formality between uncle and nephew – but on the occasion of the Ghost's brief second visit in III.iv, while he continues with *thou*, Hamlet once uses *you*, possibly conscious of his almost blunted purpose. Hamlet and Laertes hurl *thou's* at each other in the insults of the fight in Ophelia's grave ("I'll rant as well as *thou*."), but in his dying speech Laertes affectionately uses *thou* to Hamlet. Polonius, Laertes and Ophelia *you* each other (a not very united or affectionate family?) except at I.iii.57–81, Polonius's farewell to Laertes leaving for France.

It may be objected that some of the inferences I have drawn go too far, and I suspect that the *thou/you* dichotomy is not so clear-cut as some critics have argued. Consider the scene between Gertrude and Hamlet in her bedroom. He has always called her *you*, but she has varied between *thou* and *you* according to whether she wants to cajole him or is beginning to lose patience with him. So at III.vi.10:

> Hamlet, *thou* hast *thy* father much offended.

Thy father is, to her, Claudius. How nice it would be if they could all settle down and live happily ever after. Hamlet will have none of this. His immediate reply is:

> Mother, *you* have my father much offended.

Everyone gets the antithesis: *thy father* (Claudius), *my father* (old Hamlet). But Shakespeare underlines it by the switch from the affection of *thou* to the formality of *you*. I doubt, on the other hand, whether the *thou* and *you* would, by themselves, have been sufficient to signal the change of tone.[6] So while there are several fairly clear indications that the distinction could be useful to Shakespeare, we must remember that one *thou* does not constitute a glorious summer or a single *you* a winter of discontent. Nevertheless, the English language is now the poorer:

> You are a secret *thou*.
> Fumbling amongst the devalued currency
> Of 'dear' and 'darling' and 'my love'
> I do not dare to employ it –
> Not even in a poem, not even
> If I were a Quaker, any more.
> Beginning as an honorific, the unaffectionate *you*,
> For English speakers, has put *thou* out of business.
> So, in our intimate moments,
> We are dumb, in a castle of reserve.
> And He alone
> From Whom no secrets are hid, to Whom
> All hearts be open,
> Can be a public *Thou*.[7]

CONVERSION

One of Shakespeare's most exciting linguistic usages lies on the borderline between vocabulary and grammar. This is the phenomenon called either conversion or functional shift, using one part of speech as if it were another. We still do it, of course: a *key* man (noun as adjective); to *down* tools (adverb as verb); it's a *must* (auxiliary verb as noun). But it is exciting in Shakespeare because of its comparative newness. This plasticity of language would not have been easily possible before. In the heavily-inflected Old English, a noun is a noun because it has a noun-like ending. Even in Middle English, where the inflections have often decayed or even disappeared entirely, there is not much evidence of conversion.[8]

But by the Renaissance, parts of speech were often not distinguished at all by grammatical inflection. Here, surely, is Shakespeare exploiting the linguistic situation of his age. It is noteworthy that his contemporaries show fewer and individually less remarkable examples of the process than he does. Conversion seems to work through the listener's shock when he finds the word used in an unfamiliar manner. His attention is thus concentrated on that word for a moment, and this is exactly what Shakespeare wants, for his best examples are not only grammatically novel but metaphorical too. "I'll *mountebank* their loves", says Coriolanus, as he finally agrees to hide his true feelings and apologise to the plebs (III.ii.132). Fabian (*Twelfth Night* III.ii.18) tells poor Sir Andrew that Olivia is showing favour to Cesario only "to awake your *dormouse* valour" (which in Sir Andrew's case is very small and anyway asleep). The populace, almost always fickle in Shakespeare, "Goes to and back, *lackeying* the varying tide" (*Antony and Cleopatra* I.iv.46).[9] The two best examples are, I think, first Lear's description of Goneril and Regan as "those *pelican* daughters" (III.iv.72). The mother pelican will allow its young to peck its breast when desperate for food, but this sacrifice is the parent's own doing. With Lear, his daughters are deliberately tearing him to death. The other example is of Cleopatra's vivid premonition of defeat followed by something akin to the Roman triumph in which

> Antony
> Shall be brought drunken forth, and I shall see
> Some squeaking Cleopatra *boy* my greatness
> I'th' posture of a whore.

> (V.ii.218–21)

One can only marvel that there was a boy actor capable of playing Cleopatra, indeed of speaking these very lines. In fact Shakespeare occasionally goes beyond simple functional shift and the conversion becomes part of a new compound:

> Come you spirits
> That tend on mortal thoughts, *unsex* me here.

> (*Mac* I.v.38)

> Wine loved I deeply, dice dearly, and in woman *out-paramoured* the Turk.

> (*KL* III.iv.87)

> Though in this city he
> Hath widowed and *unchilded* many a one.

> (*Cor* V.vi.152)[10]

127

> If his occulted guilt
> Do not itself *unkennel* in one speech,
> It is a damned ghost that we have seen.

(Ham III.ii.90)

The prefix *un-* was a favourite with Shakespeare. It is pointless to speculate why, unless it was that it helped to break the bonds of convention to show heroes (and villains) hitherto capable of being imagined by the dramatist but hardly satisfactorily created through his language. Just as conversion breaks through the fetters of Elizabethan grammar.

Notes and References

1. For negation, see Blake (1988).
2. Samuels (1965). See also Samuels (1972), pp. 173–6.
3. Taylor (1976), reprinted in Salmon and Burness, pp. 349–69.
4. Cusack (1970), reprinted in Salmon and Burness, pp. 23–34.
5. Doran (1976), p. 132. For further examples of *thou* and *you*, see McIntosh (1963), Mulholland (1967), Barber (1981), Gurr (1982) and Wales (1983).
6. Cf. Goneril's declaration of love for Edmund: (quoted by Eagleson, 1971).

   > Decline *your* head: this kiss, if it durst speak,
   > Would stretch *thy* spirits up into the air.

   (KL IV.ii 22–3)

7. John Heath-Stubbs, *Selected Poems* (1965), p. 103. I owe this reference to the late Professor S.B. Greenfield.
8. Some remarks on conversion in Chaucer are included in Donner (1978).
9. Other notable examples of conversion are : He *childed* as I *fathered* (*KL* III.vi.108); *womaned* (*Oth* III.iv.191); *maggot* (*LLL* V.ii.410); *candy* (*I Hen IV* I.iii.247), *discandy* (*AC* IV.xii.22) and *discandying* (*AC* III.xiii.165); *pageants* (*TC* I.iii.151); *cormorant* (*TC* II.ii.6 and *Cor* I.i.119); *bower* (*RJ* III.ii.81); *sharked up* (*Ham* I.i.98); *prank* (*Cor* III.i.23); *vinegar* (*MV* I.i.54); *furnaces* (*Cym* I.vi.66). But any moderately careful reader can compile his own list. Noun to verb and verb to noun are especially common.
10. Wales (1978) notes that the *-ed* suffix may be either adjectival and (usually) stative or participial and dynamic; she compares *KL* III.iv. 31 where *windowed* is adjectival with *AC* IV.xiv.72 where it is participial.

CHAPTER SEVEN
Register and Style

STYLE, REGISTER AND OCCASION

The reader who has borne with me thus far will realise that the techniques of lexical and syntactical and rhetorical expansion, illustrated in the early chapters, are far from being innovations by Shakespeare. He produced better examples than his contemporaries, usually tailored to his context in a way that theirs were often not. He learnt a good deal about his art from the writing (and reading) of narrative and occasional poetry. What we are evidently concerned with is a number of group styles available to Elizabethan dramatists from the 1590s onwards and eventually developed by Shakespeare to an extent his contemporaries were either incapable of imagining or incapable of expressing. We are far from reality if we imagine Shakespeare scratching his head with the end of a quill pen waiting for the appropriate language to come. For one thing the hunger of the Elizabethan audience for new plays would make this picture unlikely. The second part of this book will attempt to show Shakespeare exploiting some of these accepted styles in his middle and later career. The styles I try to characterise are far from being the only ones, but they are among the most important and their description may help to sharpen the reader's or theatre–goer's awareness of what was increasingly taken for granted by the more experienced and sophisticated members of the Elizabethan audience. *Hieronimo* and *Andronicus* became shorthand terms for the flamboyance and exaggeration of one sort of tragic style and acting. In Beaumont's *Knight of the Burning Pestle* (produced 1607) the Citizen and his wife keep up a running commentary on the action, constantly intervene, and once or twice change the course of the play. Thereby they reveal not only their social pretensions but their almost complete lack of literary sophistication: they simply want a re-run of their favourite scenes from previous plays. Yet the same play burlesques different types of Elizabethan literature and therefore their appropriate styles. A barber is described like a giant from romance and is challenged and beaten by a 'knight' who is a grocer's apprentice; another apprentice disguises himself as his own ghost.

I have been talking about Elizabethan 'styles', but style is predominantly something we recognise on the page. Where it reflects a type of language according to use, depending less on the speaker than on the occasion, a better word might be *register*. This is a comprehensive term for a number of features of both vocabulary and syntax commonly associated with particular subjects or events, so easily recognised that we speak confidently of a legal register, say, or a military register, or a religious register, the kind of language we expect from people and situations 'like that'. If we turn from life to literature, certain genres (epic, pastoral) bring an expectation of certain kinds of writing, since literary language has already consciously selected from normal usage, so that here register and style overlap.[1] *Idiolects* reflect the character of the speaker by representing his own distinctive selection of language features. But there is perhaps rather less of this individuality in Shakespeare than is sometimes supposed. In the final chapter of his book *The Language of Shakespeare*, G. L. Brook discusses the idiolects of Gower (in *Pericles*), the Host of the Garter (*Merry Wives of Windsor*), Armado, Mistress Quickly, Pistol and Falstaff.[2] Opinions will naturally differ about what is distinctive, but while I shall later try to illustrate something of the language of the Host and of Pistol, I would exclude Gower and Armado from the list. The choruses spoken by Gower contain several archaisms from Middle English but nothing especially characteristic of the style of Gower himself. The intention is presumably to create an atmosphere of far away and long ago thought suitable for romance (Gower had told this story too), but eventually octosyllabics give way to blank verse so that a line like "That even her art sisters the natural roses" (Chorus V.7) is thoroughly Renaissance in content, metre and its use of the conversion *sisters*. The Quarto of *Love's Labour's Lost* refers sometimes to Armado but sometimes to 'Braggart', suggesting something of a stock figure whose linguistic usages are largely exaggerations of a style fairly easily paralleled elsewhere. Quickly and Falstaff are debatable cases. The former is an extreme example, in one person, of the malapropisms, mispronunciations and repetitive syntax characteristic of other lower–class comic characters: possibly the accumulation of all these does indeed constitute an idiolect. Falstaff's *use* of elaborate syntactical structures to avoid accepting responsibility for his previous actions and of certain lexical features (such as the outrageous compounds normally used for insults but in his case also as terms of affection to Hal) again seems to be sufficiently distinctive.

The most subtle exponent of registers in Renaissance drama is, perhaps, not Shakespeare but Jonson. What really interested him was the connection between language and manners. His is not the world of *Love's Labour's Lost* but the language of 'real life' Jacobean London: "deeds and language *such as men do use*" or, in the Prologue to *Bartholomew Fair*:

> Your Majesty is welcome to a Fair;
> Such place, such men, *such language* and such ware,
> You must expect.

Plays like *Bartholomew Fair* or *The Alchemist* demand not one but a number of specialised dictions: alchemy, fencing, the military profession, the canting terms used earlier by Greene's thieves and vagabonds (*doxy, foist, shark, firk* and others occur in *The Alchemist*) – in fact, several questionable ways of making a living ("the grammar and logic / And rhetoric of quarrelling", *Alchemist* IV.ii.64 for example). In Jonson, the jargon is most often spoken by the knaves who are opportunist enough to use it to persuade and cheat the fools who seem pathetically eager to imitate these cult languages.

The various Jonsonian registers are not simply employed to create an air of verisimilitude. The technical terms of alchemy itself ("What a brave language here is! next to canting", exclaims Surly) is naturally found throughout the play, but Subtle and Face, in the opening scene, actually quarrel in alchemical terms,:

> Raised thee from brooms and dust and wat'ring-pots?
> Sublimed thee and exalted thee, and fixed thee
> I' the third region, called our state of grace?
> Wrought thee to spirit, to quintessence, with pains
> Would twice have won me the Philosopher's Work?
>
> (*Alchemist* I.i.67–71)

Later Subtle and Face engage in a sort of alchemical catechism to deceive Ananias (II.ii). The simple-minded Ananias believes alchemy is inappropriate to puritanism, that the means are not justified by the ends, so his superior, Tribulation Wholesome, needs to use the technical puritan vocabulary to persuade him:

> Whenas the work is done, the Stone is made,
> This heat of his may turn into a *zeal*,
> And stand up for the *beauteous discipline*
> Against the *menstruous cloth and rag of Rome*.
> We must await his *calling*, and the *coming*
> *Of the good spirit.* You did fault, t' upbraid him
> With the *Brethren's* blessing of Heidelberg, weighing
> What need we have to hasten on *the work*,
> For the restoring of the *silenced Saints*,
> Which ne'er will be but by the Philosopher's Stone.
>
> (III.i.30–9)

The hypocrisy of the Puritans is revealed in another play when Zeal-of-the-Land Busy 'proves' that the eating of pig may indeed be made acceptable, even in the tents of Bartholomew Fair:

> Surely it may be otherwise, but it is subject to construction – subject,
> and hath a face of offence with the weak, a great face, a foul face, but
> that face may have a veil put over it, and be shadowed, as it were,
> it may be eaten, and in the Fair, I take it, in a booth, the tents of the
> wicked. The place is not much, not very much; we may be religious
> in midst of the profane, so it be eaten with a reformed mouth, with
> sobriety, and humbleness; not gorged in with gluttony or greediness;
> there's the fear: for, should she go there, as taking pride in the place, or
> delight in the unclean dressing to feed the vanity of the eye or the lust
> of the palate, it were not well, it were not fit, it were abominable, and
> not good.
>
> (I.vi.67–78)

Here the satire is not merely a matter of appropriate diction (*the weak, the tents of the wicked, sobriety, and humbleness, the vanity of the eye or the lust of the palate*); the syntax is deliberately repetitive and the dogmatism is that of the jack-in-office ("He was a baker, sir, but he does dream now, and see visions: he has given over his trade."). Again, in Busy's opinion, "it were a sin of obstinacy, great obstinacy, high and horrible obstinacy" not to follow the delicious aroma of roasting pork (III.ii.76). The opposite style, abrupt, often disconnected speech, extreme Senecanism, is fitting for angry characters, such as Kastril or Wasp.

SHAKESPEARE AND COLLOQUIALISM

Shakespeare did not examine the seamier side of Elizabethan London, except, to some extent, in the Eastcheap scenes of *Henry IV*. Nor does he write more obviously 'city' comedies, in the manner of Dekker's

Shoemaker's Holiday (1599 – 'A Pleasant Comedy of the Gentle Craft') or *Eastward Ho!* (1605), a collaborative work by Jonson, Chapman and Marston, with a good deal of obviously colloquial and proverbial language, a firm sense of its London riverside setting, several joking references to previous plays (including some of Pistol's lines) and a sustained alchemical metaphor in the characters Touchstone, Quicksilver and Golding. All this was presumably meant to appeal to the more literate private theatre audience. *The Merry Wives of Windsor* (? 1597) is not city comedy in this sense; it is set in a country town and much of its imagery is correspondingly domestic and 'natural'. Its interests are, however, wider than this: the discomfiture of Falstaff, Quickly's malapropisms, Evans and Caius who "make fritters of English", and the sheer normality of Ford and Page and their wives.

The swaggering bully Pistol wanders in and out of *2 Henry IV, Henry V* and *The Merry Wives of Windsor*, his mind crammed with half-remembered or misremembered scraps of old plays, his manner that of the braggart and coward who will turn to any kind of cheating or trickery that seems to promise easy pickings, his language spattered with contractions, inversions and outdated usage. The general impression is clear. But how is it achieved? How much is colloquial, obsolescent or even meant to be easily intelligible? This is a question difficult to answer precisely, since it would involve recreating the whole linguistic climate of the Elizabethan age to an extent that may be beyond us now. Through the pamphlets of Greene, we can recapture a good deal of the coney-catching background and some of the argot. The Boy in *Henry V* says Pistol *breaks words, and keeps whole weapons* (III.ii.35) and calls him *this roaring devil i' th' old play* (IV.iv.69). His very name is appropriate, for a pistol was still at the experimental stage, erratic and apt not to go off at all, but, if it did, to cause a notable explosion and almost as likely to injure its owner as his enemy. A stage direction in *The Atheist's Tragedy* makes Borachio's pistol give *false fire*. Or, as Jorgensen says,[3] the name might alternatively derive from Italian *pistolfo* which Florio's dictionary of 1611 defines as "a roguing begger, a cantler, an vpright man that liueth by cosenage". But this brings us into the somewhat murky areas of colloquial language and semantic change, for why should an *upright* man live by cosenage? The second chapter of Thomas Harman's *A Caveat for Common Cursitors* enlightens us:

> An upright man, the second in sect of this unseemly sort, must be next placed, of these ranging rabblement of rascals; some be servingmen, artificers, and labouring men traded up in husbandry. These, not minding to get their living with the sweat of their face, but casting off all

pain, will wander, after their wicked manner, through the most shires of this realm. These upright men will seldom or never want; for what is gotten by any mort, or doxy, if it please him, he doth command the same . . . Here you see that the upright man is of great authority. For all sorts of beggars are obedient to his hests, and [he] surmounteth all others in pilfering and stealing.[4]

So an upright man is not 'upright' at all, in our sense of the word, but aggressive and domineering.

Near the beginning of *The Merry Wives of Windsor*, Slender calls Bardolph, Nym and Pistol *coney-catching rascals*. Even Falstaff sees himself coney-catching as a last desperate remedy:

> There is no remedy. I must cony-catch, I must shift.
>
> (I.iii.32)

> I myself sometimes, leaving the fear of God on the left hand and hiding mine honour in my necessity, am fain to shuffle, to hedge, and to lurch.
>
> (II.ii.23–6)

Although *shuffle, hedge* and *lurch* are part of the coney-catchers' vocabulary (all three meaning 'cheat' or 'steal'), Shakespeare does not use very much of this special register, canting language, as it came to be called. The audience, however, is obviously familiar with this type of ragged, cheating scoundrel, for Autolycus in *The Winter's Tale* is another example. These 'sturdy beggars' seem to have been recruited from ex-soldiers, such as Pistol himself who laments at the end of *Henry V*:

> Old I do wax, and from my weary limbs
> Honour is cudgelled. Well, bawd I'll turn,
> And something lean to cutpurse of quick hand.
> To England will I steal, and there I'll – steal;
> And patches will I get unto these cudgelled scars,
> And swear I got them in the Gallia wars.
>
> (V.i.80–5)

or discharged serving-men, or tenants evicted as a result of the change from arable to sheep-farming which required fewer hands. The elite of the coney-catchers (*coney* meant rabbit, but in this argot 'dupe') formed a fraternity with a strong element of 'professional' training and a jargon of its own, partly to conceal from any eavesdropping worthy citizen the thievery intended, but partly also as a status symbol. The best and most readable of the literature of coney-catching is the collection of pamphlets (1591–2) by Robert Greene. Greene's criminals hardly ever work alone; a con-man set-up involving three or four of them is quite common. The subject-matter is fascinating in itself: *The Second Part of Coney-Catching* covers horse-stealing, cheating at bowls and at cards, the activities of the nip and the foist (cutpurse and pickpocket), shoplifting and burglary (including casing the premises first). Greene clearly enjoys his exposé, and one imagines that his middle-class audience had the comforting feeling of knowing about the practice while remaining at a comfortable distance from it (as with modern newspaper 'revelations' of, say, the drug scene).[5] Stylistically, though, this is the literary exploitation of one kind of colloquial vocabulary and speech rhythm not used hitherto. This extract demonstrates not only Greene's journalistic, coordinate style, full of *and's*, *but's*, *then's* and *for's* but also the clear definition of the function of each of the villains:

> . . . and the whiles he begins to resolve which of them most fitly may be lifted, and what garbage (for so he calls the goods stolen) may be most easily conveyed, then he calls to the Mercer's man and says, 'Sirrah, reach me that piece of velvet or satin, or that jewel, chain or piece of plate', and whilst the fellow turns his back, he commits his garbage to the marker: for note, the lift is without his cloak, in his doublet and hose, to avoid the more suspicion. The marker, which is the receiver of the lift's luggage, gives a wink to the santar that walks before the window, and then the santar going by in great haste, the marker calls him and says, 'Sir, a word with you; I have a message to do unto you from a very friend of yours and the errand is of some importance'. 'Truly, sir', says the santar, 'I have very urgent business in hand, and as at this time I cannot stay'. 'But one word and no more', says the marker, and then he delivers him whatsoever the lift hath conveyed unto him, and then the santar goes his way, who never came within the shop and is a man unknown to them all. Suppose he is smoked and his lifting is looked into, then are they upon their pantofles, because there is nothing found about them. They defy the world for their honesty, because they be as dishonest as any in the world, and swear as God shall judge them they never saw the parcel lost; but oaths with them are like wind out of a bellows, which being cool kindleth fire. So their vows are without conscience, and so they call for revenge.[6]

Smoked is 'discovered' (smoked out) and *upon their pantofles* means 'on their dignity'; pantofles were exotic, high-heeled slippers (as it happens Shakespeare does not use the word, preferring *chopines*). All the rest of the technical language is explained within the passage, and to punctuate the extract for Modern English, adding inverted commas for example, destroys much of Greene's breathless manner.

Coney-catchers had made their appearance in drama a few years before Pistol and his cronies. In *Arden of Feversham* (published 1592)[7] Black Will and Shakebag are coney-catchers but they do not use the argot. They do begin by speaking prose, but at iii.83, and for no apparent reason, move into verse. Occasionally they display something of the braggadocio that was to become the fustian style of Pistol and is already suspect:

> And therefore thus: I am the very man,
> Marked in my birth-hour by the destinies,
> To give an end to Arden's life on earth;
> Thou but a member but to whet the knife
> Whose edge must search the closet of his breast.
>
> (iii. 153–7)

> Black night hath hid the pleasures of the day,
> And sheeting darkness overhangs the earth,
> And with the black fold of her cloudy robe
> Obscures us from the eyesight of the world,
> In which sweet silence such as we triumph.
> The lazy minutes linger on their time,
> As loath to give due audit to the hour,
> Till in the watch our purpose be complete,
> And Arden sent to everlasting night.
>
> (v. 1–9)

But Arden will be safe: no one who spends time talking like that is going to be capable of giving a mortal wound, however dark the night and however sharp the weapon. Pistol, while just as much a coward, is far more flamboyant and far less poetical.

Towards the close of 2 *Henry IV*, he arrives in Gloucestershire with news from court:

PISTOL	Sweet knight, thou art now one of the greatest men in this realm.
SILENCE	By'r lady, I think 'a be, but goodman Puff of Barson.
PISTOL	Puff?
	Puff i'thy teeth, most recreant coward base!
	Sir John, I am thy Pistol and thy friend,
	And helter-skelter have I rode to thee,
	And tidings do I bring, and lucky joys,
	And golden times, and happy news of price.
FALSTAFF	I pray thee now, deliver them like a man of this world.
PISTOL	A foutre for the world and wordlings base!
	I speak of Africa and golden joys.
FALSTAFF	O base Assyrian knight, what is thy news?
	Let King Cophetua know the truth thereof.
SILENCE	And Robin Hood, Scarlet, and John.
PISTOL	Shall dunghill curs confront the Helicons?
	And shall good news be baffled?
	Then, Pistol, lay thy head in Furies' lap.

(V. iii. 87–106)

When Silence cannot understand the significance of Falstaff's elevation, Pistol turns on him in his usual ranting style, composed of four parts aggression to every one of sense. *Recreant*, 'one who has yielded in battle', has the proper military ring which is made to sound even more impressive by the inversion in *coward base*. *Lucky joys/And golden times* is not in his usual vein, but the phrases are probably traditional collocations. A *foutre* is indecent and almost certainly accompanied by the appropriate gesture. Falstaff joins in with a parody of Pistol's style in which there is no real sense in the linking of *Assyrian knight* (the Elizabethans regarded Assyrians as brigands) and the old ballad of King Cophetua and the beggar maid. Helicons and Furies are much more Pistol's stock-in-trade, and *baffled*, which seems odd, even for Pistol, was possibly a new word. Olivia's "Alas, poor fool, how have they *baffled* thee" and Richard II's "I am disgraced, impeached and *baffled* here" suggest that Pistol may mean 'confounded' and be wrongly applying the word to *news*.[8] Later news, however, is not so good:

> My knight, I will inflame thy noble liver,
> And make thee rage.
> Thy Doll, and Helen of thy noble thoughts,
> Is in base durance and contagious prison,
> Haled thither
> By most mechanical and dirty hand.
> Rouse up Revenge from ebon den with fell Alecto's snake,
> For Doll is in. Pistol speaks naught but truth.
>
> (V.v.31–9)

Base durance, contagious prison and *haled* are once again predictable phrases for him. Doll Tearsheet is scarcely a Helen; his later epithet ("the lazar kite of Cressid's kind", *Hen V* II.i.73) is more appropriate. But Revenge might well come from some kind of *ebon den*; he emerges from the underworld in some contemporary tragedies ("Enter the Ghost of Andrea, and with him Revenge").[9] Alecto is one of the Furies who were indeed represented with snakes in their hair, and the last line is, surprisingly, straight information.

To penetrate the layers of Pistol's mind would need not a psychologist so much as an archaeologist, for phrases and characters from old plays are overlaid with scraps of colloquial Elizabethan English. It is possibly futile to try. Alliteration occasionally appears together with archaisms, not to mention *Couple a gorge*, one of the few French phrases he thinks he knows:

> PISTOL   An oath of mickle might, and fury shall abate.
> Give me thy fist, thy forefoot to me give;
> Thy spirits are most tall.

137

> NYM   I will cut thy throat one time or other, in fair terms,
> that is the humour of it.
> PISTOL   *Couple a gorge!*
> That is the word. I thee defy again!
>
>   (*Hen V* II.i.63–9)

He is inclined to invert not only adjective and noun but also verb
and object (*thy forefoot to me give; I thee defy*). *Tall*, 'valiant' was
still used of warriors, although less and less often as our sense,
'of great height' (not recorded before 1530) became established.
Falstaff is, to Bardolph at least, *a tall gentleman* (*2 Hen IV* III.ii.60).
In the mechanicals' play in *A Midsummer Night's Dream*, Pyramus is
sweet youth and tall (V.i.143). The Second Murderer of *Richard III*
encourages his companion: "Spoke like a *tall* man that respects thy
reputation" (I.iv.154). The Clown in *The Winter's Tale* offers, four
times over, to swear that Autolycus is a *tall fellow* (V.ii.160–9). But
nobody – except Pistol – seems to speak of *tall spirits*. He cannot
even announce himself without a departure from normal word-order:
"My name is Pistol called" (*Hen V* IV.i.62), and this too is probably
old-fashioned usage. Elsewhere the grand gesture is what counts:

> Let floods o'erswell, and fiends for food howl on!
>
>   (*Hen V* II.i.89)

> Perpend my words, O Signieur Dew, and mark.
> O Signieur Dew, thou diest on point of fox.
>
>   (*Hen V* IV.iv.8–9)

> Let gallows gape for dog; let man go free,
> And let not hemp his wind-pipe suffocate.
>
>   (*Hen V* III.vi.41–2)

Heroic-sounding phrases (whatever they may *mean*) jostle with the
language of coney-catchers: *gourd and fullam* and *high and low* both
refer to loaded dice:

> Let vultures gripe thy guts! For gourd and fullam holds,
> And high and low beguiles the rich and poor.
>
>   (*MWW* I.iii.85–6)

No doubt the audience's delight, if the editor's despair. With Pistol,
Shakespeare goes far beyond the register of rogues and vagabonds
and creates a genuine dramatic idiolect.

In Shakespeare's own day one of the best and most amusing
examples of a deliberate clash of registers and styles is Dekker's *The
Gull's Horn Book* (1609). A horn-book was originally a leaf of paper
containing the alphabet, some basic spelling, the Lord's prayer, and
so forth, protected by a thin plate of translucent horn. It is therefore

an elementary book of instruction, a primer. A gull is a credulous person, someone easily imposed upon. Dekker gives directions on how the would-be gentleman setting up in London should behave throughout the day. It is a spoof guide to the high life of London for provincial people, a parody of contemporary courtesy books but also a moral work showing the worthlessness of such a style of life by his exposé of it. The deliberate contrast between the middle style (with high style phrases) of the gull, with his social aspiration of becoming a dandy, and the low style reality of his vanity and penury is the source of Dekker's irony. In this passage the gull visits the middle aisle of St Paul's, a favourite meeting-place:

> Now for your venturing into the Walk, be circumspect and wary what pillar you come in at and take heed in any case, as you love the reputation of your honour, that you avoid the Servingman's Log, and approach not within five fathom of that pillar but bend your course directly in the middle line, that the whole body of the church may appear to be yours. Where in view of all, you may publish your suit in what manner you affect most, either with the slide of your cloak from the one shoulder (and then you must, as 'twere in anger, suddenly snatch at the middle of the inside if it be taffeta at the least, and so by that means your costly lining is betrayed) or else by the pretty advantage of compliment. But one note by the way do I especially woo you to, the neglect of which makes many of our gallants cheap and ordinary: that by no means you be seen above four turns, but in the fifth make yourself away either in some of the sempsters' shops, the new tobacco office or amongst the booksellers where, if you cannot read, exercise your smoke and enquire who has writ against 'this divine weed', etc. For this withdrawing yourself a little will much benefit your suit, which else by too long walking would be stale to the whole spectators.
>
> But howsoever, if Paul's jacks be once up with their elbows and quarrelling to strike eleven, as soon as ever the clock has parted them and ended the fray with his hammer, let not the Duke's Gallery contain you any longer, but pass away in open view. In which departure if by chance you either encounter or aloof off throw your inquisitive eye upon any knight or squire being your familiar, salute him not by his name of 'Sir Such-a-One' or so but call him 'Ned' or 'Jack', etc.: This will set off your estimation with great men. And if (though there be a dozen companies between you, 'tis the better) he call aloud to you (for that's most genteel) to know where he shall find you at two o'clock, tell him at such an ordinary or such (and be sure to name those that are dearest and whither none but your gallants resort). After dinner you may appear again, having translated yourself out of your English cloth cloak into a light Turkey grogram (if you have that happiness of shifting) and then be seen for a turn or two to correct your teeth with some quill or silver instrument and to cleanse your gums with a wrought handkerchief. It skills not whether you dined or no (that's best

known to your stomach) or in what place you dined, though it were
with cheese of your own mother's making in your chamber or study.[10]

The firm sense of place is evident: St Paul's Walk, the Servingman's
Log (the bench where the servants gossiped), the new tobacco office,
the booksellers, the ordinary (eating-house). The high, literary style
of *venturing, circumspect, bend your course, pretty advantage of compliment*,
the figures having *ended the fray* as the clock strikes, *aloof off throw your
inquisitive eye* (with its reversal of normal word-order), *correct your
teeth*, shows the gallant. The colloquialisms, such as *'twere, by the way,
by no means, etc., or so*, and in particular the parentheses (*as 'twere in
anger, for a turn or two, for that's most genteel, of your own mother's making*)
which at times approach stage-directions, undercut this fashionable
pose by showing that it is all play-acting. The mock-conversational
style, with its use of *you* and its several imperatives, creates a close
relationship with the reader, and the clothing puns (*publish your suit,
your costly lining is betrayed, translated yourself, if you have that happiness
of shifting*) reveal that these fine feathers conceal a very close-plucked
bird.

The Gull's Horn Book achieves its double approach to the character
of the would-be man-about-town by its regular and deliberate juxtaposition of different registers and styles. Shakespeare sometimes
achieves the same effect in the Sonnets. Sonnet 46 is a case in point:

> Mine eye and heart are at a mortal war
> How to divide the conquest of thy sight;
> Mine eye my heart thy picture's sight would bar,
> My heart mine eye the freedom of that right.
> My heart doth plead that thou in him dost lie,
> A closet never pierced with crystal eyes;
> But the defendant doth that plea deny,
> And says in him thy fair appearance lies.
> To 'cide this title is empanelled
> A quest of thoughts, all tenants to the heart;
> And by their verdict is determined
> The clear eye's moiety, and the dear heart's part:
>> As thus – mine eye's due is thy outward part,
>> And my heart's right thy inward love of heart.

The lexical set *war, divide the conquest, bar, freedom* is confined to the
first quatrain, and is succeeded in the second and third quatrains by
a new set of terms: *plead, defendant, plea, deny, title, impaneled, quest,
tenants, verdict, determined, moiety, part*. But is not law, too, a kind of
warfare, and ought love to be discussed in terms of either? *Eye and
heart*, together in line one, have been drifting more and more apart
throughout the sonnet, and are contrasted in the concluding couplet.

Sonnet 134 also, with its mention of *mortgaged, forfeit, surety-like, bond, statute, sue*, suggests a love which, on the woman's side, is devoid of affection and is characterised by materialistic, business-like relationships.

Drama does not readily lend itself to a continuous use of this technique. What Shakespeare often does is to deflate rather obviously poetic language by a deliberate colloquialism. Hubert of Angers suggests that if King John's niece, Blanche of Spain, will marry Lewis the Dauphin, the city need not be destroyed. The Bastard Fauconbridge is magnificently unimpressed by his rhetoric. Incensed at having been *bethumped with words*, he reasserts reality by his deliberately bathetic and monosyllabic concluding line:

> He speaks plain cannon-fire and smoke and bounce;
> He gives the bastinado with his tongue.
> Our ears are cudgelled; not a word of his
> But buffets better than a fist of France.
> Zounds! I was never so bethumped with words
> Since I first called my brother's father dad!
>
> (*KJ* II.i.462–7)

At the King's final appearance, he prepares for death in a line whose colloquialisms do not detract from the solemn setting:

> Ay, marry, now my soul hath elbow-room.
>
> (V.vii.28)

Unfortunately, he follows this with several sentimental conceits. Shakespeare had not yet learned to allow direct, monosyllabic language to make its own point about the necessary simplicity of dying:

> Finish, good lady; the bright day is done,
> And we are for the dark.
>
> (*AC* V.ii.193–4)

Or a speech in *2 Henry IV*, which, despite lines like "The beachy girdle of the ocean / Too wide for Neptune's hips", reaches its climax (in the Quarto, the lines are not in F1) simply and monosyllabically:

> O, if this were seen,
> The happiest youth, viewing his progress through,
> What perils past, what crosses to ensue,
> Would shut the book, and sit him down and die.
>
> (III.i.53)

Or Hamlet, planning to make his *quietus* with a bare bodkin. However, the advantages of plainness are beginning to be realised in a play perhaps a year earlier than *King John*:

> Well, Juliet, I will lie with thee tonight.
>
> (*RJ* V.i.34)

> O true apothecary.
> Thy drugs are quick.
>
> (V.iii.119)

These lines contrast – although the contrast is not yet made fully explicit – with the extravagant language of the early part of the play, and even with the style of Paris in Act V. *Macbeth* regularly makes the contrast between surface appearance and sordid reality by the juxtaposition of two kinds of diction:

> Is't night's *predominance* or the day's *shame*
> That darkness does the face of earth *entomb*
> When living light should *kiss* it?
>
> (II.iv.8–10)

> Good things of day begin to *droop and drowse,*
> Whiles *night's black agents to their preys do rouse.*
>
> (III.ii.52–3)

So does *Antony and Cleopatra*:

> Welcome, dear madam.
> Each heart in Rome does love and pity you.
> Only th'adulterous Antony, most large
> In his abominations, turns you off
> And gives his potent regiment to a trull
> That noises it against us.
>
> (III.vi.91–6)

where *adulterous, large in his abominations, potent regiment* are negatived by the colloquialisms *turns you off, trull* and *noises it.*

PUNS

Puns (which Dekker employed as one means of irony) are common in Shakespeare. The Hostess addresses Pistol as "Good Captain Peesel", *2 Hen IV* II.iv.156, and the spelling indicates a pun on *pizzle* ('bull's penis'), a word which Falstaff uses elsewhere (*1 Hen IV* II.iv.241); the same pun occurs when Falstaff says "She [the hostess] is pistol-proof" (112).[11] A little later still, Doll Tearsheet calls Pistol *you cutpurse rascal, you filthy bung* (124). In one meaning of *bung* (something that stops a hole) the earlier indecent pun is again in evidence, but *cutpurse* suggests the slang use of *bung* as pickpocket, for in thieves' language *bung* meant purse. Indecent puns are not limited to the Falstaff plays, or indeed to lower-class characters, for Mercutio, Leontes and Beatrice all have their share. The curious may consult Eric Partridge's *Shakespeare's Bawdy* or a glossary for entries under *appetite, charge, hit, hole, lap, lie, occupy* ("an excellent good word before it was ill-sorted"), *stand to it, stewed prunes, tail / tale, tailor, top, weapon* and *will*. Perhaps we see too many examples of word-play, just as we are ready to recognise too many recurrent images.[12] But puns are by no means confined to the funny situations. Gaunt in *Richard II* puns on his name as he lies on his deathbed, as does Donne in *A Hymn to God the Father*:

> And having done that, *Thou hast done*,
> I fear no more.

Lady Macbeth, trying to recall her husband to practicalities as he begins to realise the enormity of his murder of Duncan, makes what to us would be an unacceptable pun:

> I'll gild the faces of the grooms withal,
> For it must seem their guilt.

(Mac II.ii.56–7)

Hamlet's very first words are a pun:

KING	But now, my cousin Hamlet, and my son –
HAMLET	(*aside*) A little more than kin, and less than kind!
KING	How is it that the clouds still hang on you?
HAMLET	Not so, my lord. I am too much in the sun.

(I.ii.64–67)

Claudius, in a bid to gain Hamlet's support for the new regime and his own marriage to Gertrude, addresses him as *cousin* ('kinsman') but also as *son*. Hamlet acknowledges the fact of relationship (*kin*) but repudiates any closer tie or any shared feelings, since *kind* was often used of close blood relations such as members of the same family: Lear calls Goneril and Regan "these *unkind* daughters". Claudius's second attempt at friendship meets with a further pun on *sun* and *son*. The melancholic's favourite position on the fringes of society (the 'shade') and his dark clothes (his "inky cloak" and "customary suits of solemn black" of the immediately following lines) would lead Hamlet to refuse the proffered 'sunshine' of royal favour, the more so as this king has made an incestuous marriage with Hamlet's own mother. Later on Hamlet takes some of Polonius's words in another sense:

POLONIUS	What do you read, my lord?
HAMLET	Words, words, words.
POLONIUS	What is the matter, my lord?
HAMLET	Between who?

POLONIUS   I mean the matter that you read, my lord.

(II.ii.191–6)

as he does those of Rosencrantz and Guildenstern:

GUILDENSTERN Happy in that we are not over-happy.
                        On Fortune's cap we are not the very button.
HAMLET   Nor the soles of her shoe?
ROSENCRANTZ Neither, my lord.
HAMLET   Then you live about her waist, or in the middle
                        of her favours?
GUILDENSTERN Faith, her privates we.
HAMLET   In the secret parts of Fortune? O, most true!
                        She is a strumpet.

(II.ii.228–35)

To their despair:

GUILDENSTERN Good my lord, put your discourse into some
                        frame, and start not so wildly from my affair.

(III.ii.316–17)

but Hamlet's puns both show that he recognises that all three are the King's spies and also indulge his intellect as a substitute for direct action.

In the best general treatment of the subject, *Shakespeare's Word-play*, M. M. Mahood argues further: that Shakespeare's imagination sometimes worked through puns, and that the puns frequently have not only a local significance but a wider dramatic function such as characterisation or emphasising a dominant idea in the play. The first point is really incapable of proof, but Professor Mahood may well be correct when she argues that, in the following quotation, *knave, queen, heart* produced the metaphor *packed cards* (characteristic in its use of colloquialism to express the always slightly suspect nature of Cleopatra's behaviour) and that this in turn led to *false-played* and *triumph* (the latter itself a pun meaning both 'victory' and 'trump card'):

Here I am Antony,
Yet cannot hold this visible shape, my knave.
I made these wars for Egypt; and the Queen –
Whose heart I thought I had, for she had mine,
Which, whilst it was mine, had annexed unto't
A million more, now lost – she, Eros, has
Packed cards with Caesar, and false-played my glory
Unto an enemy's triumph.

(*AC* IV.xiv.13–20)

On the wider implications of the puns, it is easy to agree with many of the examples Miss Mahood cites from the comedies. Not only do the lovers seek to out-pun one another, but the heroines sometimes bandy puns with the clown, as in the extended passage of wit which begins Act III of *Twelfth Night*:

VIOLA	Save thee, friend, and thy music. Dost thou live by thy tabor?
FESTE	No sir, I live by the church.
VIOLA	Art thou a churchman?

At the other extreme, Hamlet's puns in the play scene certainly provide a momentary relief from tension, both for him and for us. But what about Polonius's advice to Ophelia?

> Do not believe his vows. For they are brokers,
> Not of that dye which their investments show,
> But mere implorators of unholy suits,
> Breathing like sanctified and pious bawds,
> The better to beguile.
>
> (*Ham* I.iii.127–31)

Would the audience follow the fourfold pun:

brokers	(i) go-betweens	(ii) second-hand clothes dealers
dye	(i) appearance	(ii) colour
investments	(i) finances	(ii) garments
suits	(i) requests	(ii) clothing

and grasp the secondary meanings of shabby, worthless reality below the attractive surface appearance? Would it need to? Probably all four puns are intentional, although their recognition is not essential to appreciate the drift of Polonius's advice and the way in which his puns seek to ridicule Ophelia's love for Hamlet.

POPULAR LANGUAGE

Lower-class life and colloquial language often go together. But not invariably. As Fluellen drives the cowards Nym, Pistol and Bardolph forwards "into the breach", Pistol cries "Good *bawcock*, bate thy rage! Use lenity, sweet *chuck*" (*Hen V* III.ii.25). Sir Toby uses the same two words to Malvolio (III.iv.112) and Leontes uses *bawcock* and *captain* as terms of endearment to his son (I.ii.121). Antony calls Cleopatra *chuck* (IV.iv.2) and Virgilia her son *crack*, a lively youngster (I.iii.69). It is probably impossible for us now to recreate the spoken English of lower-class life in Shakespeare's time, especially its grammar and syntax – vocabulary is easier.[13] We get hints of it in the speech at the inn in *1 Henry IV* II.i: *out of all cess, stung like a tench, your chamber-lye breeds fleas like a loach, Troyans, you muddy knave* and "no foot-landrakers, no long-staff sixpenny strikers, none of these mad mustachio purple-hued maltworms". Prince Hal believes himself to be an honorary member of the fraternity of Eastcheap barmen:

> They take it already upon their salvation that though I be but Prince
> of Wales yet I am the king of courtesy, and tell me flatly I am
> no proud Jack like Falstaff, but a Corinthian, a lad of mettle, a
> good boy – by the Lord, so they call me! – and when I am King
> of England I shall command all the good lads in Eastcheap. They
> call drinking deep 'dyeing scarlet', and when you breathe in your
> watering they cry 'Hem!' and bid you 'Play it off!'
>
> (*I Hen IV* II.iv.8–16)

The fashion for classical names (*Corinthian*) is one shared by the Host of the Garter (*Merry Wives*) and Simon Eyre (Dekker's *Shoemaker's Holiday*). The Fishermen in *Pericles* are more concerned with social comment than with appropriate language; only an occasional phrase, such as *with a wanion, bots on't*, suggests real idiom. The brothel scene in the same play relies on a different register, one closer to similar settings in *Henry IV* or *Measure for Measure*. *Pooped, piece, stir you up, crowns of the sun, fitment, plucked, paced, work her to your manage, doorkeeper, ploughed, Tib*, are suggestive enough, often metaphorical or punning, as is common in such language. William and Audrey might have taken the opportunity to show us what real life – with the real dialect – in Arden was like, but instead they simply give Touchstone a chance to show off his wit.

As was the case with change of meaning, the context will usually give us a clue to the interpretation of colloquial phrases. A few of these have survived to our own times; we experience no difficulty with "I cannot tell *what the dickens* his name is", "a man of my kidney" (*MWW* III.ii.16 and III.v.113) or Maria's "at my fingers' ends" and "a horse of that colour" (*TN* I.iii.75 and II.iii.160). Other usages which have not survived still give us little trouble. When Goneril says to Regan *let us hit together* (*KL* I.i.302), she most probably means 'fit in together', and when they resolve to do something *i' th' heat* the phrase is clearly analogous to 'strike while the iron is hot'. Occasionally the origin of the phrase is clear too. Menenius says to the Volscian sentries "it is lots to blanks / My name hath touched your ears" (*Coriolanus* V.ii.10). In Elizabethan lotteries, lots won prizes and blanks didn't. Shylock wants to catch Antonio *upon the hip* (*MV*

I.iii.43); the phrase is a wrestling term ('at a disadvantage') with a possible additional reference to the dislocation of Jacob's hip in *Genesis 32*. *Godfathers* was a slang term for jury; hence Gratiano's jibe at Shylock:

> In christ'ning shalt thou have two godfathers.
> Had I been judge, thou shouldst have had ten more,
> To bring thee to the gallows, not to the font.
>
> (*MV* IV.i.395–7)

When the unpleasant Bertram refers to Helena as *my clog* (*All's Well*, II.v.53), this seems to be a metaphorical use of *clog* as a block of wood tied to an animal's leg to prevent it from straying. Don John in *Much Ado* (I.iii.30) complains that he is "trusted with a muzzle and enfranchised with a *clog*". Autolycus, who regularly uses colloquialisms, speaks of Florizel "stealing away from his father with his *clog* [Perdita] at his heels" (*WT* IV.iv.674). *Slubber* clearly means 'scamp' in *The Merchant of Venice*: "*Slubber* not business for my sake, Bassanio" (II.viii.39), but when the Duke tells Othello that, in Cyprus, he must "*Slubber* the gloss of your new fortunes with this more stubborn and boisterous expedition" (I.iii.224), 'smear' is a better equivalent. These are the only two uses of the word in Shakespeare, but a shared metaphorical sense of a hurried covering over to conceal the more worthwhile texture beneath seems evident. Metaphor is also behind "This Doll Tearsheet should be some *road*" ('whore'), Falstaff's direction to Bardolph to push Pistol downstairs, "*Quoit* him down" (*2 Hen IV*, II.ii.160 and II.iv.187 respectively), and the Nurse's switch of support to Paris: "O, he's a lovely gentleman! / Romeo's a *dishclout* to him." (*RJ* III.v.219). Even when we cannot be sure of the explanation, the idea is clear enough. Parolles (*AW* II.iii.278) laughs at the man who, instead of going to the wars, "hugs his *kicky-wicky* here at home"; this bawdy compound is unique in Shakespeare. Aufidius's "I'll *potch* at him some way" uses an apparently slang word (Onions thought a Warwickshire dialect word)[14] and one which suggests the unheroic, underhand manner in which he does finally accomplish Coriolanus's death. When the Hostess, assessing Fenton's chances of winning Anne Page, is sure "'*tis in his buttons* he will carry't", we may not be able to suggest the origin of the phrase but it presumably means 'it's obvious'. In the same play, *fap* (*MWW* I.i.172), a word often unnecessarily emended, probably means 'drunk' and may be an example from West Midland dialect.[15]

In some cases, colloquial language seems to be used as one means of characterisation. There is a good deal of it in *Twelfth Night*, almost all in the Toby-Andrew-Maria-Fabian scenes. Maria says that Sir Andrew "hath the gift of a coward to *allay the gust* (offset the delight?) he hath in quarrelling" (I.iii.28). Toby himself uses *coystril* (rogue); *I am a dog at* (very good at) *a catch; sneck up* (push off); a *beagle, true bred* (a marvellous girl); *call me cut* (a fool); *at a cold scent* (from hunting); *play at cherry pit* (be on friendly terms) *with Satan*. Maria has the delightful *Go shake your ears* (oh, shut up!) and *gull him into a nayword* (make a fool of him). Fabian speaks of *the windy side of the law* (the safe side). The racy style aptly matches their high spirits. In *Antony and Cleopatra* the purpose is rather different. Antony tells Octavia *I have not kept my square* (I have wandered from the straight and narrow) and her brother tells Antony we could not *stall* together. But the epithets applied to Cleopatra are far more interesting. To Enobarbus she is a *wonderful piece of work*, an *Egyptian dish*, and he notices that even the priests bless her when she is *riggish*. To Agrippa she is *royal wench*, to Scarus *yon ribaudred nag of Egypt*, and finally to Charmian a *lass unparalleled*. When Antony suspects her of betraying him to Caesar, he calls her a *boggler ever*, and, in the metaphor discussed above, one who has *packed cards* with Caesar. She sees herself as a *morsel for a monarch*. These do not merely contribute to the sense of abundant vitality which everyone notices in the play. They also imply that there is something about Cleopatra both unpredictable and unreliable, part of the infinite variety of the queen whom Enobarbus saw not only sailing majestically down the Cydnus but hopping forty paces through the public street.

Slang is ephemeral and, initially, sub-standard too. It aims at a colourful effect, but its very proliferation inevitably destroys much of the novelty, and the word disappears, or, in a few cases, is adopted into the standard vocabulary. Intensifiers, for instance, move in and out of fashion in different ages. How long will *right* ('a right fool', 'a right idler') last? It was certainly very common in Shakespeare's day, as a glance at the *Concordance* will show, although usually with adjective or adverb and only occasionally with noun: *right valiant, right apt, right sorry, right deadly, a right gypsy*. How long a life for *dead* ('dead easy'), not to mention *plumb* easy? *Out-and-out* ('an out-and-out liar'), *desperately* ('desperately tired') and sheer ('sheer force of habit') seem to have been around for some time. Shakespearean drama has its own favourites; not surprisingly they are most common in lower-class dialogue or the colloquial language of upper-class characters. *Whoreson* is used with its literal meaning, 'bastard', by Gloucester at the beginning of *Lear*: "there was good sport at his making, and the whoreson must be acknowledged", but the instances in *Romeo and Juliet*, "a merry whoreson" (IV.iv.20) and *Henry VIII*, "The sly whoresons / Have got a speeding trick to lay down ladies" (I.iii.39), are obviously colloquial. From there it is a short step to "Thou *whoreson* mad compound of majesty" and "Thou *whoreson* little tidy Bartholomew boar-pig" (*2 Hen IV*, II.iv.289 and 226) where the word has become an affectionate intensifier. Indeed, it is something of an Eastcheap mannerism in *2 Henry IV*, for the majority of the Shakespearean uses come from that play. Even more of a catch-phrase is *bully*. The Host in *The Merry Wives of Windsor* is especially addicted to the word (*bully* rook, *bully* stale, *bully* knight, or simply *bully* on its own). Sixteen of the twenty recorded instances in Shakespeare are his: two more are used about Bottom, a third by Pistol and the fourth by Stephano to Caliban. *Old*, another intensifier from these plays, is less frequent. Francis the Drawer looks forward to *old utis*, 'a high old time' (*2 Hen IV* II.iv.19). Once Doctor Caius appears, Mistress Quickly – who should know – fears "old abusing of God's patience and the King's English" (*MWW* I.iv.5). Moving up the social scale, Portia says "We shall have old swearing / That they did give the rings away" (*MV* IV.ii.15) and Ursula calls back Beatrice because "Yonder's old coil at home" (*MA* V.ii.86). The Porter's "If a man were porter of hell gate he should have *old* turning the key" (*Mac* II.iii.2) has a rather similar meaning, although here *old* does not quite look like an intensifier.

Passing is used as an intensifier on many occasions, in some seventeen different plays and poems. In *Titus Andronicus* poor Lavina, ignorant of her fate or that of Bassanius, has discovered the affair between Tamora and Aaron and says "This valley fits the purpose passing well" (III.ii.84). Richard III (as yet still Duke of Gloucester) suggests it is no treason to admit that Edward IV's mistress, Shore's wife, "hath a pretty foot, / A cherry lip, a bonny eye, a passing pleasing tongue" (I.i.93). Desdemona considered Othello's adventures *passing strange* (I.iii.159) and Autolycus offers one from his stock of ballads, "a passing merry one" (*WT* IV.iv.286). These, and others like *passing fair* are acceptable enough, but *passing cowardly* (*Cor* I.i.201), *passing scornfully* (*Hen V* IV.ii.40) and *passing short* (*AYLI* III.v.138) strike us as odd. For some reason, *The Taming of the Shrew* is especially fond of the word, with seven examples. *Wondrous* is, if anything, even more frequent than *passing*, but most of the collocations: *wondrous fair / strange / heavy / cold / hot / kind / rare*, are clear enough. One at least, Othello's "'twas pitiful, 'twas wondrous pitiful", is one of the best remembered lines of the play. *Monstrous, shrewdly, vengeance* and (one which we have kept) *thoroughly* are far less common. Of the two uses of *monstrous* as intensifier, one is comic, Bottom's "monstrous little voice" (*MND* I.ii.48) but the other more truly poetic: "Skill infinite, or monstrous desperate" (*AW* II.i184). *All's Well* also contributes *shrewdly vexed* (III.v.88); the other similar use of the word is *Winter's Tale* V.i.102, where *shrewdly ebbed* continues the metaphor of *flowed* earlier in the line. *Vengeance proud* (*Cor* II.ii.5; compare Menenius's "What the vengeance." III.i.261 and present day English 'with a vengeance') is emphatic and arresting, but "This fellow has a *vengeance* trick o' th' hip" (*Two Noble Kinsmen* II.ii.71) is more puzzling, since the word intensifies a noun rather than the usual adjective or adverb. Shakespeare usually spells 'thoroughly' *throughly*; it occurs four times as an intensifier. *Throughly healed* (*TGV* I.ii.115), *throughly moved* (*MWW* I.iv.89), *throughly weary* (*Cym* III.vi.36) are intelligible enough. Kent's "My point and period will be *throughly* wrought" is part of a couplet which closes a scene (*KL* IV.vii.96); he seems to mean 'things will come to a head'.

Shakespeare, then, made considerable use of features of contemporary colloquial English, many of which correspond to those of our own day. But he was also sensitive to the vocabulary and syntax of special registers. With characters like the Host of the Garter, on a small scale, and Pistol, on a much larger scale (although we have not quite finished with Pistol yet), he fused these to achieve a literary idiolect of considerable complexity but immensely attractive personality.

Notes and References

1. Katie Wales defines register as "degrees of formality, appropriate to the different social uses of language", *A Dictionary of Stylistics* (1989), p. 98. She emphasises register-switching and register-borrowing and the relationship between register and genre in literary studies.
2. Hibbard (1981), pp. 125–8, 174–81 would add the Nurse in *RJ* and Hotspur.
3. Jorgensen (1962), pp. 70–4.
4. *Coney-Catchers and Bawdy Baskets: An Anthology of Elizabethan Low Life*, ed. G. Salgado (1972), pp. 91, 94.
5. They are so natural follies, but so shown
   That even the doers may see, and yet not own.
   　　　　　　　　　　　　　　　(*The Alchemist*, Prologue, 23–4)
6. *Life and Complete Works of Robert Greene*, ed. A. B. Grosart (New York, 1964), X, pp. 118–20.
7. Included in *Minor Elizabethan Tragedies*, ed. T. W. Craik (1974).
8. Among the earlier meanings in the *OED* are "disgrace" (1548) and "hoodwink" (1590).
9. Opening to *The Spanish Tragedy*.
10. *Thomas Dekker*, ed. E. D. Pendry (1967), pp. 88–9.

11. Compare "With a pistol in his great cod-piece", *Duchess of Malfi*, II.ii.39.
12. As Colman, p. 21, says, ribald punning is often assumed without proof in "the sex-conscious and irony-loving atmosphere of the later twentieth century". We see what we want to see.
13. Salmon (1967), reprinted in Salmon and Burness (1987), pp. 37–70.
14. C. T. Onions, *A Shakespeare Glossary* (1911). See also Brook (1976), p. 180.
15. Oliver (1971), p. 13 (note).

CHAPTER EIGHT
Some Shakespearean styles

INTRODUCTION

On the face of it, the primary distinguishing feature of a passage from Shakespeare might seem to be whether it is written in prose or in verse. But it is not quite so simple. There is no prose at all in *Richard II* or in *King John*. *The Merry Wives of Windsor* contains the most prose (and its language may well be the nearest to Elizabethan colloquial English), followed by *Much Ado*, *Twelfth Night* and *As You Like It*. Other plays with marked comic elements – *1 and 2 Henry IV*, for example, in which Falstaff speaks only about a dozen lines of verse – also contain a good deal of prose.[1] Prose, therefore, is most prominent in the middle comedies and some of the histories of about the same date. The earlier comedies, as we have seen, sometimes use patterned euphuistic prose in the manner of Lyly who wrote six prose comedies and only one verse play, and we have to wait for *The Merchant of Venice* (1596) before a major character, Shylock, speaks serious prose. Only in the earliest comedy, and once or twice later (for example where Hal uses prose to Falstaff and his cronies but verse to the nobles) will we find such a clear division as in *The Taming of the Shrew* where the high life is in verse and the low life in prose. Henry V, on the night before Agincourt, speaks prose to his soldiers as he moves amongst his army in disguise. He later woos Katherine in prose; the soldier has become the lover. Yet in neither of these scenes does the prose seem natural: brief exchanges, characteristic of conversation, are interspersed with longer, more balanced, rhetorical passages:

Some, peradventure, have on them the guilt of premeditated and contrived murder; some, of beguiling virgins with the broken seals of perjury; some, making the wars their bulwark, that have before gored the gentle bosom of peace with pillage and robbery.

(IV.i.157–61)

A good leg will fall; a straight back will stoop; a black beard will turn white; a curled pate will grow bald; a fair face will wither; a full eye will wax hollow; but a good heart, Kate, is the sun and the moon – or rather, the sun, and not the moon; for it shines bright and never changes, but keeps his course truly.

(V.ii.158–63)

The low-life prose of Eastcheap has been abandoned by Henry in the face of the more serious concerns of *Henry V*.

Not all lower-class characters confine themselves to prose. Mistress Quickly and Pompey in *Measure for Measure* do, but the Nurse in *Romeo and Juliet* speaks verse of a kind, as well as her usual prose, just as the citizens in *Julius Caesar* use prose in I.i. but verse in III.ii. The norm of the plays is obviously blank verse, and Shakespeare's authoritative characters – kings, dukes and leaders generally – for the most part use a verse whose diction includes rather more than the average number of polysyllables and whose smooth flow conceals a deliberate control of syntax. Members of the aristocracy, however, sometimes "relax or condescend into prose".[2] Hamlet, for example, speaks prose to Rosencrantz and Guildenstern and also to the Players and the Gravedigger. Prose, then, appears to be used for special reasons of dramatic contrast.

One of the most obvious uses of prose to reflect something other than the norm, is to indicate madness, real or assumed. Ophelia in her madness is a wreck of her former self, and her derangement is signalled not only by the doggerel verse but also by a change to prose. Lady Macbeth's monosyllabic prose in the sleep-walking scene is another case in point. Lear, however, when mad speaks both verse and prose; perhaps the verse indicates his growing perception of reality. Edgar as Poor Tom usually speaks prose (apart from snatches of doggerel verse) but blank verse for the soliloquies at the close of II.vi. and the beginning of IV.i. In the scene where he pretends to lead the blind Gloucester to the edge of Dover cliffs, both characters speak blank verse, and Gloucester is consequently puzzled not only by his preservation but by 'two' characters:

Methinks thy voice is altered, and thou speak'st
In better phrase and matter than thou didst.

(IV.vi.7–8)

Edgar resumes his disguise of a *bold peasant*, and consequently adopts

stage Zummerset prose, for the brief altercation with Oswald, but
in Act V, once again Edgar and eventually restored to his rightful
position, he uses verse. After he decides to feign madness, Hamlet
speaks prose to everyone except to Horatio (his one confidant), to
Gertrude and the Ghost in the closet scene, and of course in his
soliloquies. But when he returns from the voyage no further pretence
of madness is necessary, and the final scene is in blank verse.

Prose, in fact, is not inferior to blank verse. Mercutio, who
had earlier been responsible for the poeticism of the Queen Mab
speech, dies in prose. It is, of course, capable of balance and wit,
and its range can be seen in a character like Falstaff, whose prose
increases in complexity as he tries (and usually succeeds) to slide
out of his responsibilities. But, as Vickers says,[3] prose-speaking
characters are not heroes, visionaries or romantics, but are sometimes
beastly (Thersites), blunt (Enobarbus, Casca) or buffoons (Parolles,
Menenius).

THE RATIONAL MAN

To this I would add a further category, the efficient, 'rational' man
whose air of common sense may be either real or assumed. Once
again, most of these characters alternate prose and verse, so the prose
is likely to be contrastive in intention. The Duke in *Measure for
Measure* begins Act III with the magnificent verse speech to Claudio,
"Be absolute for death . . .". Yet to Isabella later in the same scene,
and to Escalus in the next, he employs prose. Perhaps this is partly
to emphasise his disguise as a friar, but the balance and spareness of
this prose suggests above all a man subject to plan and to command:

> The hand that hath made you fair hath made you good. The goodness
> that is cheap in beauty makes beauty brief in goodness, but grace,
> being the soul of your complexion, shall keep the body of it ever fair.
> The assault that Angelo hath made to you, fortune hath conveyed to
> my understanding, and, but that frailty hath examples for his falling, I
> should wonder at Angelo. How will you do to content this substitute,
> and to save your brother?
>
> (III.i.182–90)

ESCALUS	What news abroad i' th' world?
DUKE	None, but that there is so great a fever on goodness
	that the dissolution of it must cure it. Novelty
	is only in request, and it is as dangerous to be aged in
	any kind of course as it is virtuous to be constant

in any undertaking. There is scarce truth enough alive to make societies secure, but security enough to make fellowships accursed. Much upon this riddle runs the wisdom of the world. This news is old enough, yet it is every day's news. I pray you sir, of what disposition was the Duke?

(III.ii.211–21)

If we were ever tempted to regard the Duke's temporary abdication as irresponsible, these passages surely remove our doubts. By the close of IV.iii. the plans are completed. Henceforth (and in verse):

> By cold gradation and well-balanced form,
> We shall proceed with Angelo.

(98–9)

Brutus, too, is efficient – or believes he is. Both before and after the funeral speech he uses verse, but the oration itself is in prose. Its rhetoric is obvious: the answers to hypothetical questions, the antitheses, the repetitions, the isocolon and parison:

> As Caesar loved me, I weep for him; as he was fortunate, I rejoice at it; as he was valiant, I honour him; but, as he was ambitious, I slew him.

(*JC*, III.ii.24–6)

It is above all reasonable; Brutus had assured the sceptical Cassius that he would show "the *reasons* of our Caesar's death". It is also brief. Antony's much longer verse rejoinder is rhetorical too: antithesis in *The evil . . . The good . . .*; the repetition of *ambitious, honourable* and *wrong*; the pretence that he is overcome by emotion; the withholding of the will; the affectation of modesty ("I am no orator, as Brutus is"), but these are not so much the figures of speech as that part of rhetoric concerned with the delivery of the speech (*pronunciatio*). At the close, Antony is well-satisfied, and his simple aside, "Now let it work" indicates his scheming. Brutus, sincere and full of integrity, had appealed in cool prose to the reason, the quality which, in Shakespeare, the populace above all lacks. His idealism comes to seem naïve, remote from reality. Intellectual prose is vanquished by passionate blank verse. If Brutus is an *orator*, Antony is the greatest actor of them all.[4] Coriolanus, too, briefly begs for the citizens' support in prose with an irony they totally fail to perceive. But he regards the whole process as dishonourable and insulting to himself, and so here prose is the mark of an assumed style. Immediately the first group of citizens has gone, Coriolanus returns to blank verse which he continues for a perfunctory appeal to two or three stragglers who must also be placated. The 'plainness' of Coriolanus, however, is best seen in his usual style which I intend to discuss later as an aspect of a deliberately created 'Roman' or 'soldierly' language.

The spare, controlled prose of Brutus is a world away from the prose we have considered hitherto: the euphuism of Lyly, the Ciceronianism of Sidney and Hooker, the looser but still expansive style of Donne. Around 1600, Ciceronianism, with its elaboration of the constituent parts of the sentence, began to lose ground in favour of the much more terse, epigrammatic, but still balanced style of Seneca and Tacitus where the ideal became "the most matter with best conceyt in fewest words".[5] (Seneca, of course, was not exactly a new author to the Elizabethans.) The distaste for over-refined Ciceronianism, with its deviousness and disproportionate attention to manner at the expense of matter, is expressed most forcibly in a well-known passage from Bacon's *Advancement of Learning* (1605):

> There be therefore chiefly three vanities in studies, whereby learning hath been most traduced. For those things we do esteem vain, which are either false or frivolous, those which either have no truth or no use: and those persons we esteem vain, which are either credulous or curious; and curiosity is either in matter or words: so that in reason as well as in experience, there fall out to be these three distempers (as I may term them) of learning: the first, fantastical learning; the second, contentious learning; and the last, delicate learning; vain imaginations, vain altercations, and vain affectations; and with the last I will begin . . . so that these four causes concurring, the admiration of ancient authors, the hate of the schoolmen, the exact study of languages, and the efficacy of preaching, did bring in an affectionate study of eloquence and copie of speech, which then began to flourish. This grew speedily to an excess; for men began to hunt more after words than matter; more after the choiceness of the phrase, and the round and clean composition of the sentence, and the sweet falling of the clauses, and the varying and illustration of their works with tropes and figures, than after the weight of matter, worth of subject, soundness of argument, life of invention, or depth of judgement.[6]

Bacon parodies the excess of eloquence and *copie* ('copiousness') which he rejects, for the passage "the choiceness of the phrase, and the round and clean composition of the sentence, and the sweet falling of the clauses, and the varying and illustration of their works with tropes and figures" is indeed artfully and elegantly expressed and contrasts with the hammer-blows of "weight of matter, worth of subject, soundness of argument, life of invention, or depth of judgement". But Bacon's own prose in *The Advancement of Learning* is still far from the impersonal prose of later scientists. We are not yet at the level of absolute plainness advocated in Sprat's *History of the Royal Society* (1667) or of Hobbes's rejection of metaphor (*Leviathan*, 1651).

The essay and the 'character', and in drama the comedies of Jonson, begin to supply the greater observation and experiment which Bacon the scientist desired. If brevity was in, copiousness was not altogether out. But, by 1600, it is more likely to be reserved for a special purpose (the insincerity of Osric or of Timon's friends) than indulged in for its own sake. One Latin model has simply been exchanged for two others, and the balance of Bacon's final phrases (abstract noun + *of* + noun) reminds us that symmetry is still appreciated even if the top-dressing of Ciceronianism is less in vogue.

The eloquent, associative, frequently redundant, sermon style of John Donne (see p. 19) may be contrasted with the pointed, staccato, economic style of Lancelot Andrewes. Andrewes's method is explication; indeed he has been called "not so much a religious thinker as a religious philologist",[7] and T.S. Eliot's metaphor of squeezing the last drop of meaning from the text is an apt one. Andrewes's style may be conveniently illustrated by an excerpt from his Christmas Day sermon, 1622, well-known for its influence on Eliot's *Journey of the Magi*:

> It is not commended, to stand *gazing up into heaven* too long, on Christ himself ascending: much less on His star. For, they sat not still gazing on the star. Their *Vidimus* begat *Venimus*; their seeing made them come; come a long journey. Venimus is soon said; but a short word: But, many a wide and weary step they made, before they could come to say *Venimus*, Lo, *here we are come; Come* and at our journey's end. To look a little on it. In this their coming, we consider, First, the distance of the place they came from. It was not hard by, as the shepherds' (but a step to Bethlehem, over the fields:) This was riding many a hundred miles, and cost them many a day's journey. Secondly, we consider the way that they came: If it be pleasant, or plain and easy: For if it be, it is so much the better. This was nothing pleasant: for through deserts, all the way waste and desolate. Nor (secondly) easy either: For over the rocks and crags of both Arabies (specially Petrea) their journey lay. Thirdly, yet if safe: but it was not; but exceeding dangerous, a lying through the middest of the black tents of Kedar, a nation of thieves and cut-throats; to pass over the hills of robbers; infamous then, and infamous to this day. No passing, without great troop or convoy. Last we consider the time of their coming, the season of the year. It was no summer progress. A cold coming they had of it, at this time of the year; just the worst time of the year to take a journey, and specially a long journey in. The ways deep, the weather sharp, the days short, the sun furthest off in *solstitio brumuli*, the very dead of Winter. *Venimus*, we are come, if that be one; *Venimus*, we are (now) come, come at this time, that (sure) is another. And these difficulties they overcame, of a wearisome, irksome, troublesome, dangerous, unseasonable journey; And for all this, they came. And came it cheerfully and quickly; As appeareth by the speed they made. It was but *Vidimus, Venimus*, with them; They

saw and they came: No sooner saw, but they set out presently.[8]

While this, with its several colloquialisms (*much less, hard by, but a step, so much the better, No passing, A cold coming they had of it, sure, No sooner*) and its short sentences (some of them without a main verb) may appear unstudied, it is really no more spontaneous than the expansiveness of Donne. His progress is a logical one (*First . . . Secondly . . . Thirdly . . . Last*). He will state a hypothesis, almost immediately to deny it: "If it be pleasant . . . This was nothing pleasant"; "yet if safe: but it was not". The balance of "The ways deep, the weather sharp, the days short, the sun furthest off" is obvious. The rhetorical figure of *gradatio* is a favourite: "made them *come*; *come* a long journey", "the time of their *coming* . . . A cold *coming*". Andrewes's method is, in his own words here, "to look a little on it", to probe what the words may mean. And the only occasion he uses copiousness is in the deliberate contrast of "a wearisome, irksome, troublesome, dangerous, unseasonable journey".

If the style of Andrewes seems too disconnected, the coordinate but nevertheless symmetrical syntax of the opening of Bacon's essay *Of Studies* is an example of Senecanism of a less extreme kind. The clauses are mostly of equal length and within them noun matches noun and infinitive answers to infinitive; antithesis is a frequent device:

> *Studies* serve for delight, for ornament, and for ability. Their chiefe use for delight is in privatenesse and retiring; for ornament, is in discourse; and for ability, is in the judgement and disposition of businesse. For expert men can execute, and perhaps judge of particulars, one by one; but the generall counsels, and the plots and marshalling of affaires, come best from those that are *learned*. To spend too much time in *studies* is sloth; to use them too much for ornament is affectation; to make judgement wholly by their rules is the humour of a scholler. They perfect nature, and are perfected by experience: for naturall abilities, are like naturall plants, that need proyning by *study*: and *studies* themselves doe give forth directions too much at large, except they be bounded in by experience. Crafty men contemne studies; simple men admire them; and wise men use them: for they teach not their owne use; but that is a wisdome without them, and above them, won by observation. Read not to contradict, and confute; nor to beleeve and take for granted; nor to finde talke and discourse; but to weigh and consider.[9]

The efficient, rational prose of such characters as Brutus, or the Duke in *Measure for Measure*, is therefore one of several clearly defined prose styles around the turn of the century. But the surface pragmatism and balance may cloak villainy beneath, as Iago well knew:

The Moor is of a free and open nature
That thinks men honest that but seem to be so.

(I.iii.393–4)

How did Iago acquire his reputation for honesty? Again, the answer lies, partly at least, in the kind of language he uses. For much of the time he speaks in prose, although the soliloquies, in which he takes the audience into his confidence, are in verse. Iago gives the impression of balancing his own (admittedly biased) imagination against Othello's natural wisdom and candour. But he is a Machiavellian villain (like Webster's Bosola and Vindice), completely and remorselessly dedicated to the winning of power for his own ends, a political realist, a man who knows, through practical experience, that men do not always by any means act in the way they purport to act and that the world often favours the shrewd operator rather than the man of principle. This is, in Ralph Berry's words, "the man in the outside lane, the New Man".[10] Such men sometimes seem to overturn accepted values and standards simply by virtue of their rational 'modern' thinking. And rational men are often honest men. Often, but not always. If Iago is to persuade Othello that seeing is believing (a typically Machiavellian viewpoint), he starts with the advantage of appearing a rational man.

So does another villain, Edmund, who likewise links credulity and honesty:

A credulous father and a brother noble,
Whose nature is so far from doing harms
That he suspects none; on whose *foolish honesty*
My practices ride easy.

(I.ii.175–8)

Edmund is, like other Shakespearean villains, a manipulator of language. He uses both prose and verse, but the balance of his prose to Gloucester is speciously logical:

I do not well know, my lord. If it shall please you to suspend your indignation against my brother till you can derive from him better testimony of his intent, you should run a certain course; where, if you violently proceed against him, mistaking his purpose, it would make a great gap in your own honour and shake in pieces the heart of his obedience. I dare pawn down my life for him that he hath writ this to feel my affection to your honour and to no other pretence of danger.

(I.ii.80–8)

His contempt, in the same scene, for Gloucester's astrological explanations of his *goatish disposition* is also that of the 'new' Machiavellian man ("Fut! I should have been that I am had the

maidenliest star in the firmament twinkled on my bastardizing.").
When he speaks verse his style is equally pared-down and business-like
(e.g. II.i.48–55, V.i.55–69), as is that of Goneril and Regan who,
interestingly enough, both assume the masculine role in marriage and
to whom Edmund becomes attached. Lear's poetic eloquence in the
opening scene is brought to earth by the unemotional and calculating
prose of Goneril and Regan in the final lines (" 'Tis the infirmity of his
age. Yet he hath ever but slenderly known himself.").

An earlier essay in the balanced language of deceit is Don John
in *Much Ado*. He is an uncomplicated villain, but his prose, too, is
symmetrical, even rigid:

> I had rather be a canker in a hedge than a rose in his grace, and it better
> fits my blood to be disdained of all than to fashion a carriage to rob
> love from any. In this, though I cannot be said to be a flattering honest
> man, it must not be denied but I am a plain-dealing villain. I am trusted
> with a muzzle and enfranchised with a clog; therefore I have decreed
> not to sing in my cage. If I had my mouth, I would bite; if I had my
> liberty, I would do my liking. In the meantime, let me be that I am,
> and seek not to alter me.

(I.iii.25–34)

and, as with Iago, seeing is believing:

> If you dare not trust that you see, confess not that you know. If you
> will follow me, I will show you enough; and when you have seen more
> and heard more, proceed accordingly.

(III.ii.107–10)

THE LANGUAGE OF INSULTS

These various illustrations will not explain all the uses of prose
by Shakespeare, for instance the curious scene in prose (where
verse might normally be expected) between Autolycus and the
three 'Gentlemen' (*Winter's Tale* V.ii). Probably the prose here is
meant simply to convey information in a play whose verse syntax
is notoriously difficult. It may be useful, however, to conclude
this discussion of prose with an examination of the kind of prose
used for insults and scurrilous comment, not least because it shows
Shakespeare developing a different kind of compound. If we were
inclined to think that all Shakespeare's compounds are 'poetical',
several of the examples in the *Henry IV* plays and in *Troilus and
Cressida* will soon disillusion us. Falstaff roars into action in the
Gadshill robbery:

Strike, down with them, cut the villains' throats! Ah, whoreson caterpillars, bacon-fed knaves!

(1 Hen IV II.ii.82–3)

His creditors are, to him, equally unreasonable:

A whoreson Achitophel! A rascally yea-forsooth knave, to bear a
gentleman in hand, and then stand upon security! The whoreson
smoothy-pates do now wear nothing but high shoes and bunches of
keys at their girdles.

(2 Hen IV I.ii.34–6)

His pressed soldiers are no better than "toasts-and-butter, with
hearts in their bellies no bigger than pins' heads" (*1 Hen IV*
IV.ii.20), but Falstaff himself is to Prince Hal "this bed-presser,
this horse-back-breaker" (*1 Hen IV* II.iv.238) or "You whoreson
candle-mine you" (*2 Hen IV* II.iv.295). Bardolph is "that arrant
malmsey-nose knave" (*2 Hen IV* II.i.37) and Pistol "you bottle-ale
rascal, you basket-hilt stale juggler, you!" (*2 Hen IV* II.iv.127).
To the beadle, carrying her off to be whipped, Doll Tearsheet
screams:

Nut-hook, nut-hook, you lie! Come on, I'll tell thee what, thou
damned tripe-visaged rascal, an the child I go with do miscarry, thou
wert better thou hadst struck thy mother, thou paper-faced villain.

(2 Hen IV V.iv.7–10)

Thersites ("Who's there? Good Thersites, come in and *rail*.") speaks
of his own *spiteful execrations*, and *Troilus and Cressida* provides
an impressive list: *thou mongrel, beef-witted lord; thou sodden-witted
lord; thou scurvy-valiant ass* (all to Ajax); *short-armed ignorance; idol of
idiot-worshippers; clapper-clawing; that stale old mouse-eaten dry cheese,
Nestor, and that same dog-fox Ulysses*, and his pièce-de-résistance:

Now, the rotten diseases of the south, the guts-griping ruptures, ca-
tarrhs, loads o' gravel in the back, lethargies, cold palsies, raw eyes,
dirt-rotten livers, wheezing lungs, bladders full of imposthume, sci-
aticas, lime-kilns i' the palm, incurable bone-ache, and the riveled fee-
simple of the tetter, and the like, take and take again such preposterous
discoveries!

(V.i.17–24)

Elsewhere in the same play, *bed-work, cob-loaf, overproud and under-honest,
enlard his fat-already pride, boy-queller, great-sized coward, the hold-door trade*
keep up the level of insults which so often seem a substitute for action.
But it is easy to find lists in other plays: Berowne in *Love's Labour's
Lost* (V.ii.464–5), Aaron in *Titus Andronicus* (IV.ii.97–8), Capulet to

161

a Juliet who refuses to marry Paris (*RJ* IIII.v.156–7), Kent insulting Oswald (*KL* II.ii.13–22) and, most interestingly, Macbeth's outburst to the unfortunate servant, which expresses his rising panic:

> The devil damn thee black, thou cream-faced loon!
> Where got'st thou that goose look? . . .
> Go prick thy face and over-red thy fear,
> Thou lily-livered boy. What soldiers, patch?
> Death of thy soul! Those linen cheeks of thine
> Are counsellors to fear. What soldiers, whey-face?
>
> (V.iii.11–17)

Not quite all of these are in prose, although most are. What they have in common is their outrageous nature. They are coined for this particular occasion, neologisms, unlikely perhaps to be used again. Here Shakespeare's mentor – if he needed one – was probably Nashe. Nashe was one of the new university-trained men who had to make a living by his pen. He was twenty-seven when he wrote *The Unfortunate Traveller* which has been called the first picaresque novel in English, but most of his work was in the form of pamphlets, usually controversial, always eye-catching, essentially ephemeral. Nashe, in short, was a journalist before his time, and his extravagant, deliberately shocking, exhibitionist style, which often seems to challenge the reader to do better if he can, is part of his stock-in-trade. Almost any page of Nashe will provide illustrations, but here is a random list: *scholastical squitter-books* (scribblers); *the shop-dust of the sights I saw in Rome; old excellent he was at a bone-ache* (a torturer); *this supereminent principal metropolis of the red fish* (Yarmouth); *shame-swollen toad to have the spit-proofed face* (of one of his opponents in the pamphlet war); *such gargantuan boisterous galliguts* (the Spanish Armada). To those who complained of the harshness of his diction, Nashe retorted:

> To the second rancke of reprehenders, that complain of my boystrous
> compound wordes, and ending my Italionate coyned verbes all in *Ize*,
> thus I replie: That no winde that blowes strong but is boystrous, no
> speech or wordes, of any power or force to confute or perswade,
> but must bee swelling and boystrous. For the compounding of my
> wordes, therein I imitate rich men, who, hauing gathered store of white
> single money together, conuert a number of those small little scures
> into great peeces of gold, such as double Pistols and Portugues. Our
> English tongue, of all languages, most swarmeth with the single money
> of monasillables, which are the onely scandal of it. Bookes written
> in them, and no other, seeme like Shop-keepers boxes, that containe
> nothing else saue halfe-pence, three farthings and two-pences. There-
> fore, what did me I, but hauing a huge heape of those worthelesse
> shreds of small English in my *Pia mater's* purse, to make the royaller

shew with them to mens eyes, had them to the compounders immediately, and exchanged them foure into one, and others into more,
according to the Greek, French, Spanish, and Italian.[11]

This is another variety of the prose of the 1580s and 1590s to
place beside Euphuism, Ciceronianism, or the more realistic style
of Dekker. Add the Senecan style of the turn of the century, and it is
clear that, in his prose, no less than in his dramatic verse, Shakespeare
could select any of several well–established styles.

THE PLAY WITHIN THE PLAY

Pistol was surely a playgoer. Some of his heroic-sounding phrases
derive from the more melodramatic speeches in earlier drama, from
Marlowe or from Peele (*2 Hen IV* II.iv.158,174). Noun phrases like
lungs military or hand terrestial (both from the Host of the Garter,
not Pistol) raise the question whether this portentous style was
deliberately used to satirise older-style dramatic verse. If we were
asked to identify *tristful visage*, we might well guess Kyd or Marlowe
rather than Hamlet in the closet scene:

> Yea, this solidity and compound mass
> With tristful [heated, Q2] visage, as against the Doom,
> Is thought-sick at the act.
>
> (III.iv.50–52)

It is a curious conceit: Hamlet seems to be saying that the earth
would be as appalled as the heavens at an act like this. Perhaps
the pathetic fallacy spawned the old-fashioned phrase. There are,
however, a few distinct 'inset devices', as they have sometimes been
called, in Shakespeare. Two, the pageant of the worthies in *Love's
Labour's Lost* and the mechanicals' play in *A Midsummer Night's Dream*,
are expected to be ludicrous because of their performers. The first is
given an unkind reception by the wits of Navarre. What the Athens
artisans themselves call "A tedious brief scene of young Pyramus"
and Theseus (having seen it) "This palpable-gross play", is less subject
to aristocratic interruption, and so we get more of its individual
flavour. *Dreadful dole* and *Come blade, my breast imbrue* and some of
Bottom's frequent apostrophes:

> O grim-looked night, O night with hue so black,
> O night which ever art when day is not!
>
> (V.i.167–8)

would not have disgraced Pistol. Elsewhere alliteration, one or two archaisms (*hight; an*, 'if'), an excessive use of *do* as tense-marker, an inversion or two (*lion vile, lion rough*) more often give the impression of well-meaning rustic performers than deliberate parody of earlier drama, but the best in this kind are but shadows.

The extreme reaction to Juliet's supposed death (IV.v.) is almost a 'play within a play' of quite another kind. The exaggerated exclamations of the Nurse ("O lamentable day!"), Lady Capulet ("Accursed, unhappy, wretched, hateful day!"), Capulet ("Death is my son-in-law. Death is my heir.") and Paris ("Beguiled, divorced, wronged, spited, slain!") represent the ritualised grief of uncomprehending Verona. The Friar's motives are good and his theology impeccable, but his conceits on *promotion* and *married* seem too mannered. Only the musicians ("Faith, we may put up our pipes and be gone") show the correct and dignified response. The masque of Herne the Hunter in *The Merry Wives* is in verse – in a play predominantly in prose – as is proper to fairies. The more elevated style of the wedding masque in *The Tempest*, with its many adjectives and compounds, is proper to goddesses. It is narrative rather than dramatic poetry, but "a most majestic vision, and / Harmonious charmingly" is in any event unlikely to be satirical. There is a great deal of pageantry in *Henry VIII*, but neither Henry's masque nor Katherine's dying vision ever really gets under way.

Which leaves *Hamlet*, both *Aeneas' Tale to Dido* and *The Murder of Gonzago*. *Aeneas' Tale to Dido* certainly seems a part for the First Player to tear a cat in. Yet Hamlet, and "others whose judgement in such matters cried in the top of mine" think it an excellent play. How *could* he countenance such phrases as *total gules* (II.ii.455), *baked and impasted* (457), *o'er-sized with coagulate gore* (460), *whiff and wind of his fell sword* (471), *declining on the milky head / Of reverend Priam* (476), *Mars's armour, forged for proof eterne* (488), *threatening the flames/With bisson rheum* (503)? Are not these little better than some of the phrases Pistol uses? Well, not quite. They are, at least, coherent, part of a set speech, even if they are turgid and over-elaborate. Pistol's are disjointed scraps which together make little sense and, however comic, are presumably his comments on a real-life situation. *Aeneas' Tale to Dido* is regarded as fiction. This is the whole tenor of Hamlet's following soliloquy: "What would he do / Had he the motive and the cue for passion / That I have?" Hamlet considers it a good *play*, and Elizabethans saw rhetoric as appropriate language: you didn't come across a rugged Pyrrhus every day.

Before *The Murder of Gonzago* comes Hamlet's advice to the

players. Hamlet is being his own Master of the Revels, auditioning the performers, selecting a play appropriate for the court of Elsinore (as if for the court at Whitehall), suggesting changes in the text, and giving orders for its production. The players are the chief actors of a standard Elizabethan public repertory company, with a king, a boy playing the Lady, an 'adventurous knight' and a humorous man (i.e. the character actor).[12] If the speech (III.ii.l) is the one Hamlet has composed specially, he may mean only that he does not want it disproportionately stressed.

He evidently accepts "the very torrent, tempest, and, as I may say, whirlwind of your passion" if the material justifies it; he does not accept ham acting just to please the groundlings or to draw unnecessary attention to the actor. *The Murder of Gonzago*, when it arrives, is if anything more unreal than *Aeneas' Tale to Dido*. It is preceded by a dumb-show. There were dumb-shows on the Elizabethan stage, but not, so far as we know, followed by a repetition of the same action within the play proper. (Why did not Claudius react to the dumb show? He later asks Hamlet "Have you heard the argument? Is there no offence in it?") *The Murder* is distinguished from the style of *Hamlet* proper by its rhymed couplets, its sententiae, its long-winded repetition, a few unusual words (*commutual, operant, enactures, confederate season*), some inversions (*Thoughts black, hands apt*), but the language of most of this inset is not very difficult. The opening speech of the Player King and the short speech of Lucianus which finally alarms Claudius (each of them only six lines long) are the only two passages obviously ritualistic and rhetorically strained. As Claire Replogle points out,[13] the audience (both at Elsinore and at the Globe) must not be unnecessarily distracted from the events of the play: the point of the performance is, after all, to spring Claudius's guilt. Hamlet constantly criticises exaggerated acting ("pox, leave thy damnable faces, and begin") but not the style. What we have here is archaism maybe, exaggerated rhetoric maybe, theatricality maybe – but certainly not nonsense and hardly burlesque.

Nevertheless, as A. B. Kernan has remarked, Shakespeare seems oddly patronising in his portrayal of his own profession:

> He was, after all, a professional writer for what was by all accounts a skillful professional company playing in an excellent London theater, while the players he portrays in his plays are either members of a touring road company or amateurs performing old-fashioned entertainments and dramatisations of 'moldy tales' in a pavilion in an open park, the dining hall of a great house, and the presence chamber of a court.[14]

Was he contemptuous of the kind of drama which had preceded him, of things he could by now do so much better, biting the hand that had fed him? More likely, I think, he realised, once again, that a demonstratable clash of styles is one of the best ways of achieving dramatic contrast.

AFFAIRS OF STATE

Of the different Shakespearean styles which might be distinguished with some confidence, perhaps the most obvious is the heightened language of affairs of state. Important events concerning important persons require important-sounding language, a kind of linguistic flourish of trumpets. A few of Shakespeare's plays begin with a formal Chorus or Induction: *Romeo and Juliet, 2 Henry IV, Henry V, Troilus and Cressida*. In the short introductory chorus to *Romeo and Juliet*, the compounds (*star-crossed* lovers, *death-marked* love), the empty tense-marker (*doth . . . bury*), the elevated diction (*civil blood, fatal loins, misadventured piteous overthrows*) and the distorted syntax ("Which, but their children's end, naught could remove"; "What here shall miss, our toil shall strive to mend") – all these combine to suggest that this is not just a love story, for Romeo and Juliet are members of the two leading families in Verona whose quarrels will determine their tragic love and tragic death. But a better example is the Prologue to *Troilus and Cressida* which does not even mention Troilus and Cressida but concentrates on the war:

> In Troy there lies the scene. From isles of Greece
> The princes orgulous, their high blood chafed,
> Have to the port of Athens sent their ships,
> Fraught with the ministers and instruments
> Of cruel war. Sixty and nine, that wore
> Their crownets regal, from th' Athenian bay
> Put forth toward Phrygia; and their vow is made
> To ransack Troy, within whose strong immures
> The ravished Helen, Menelaus' queen,
> With wanton Paris sleeps – and that's the quarrel.
> To Tenedos they come,
> And the deep-drawing barks do there disgorge
> Their warlike fraughtage. Now on Dardan plains
> The fresh and yet unbruised Greeks do pitch
> Their brave pavilions. Priam's six-gated city,
> Dardan, and Timbria, Helias, Chetas, Troien,
> And Antenonidus, with massy staples

> And corresponsive and fulfilling bolts,
> Sperr up the sons of Troy.

Immures, not walls; *fraughtage*, not freight; *corresponsive and fulfilling bolts / Sperr up*, rather than 'tightly fitting bolts shut in'. *Ministers and instruments* and *fresh and unbruised* form doublets. *Deep-drawing* barks jostle beneath the *six-gated* city. Grammatically the periphrasic *do . . . disgorge* and *do pitch* achieve a suitable air of formality, as do the phrases *princes orgulous* and *crownets regal* with their un-English word–order of noun plus adjective. Occasional alliteration and sonorous proper names, in the manner of Marlowe before and Milton afterwards, simply increase the air of impressiveness and importance appropriate to the description of perhaps the greatest event of the classical world.

Not surprisingly, this style occurs most frequently in the history plays and the Roman plays. In *1 Henry IV* the opening speech is given by King Henry himself. It is less usual for the monarch to adopt this role, but Henry's language here is characteristic of the 'prologue' style. In addition to the features of diction and syntax mentioned above, he introduces the image of the clashing meteors (*a troubled heaven* reflects a troubled state) and the matter of his postponed pilgrimage to the Holy Land (once the rebellious English are settled he can transfer his attention to God's enemies). *2 Henry IV*, however, opens with an Induction: *Enter Rumour, painted full of tongues*. Rumour is a symbolic figure, not a particularised one, and both his name and his appearance recall *Aeneid IV* and Chaucer's *House of Fame*. In 1553, the Revels Office actually bought a coat and cap painted with eyes, tongues and ears. The *fearful musters* of line 12 might well recall those recently made in the late 1590s to oppose an expected Spanish invasion.[15] A few lines from the middle of the speech will illustrate its copiousness, partly of diction, partly of imagery:

> And who but Rumour, who but only I,
> Make fearful musters, and prepared defence,
> Whiles the big year, swollen with some other grief,
> Is thought with child by the stern tyrant War,
> And no such matter? Rumour is a pipe
> Blown by surmises, jealousies, conjectures,
> And of so easy and so plain a stop
> That the blunt monster with uncounted heads,
> The still-discordant wavering multitude,
> Can play upon it.

But the less admirable aspect of Rumour, its fickleness and coarseness, is indicated by the occasional plain style intrusion ("And no such matter"; "*Stuffing* the ears of men with false reports").[16]

In this, and other plays, a similar high style is characteristic of those who speak of public affairs. They are frequently minor characters: Gentlemen, Messengers and old men without a name; the Bloody Sergeant in *Macbeth* and the Gardeners in *Richard II* (with their allegory of England as an overgrown garden) with a profession only. Who they are is not significant; what they say and the way in which they say it is. An extension of this 'prologue' style is used in some obvious set pieces, such as Gertrude's account of Ophelia's death or Enobarbus describing Cleopatra in her barge on the river Cydnus. It does not seem important that it is Gertrude who brings the news of Ophelia's suicide: her function here is simply that of messenger. Her initial statement is completely straightforward: "Your sister's drowned, Laertes"; only then does she begin to speak of *pendent boughs, crownet weeds* and the *envious sliver*. The high-style epitaph ended, the text returns to the factual, plain style:

> LAERTES   Alas, then, she is drowned?
> QUEEN   Drowned, drowned.

Nor is it significant that it is John of Gaunt who makes the great patriotic speech about *This England*. From "This royal throne of kings" (*Richard II* II.i.40) to "this dear dear land / Dear for her reputation through the world" (line 58) is one huge subject, containing within itself lower levels of subordination but kept afloat by the repeated *This*. The predicate "Is now leased out" does not occur until line 59. How many people who can recite the long high-style opening sequence also know the contrastive plain-style conclusion "leased out . . . like to a tenement or pelting farm"? The remainder of the opening scene of *2 Henry IV*, following Rumour's Induction, is still concerned with affairs of state, and Morton adopts an appropriately heightened style to describe the death of Hotspur at the hands of Prince Hal with the resultant rout of the rebels. But he concludes in the plain style of places, facts and figures:

>   The sum of all
> Is that the king hath won, and hath sent out
> A speedy power to encounter you, my lord,
> Under the conduct of young Lancaster
> And Westmorland. This is the news at full.

>   (I.i.131–5)

I.ii., in deliberate contrast with I.i., opens in a much lower style, with Falstaff and his page. Another example of deliberate style-switching – this time from outside the history plays – occurs early in *Hamlet*. Marcellus asks for an explanation of the military preparations going forward in Denmark and of the general air of anxiety and foreboding: "Who is't that can inform me?" Horatio replies in the low style:

> That can I.
> At least the whisper goes so.
>
> (I.i.79–80)

but immediately changes to a much higher style to explain the national emergency (*emulate pride, sealed compact, seised, moiety competent, gaged, Sharked up, terms compulsatory, Did slay, Did forfeit, doth . . . appear,* the Latinate *which* in lines 91 and 100). He concludes, however, in the same colloquial style as he had begun:

> And this, I take it,
> Is the main motive of our preparations,
> The source of this our watch, and the chief head
> Of this posthaste and romage in the land.
>
> (I.i.104–7)

so that the 'public' material is sandwiched between two short conversational passages.

I should like now to consider a rather more extended use of this style for affairs of state, the opening scene of *King Lear*. Lear does not merely divide his kingdom, he does it in the grand manner:

> Tell me, my daughters,
> Since now we will divest us both of *rule*,
> *Interest of territory, cares of state*,
> Which of you shall we say *doth love* us most,
> That we our largest bounty may extend
> Where nature *doth* with merit *challenge*.
>
> (I.i.48–53)

(Even before this, the doublet *cares and business*, the reference to France and Burgundy's *amorous sojurn* and the Latinism *we unburdened* set the tone.) Goneril is given her ample third of the territory:

> Of all these bounds, even from this line to this,
> With shadowy forests and with champains riched,
> With plenteous rivers and wide-skirted meads,
> We make thee lady. To thine and Albany's issues
> Be this perpetual.
>
> (I.i.63–7)

Here the syntax achieves most of the desired effect: the inversion of adjective and noun (a loan-word, anyway) in *champains riched*; the construction *Of all these bounds . . . We make thee lady*; the grandeur of *Be this perpetual*, with the heavy mid-line pause.

And so throughout the first half of the play, especially Act I. Consider, for example, the 'placing' of the Latin borrowings *felicitate* (I.i.75), *Propinquity* (I.i.114), *derogate* (I.iv.277) and *cadent* (I.iv.282). This is Lear's conception of his own role: *every inch a king; the name and all th'addition to a king.* He keeps it up for some time, even in the early part of the storm scene (e.g. III.ii.49–60) where the imperatives are now directed to the elements instead of to his subjects. But at III.ii.67 "My wits begin to turn", and the appearance of Edgar as Poor Tom in III.iv. seems finally to make Lear lose hold of his sanity. So far as we know, Lear's madness and the figure of Poor Tom are Shakespeare's own contribution to the story. At one point language almost disintegrates, certainly as a tool for communication. Tom's language reflects simply the concerns of his private world and Lear in his turn can understand it only with reference to *his* world: "What, has his daughters brought him to this pass?"[17] When Lear finally achieves true knowledge of himself and of events, the exaggerated simplicity of his diction – too simple, surely, for any 'real' speech – with its predominantly monosyllabic cast, and of his syntax, with its short, coordinate clauses, incorporates the change:

LEAR   Pray do not mock me.
    I am a very foolish fond old man,
    Four score and upward, not an hour more nor less,
    And, to deal plainly,
    I fear I am not in my perfect mind.
    Methinks I should know you, and know this man;
    Yet I am doubtful; for I am mainly ignorant
    What place this is; and all the skill I have
    Remembers not these garments; nor I know not
    Where I did lodge last night. Do not laugh at me,
    For, as I am a man, I think this lady
    To be my child Cordelia.
CORDELIA   And so I am, I am.
LEAR   Be your tears wet? Yes, faith: I pray, weep not.
    If you have poison for me I will drink it.
    I know you do not love me, for your sisters
    Have, as I do remember, done me wrong.
    You have some cause; they have not.
                                      (IV.vii.59–75)

The course of the plot is therefore reflected in the changing style. In this last extract even the blank verse is instinctive, not regular. It is no accident that, at the very end of the play, Edgar's recipe for the new regime is to "Speak what we feel, not what we ought to say".

A ROMAN STYLE?

It is sometimes suggested that Shakespeare developed a distinctively 'Roman' style for characters like Brutus, Coriolanus or Octavius and that Antony contrasts with this. I should prefer to speak of a 'soldierly' style where, by convention, a plain manner of speech comes to be equated with integrity of character. This extension would allow us to incorporate characters from the English history plays, and others like Claudius and Kent. Such a style – if we can establish it – might show occasional affinities with that used for affairs of state, for these soldiers are frequently involved with matters of great moment, and, since they often use prose, a rather greater correspondence with the balanced prose style previously described. Brutus is the most obvious exponent of balance in his speech, although the clarity and austerity of the style of *Julius Caesar* as a whole owes something to its source in North's Plutarch. Brutus's verse is usually as balanced as his prose (I.ii.161–9 is a good example). An exception is the soliloquy at II.i.10, "It must be by his death . . .". Cassius is more imaginative than Brutus, more impulsive and histrionic – in his prompt acceptance of Caesar's challenge at swimming or in his offer (IV.ii) to let Brutus stab him to death. He consequently uses more figurative language, although this never obtrudes. Caesar's own style is rather colourless, and it has often been remarked that we really see him only through the opinions of others. Although he sometimes shows evidence of real political judgement, he is perhaps beginning to live the Caesar legend, to listen to flatterers and to speak of himself in the third person. The short syntactical units he prefers emphasise his authority and efficiency.

Cassius pretends to be contemptuous of his opponents, Octavius and Antony:

> A peevish schoolboy, worthless of such honour,
> Joined with a masquer and a reveller.
>
> (V.i.61–2)

Antony makes little impression until after the murder and Octavius does not appear until Act V. What one critic calls Antony's "easy rhetoric"[18] is evident in the funeral oration, although, as with Goneril and Regan at the end of the first scene of *King Lear*, the exaggerated and hypocritical nature of much of what has just happened is emphasised by the flat business-like exchange between Antony and his servant immediately afterwards. The true expansiveness of Antony's style becomes evident in *Antony and*

Cleopatra, and the very fact that he so seldom shares in the 'Roman' style is no small part of his attractiveness. In this play Egypt stands for indulgence and Rome for the hard work of running the Empire. In the East Antony's pleasure lies, but *business* (his own word) calls him away. On another occasion:

> He was disposed to mirth; but on the sudden
> A Roman thought hath struck him.

> (I.ii.83–4)

To Pompey he is "this amorous surfeiter" (II.i.33) and, according to Enobarbus, "He is already [III.vii.12] / Traduced for levity" in Rome. The death of Fulvia is only one of several reasons why he feels he must return to Rome. Her death is a matter for laconic regret, but is still more a reminder of the contrast between Rome and Egypt:

> She's good, being gone:
> The hand could pluck her back that shoved her on.
> I must from this enchanting queen break off.

> (I.ii.127–9)

Rome seems to recall the younger, more military-minded Antony and the syntax becomes correspondingly more taut:

> You do mistake your business. My brother never
> Did urge me in his act. I did inquire it,
> And have my learning from some true reports
> That drew their swords with you. Did he not rather
> Discredit my authority with yours,
> And make the wars alike against my stomach,
> Having alike your cause? Of this, my letters
> Before did satisfy you. If you'll patch a quarrel,
> As matter whole you have to make it with,
> It must not be with this.

> (II.ii.49–58)

It is no accident that this is part of an exchange with Octavius.

Octavius is developed more fully than in *Julius Caesar.* His austere and rather joyless style remains; D. M. Burton notices[19] the marked word order sustained over several sentences, each beginning with an adjunct phrase:

> OCTAVIUS   *I'th' market-place on a tribunal silvered,*
> Cleopatra and himself in chairs of gold
> Were publicly enthroned; *at the feet* sat
> Caesarion, whom they call my father's son,
> And all the unlawful issue that their lust
> Since then hath made between them. *Unto her*

```
                He gave the stablishment of Egypt; made her
                Of lower Syria, Cyprus, Lydia,
                Absolute queen.
MAECENAS        This in the public eye?
OCTAVIUS        I'th' common showplace, where they exercise.
                                                (III.vi.3–12)
```

But Octavius uses a surprising number of polysyllabic words too, so that his disciplined style is likely to be an instrument of deliberate policy, to be used as occasion serves. Cleopatra, at least, comes to recognise this:

```
        He words me, girls, he words me, that I should not
        Be noble to myself.
                                                (V.ii.191–2)
```

Enobarbus, less puritanical than some of the Roman soldiers, recognises both the discipline of Rome and the attraction of Egypt. His early air of disillusionment makes him the ideal character to describe the magnificence of Cleopatra on her barge (just as the blunt Casca is chosen to relate the marvels seen on the streets of Rome on the night before Caesar's murder). He does, it, furthermore, in blank verse, whereas hitherto he has used more prose than verse. It is a measure of how much Cleopatra inspires him, even though to her face he is unsparing of her faults. But as self-interest gradually overcomes his loyalty to Antony, Enobarbus, in Burckhardt's phrase "the man who leaves before the play is over",[20] increasingly uses a verse marked by both aphorism and colloquialism:

```
        Yes, like enough, high-battled Caesar will
        Unstate his happiness and be staged to th' show
        Against a sworder! I see men's judgements are
        A parcel of their fortunes, and things outward
        Do draw the inward quality after them,
        To suffer all alike. That he should dream,
        Knowing all measures, the full Caesar will
        Answer his emptiness! Caesar, thou hast subdued
        His judgement too.
                                                (III.xiii.29–37)
```

Finally, overcome by Antony's generosity in sending him his treasure, he dies, in a ditch, "a master-leaver and a fugitive", in a Roman manner but in a most un-Roman style.

In many ways *Coriolanus*[21] maintains the quintessence of Romanness. Almost one-quarter of the text is in prose, an unusually high proportion for a comparatively late play. The hero – like Caesar – is apt to speak of himself in the third person. There is little Latinate diction, however. When Coriolanus speaks of *acclamations hyperbolical*, he is being sarcastic to the plebeians. Of Menenius's two coinages, one, *bisson conspectuities* (II.i.60), is addressed to the tribunes and the other, *empiricutic* (II.i.112), is a mark of high spirits at receiving a letter from Coriolanus. The only phrase of this kind that jars is *Th'apprehension of his present portance*, used by Sicinius to the citizens who seem much more literate than their counterparts in *Julius Caesar*. The tribunes, too, are more adroit politicians than plain men. Coriolanus has only three soliloquies, none very long, and the third – as he watches his family approach to sue for peace – may more properly be termed an aside. His syntax sometimes shows the balance that in the Roman plays suggests strength and reserves of power. Early in the play he seeks support for yet another battle:

> If any such be here –
> As it were sin to doubt – that love this painting
> Wherein you see me smeared; if any fear
> Lesser his person than an ill report;
> If any think brave death outweighs bad life,
> And that his country's dearer than himself;
> Let him alone, or so many so minded,
> Wave thus to express his disposition,
> And follow Martius.
>
> (I.vi.67–75)

The repeated *if*, in initial position, emphasises the rhetorical construction. Madeline Doran notes the antitheses and paradox in a later speech:

> If he [Sicinius] have power,
> Then vail your ignorance; if none, awake
> Your dangerous lenity. If you are learned,
> Be not as common fools; if you are not,
> Let them [the tribunes] have cushions by you. You are plebians,
> If they be senators; and they are no less,
> When, both your voices blended, the great'st taste
> Most palates theirs.
>
> (III.i.97–104)[22]

Once again this is the language of command and of argument between equals which (despite its metaphors) has been pared down to essentials. A similar syntax characterises Titus Lartius (I.vii.1–5), the brief, coordinate clauses of Comenius's eulogy of Coriolanus before the Senate (II.ii.80–120), and the parallel verbs in Aufidius' speech at V.vi.29–41 (*took . . . made . . . gave . . . let . . . served . . . holp . . . took . . . seemed . . . waged . . .*). These are all soldiers, all men whom Coriolanus admires.

Of course Coriolanus's ruin is brought about by his failure to flatter the plebeians in the appropriately fulsome language:

> I would not buy
> Their mercy at the price of one fair word.

(III.iii.90–1)

He is no Bolingbroke *wooing poor craftsmen*. Certainly he is, as Menenius points out, *ill-schooled in bolted* [refined] *language*. He himself admits that he *fled from words*. He calls Virgilia *my gracious silence*. But it would be wrong to see him as inarticulate or taciturn, although he is often embarrassed or angry. He is eloquent as well as scathing about the attitudes of the plebs in the opening scene and again in III.i. when they change their minds about supporting him for the consulship. In this latter scene, people want to *stop* him talking: *No more words*, says a senator; *Come, enough*, from Menenius; *he has said enough*, from Brutus. What he detests is cowardice, hypocrisy, and undue flattery which he interprets as hypocrisy. It is this which produces brusqueness and occasionally downright rudeness: "I will go wash." (I.ix.67), "Will the time serve to tell? I do not think. / Where is the enemy?" (I.vi.46–7). When his obduracy is finally overcome by Volumnia's double appeal to his patriotism and his regard for his mother, the change is marked by a new style:

> Hail Lords! I am returned your soldier,
> No more infected with my country's love
> Than when I parted hence, but still subsisting
> Under your great command. You are to know
> That prosperously I have attempted and
> With bloody passage led your wars even to
> The gates of Rome. Our spoils we have brought home
> Doth more than counterpoise a full third part
> The charges of the action. We have made peace
> With no less honour to the Antiates
> Than shame to th' Romans. And we here deliver,
> Subscribed by th' consuls and patricians,
> Together with the seal o' th' Senate, what
> We have compounded on.

(V.vi.71–84)

When previously did Coriolanus speak in such generalities, with subordinate clauses, with *we* and not *I*? He has finally learned to talk like a politician, to present a defeat as a victory, but in so doing he debases himself. For all his previous inflexibility, we admired him more when he spoke like a Roman. Plutarch's Coriolanus had been "thought no less eloquent in tongue than warlike in show", but if you trim your hero's style too drastically, you stop the play.

There is a limit even to the reticence of an extreme Roman style, and intransigence eventually gives way to maternal pressure and to necessity.

With some qualifications, then, it seems possible to distinguish a basic Roman style,[23] although it is hard to find major characters (except perhaps Brutus) who can be characterised adequately in this manner. Others adapt or temporarily relinquish the style according to situation or audience. The Roman plays do not form a series like the English history plays, however much Rome may have been viewed as the civic model for the Elizabethans. But their central theme does seem to be the relationship between the individual and the state and usually (although not with Antony) the state wins. Public good is placed above private good, and public good demands control, austerity, decisiveness. The comparative restriction of stylistic range – although it does not appear quite in this light when we read the Roman plays – means that the hero, not needing to universalise his situation, makes little use of devices like soliloquy, and when soliloquies occur they are simpler in diction and syntax than in the great tragedies. Traces of the plain, impersonal, sometimes clipped manner of the 'Roman' style can be seen in the English histories and, adapted to rather different purposes, in one or two other plays.

In a negative way it appears in Hotspur's rejection of 'poetic' language as manifested in Glendower's Celtic charm:

> I had rather be a kitten and cry 'mew'
> Than one of these same metre ballad-mongers.
> I had rather hear a brazen canstick turned,
> Or a dry wheel grate on an axle-tree,
> And that would set my teeth nothing on edge,
> Nothing so much as mincing poetry.
> 'Tis like the forced gait of a shuffling nag.
>
> (*1 Hen IV* III.i.123–9)

although Worcester had shrewdly noticed that honour is apt to make Hotspur wax lyrical:

> He apprehends a world of figures here,
> But not the form of what he should attend.
>
> (*1 Hen IV* I.iii.207–8)

The Bastard Fauconbridge in *King John* shows some of the same irreverence, although his contempt is for power politics, but later he is driven, despite himself, to become more involved in the political struggle. As yet (1596?) his mental attitude does not seem to produce an individual style. Horatio's integrity, too, is more a passive than an active virtue: he is the reverse of Hamlet in apparently having no problems at all. Bolingbroke, however, is an altogether different case. He is said by Gaunt to *hoard words*, and we are surely meant to watch the gravitation of power from a king who attitudinises and poeticises to a man who has no time to waste on unnecessary refinements of language. It has recently been argued, however, that this contrast can be overstated. On occasion Bolingbroke can be as polished as Richard, both in diction and in syntax, while Richard is capable of using a plain style (e.g. at III.iii.200–8 and V.i.59–68). Moreover, Richard's conceits are most numerous in the second part of the play, whereas he had earlier shown some signs of an ability to control events.[24] Stephen Booth believes that the excessive subordination in Richard's early speeches mirrors his ineffectual behaviour, for example the long periphrasis between "Draw near / And list what with our council we have done" and "Therefore we banish you our territories" (I.iii.123–39). He might also have cited the heavy modification of noun phrases in this speech, often by 'poetic' compounds. After Richard returns from Ireland in III.ii., Booth notices that, however extravagant his images, his *syntax* is more easily intelligible.[25] Surely the overriding difference between Richard and Bolingbroke is that the latter is an accomplished politician? As spectators we remain uncertain and uncommitted about him: he is a usurper, yet he is also acting to defend his inheritance. (Something of the same deviousness of character continues after he becomes Henry IV.) He does not make the same single, unconvincing shift as Mortimer in Marlowe's *Edward II*, from plain-speaking rough baron and upholder of justice to the Machiavellian protector and lover of Isabella, who can quote Latin and philosophise about Fortune. As Edward II is not Richard, so Mortimer is not yet Henry Bolingbroke: hoarding words was far from being Marlowe's genius. Bolingbroke's variations in style seem always motivated by expediency. As do Octavius's and Claudius's in later plays. All three go about getting their own way by a kind of linguistic stealth.

SONNETS AND SOLILOQUIES

Sonnets and soliloquies are both undramatic: the sonnet obviously so, the soliloquy in privileging us to share the speaker's innermost thoughts in a way the other characters cannot. Anne Ferry remarks[26] that we have specialised vocabularies, often derived from social psychology, to describe a character such as Hamlet. *Psychological, introspective, self-conscious, persona* are words which did not exist in English before the sixteenth century. *Feelings*, too, does not occur in the sense of 'emotions': *affections* and *passions* were used instead. Even *individual* is a rare word, and the idea of a sense of self-identity seems to appear first in 1633; *individuality* came still later, in 1645. Shakespeare, like Sidney, was aware of a courtly world with its frequent affectation and dissimulation and of the individual's need to escape from that world into an interior world, more sincere, more 'real', if also sometimes more puzzling:

> . . . the speaker in Shakespeare's sonnets is a dramatic creation like Hamlet. His language gives the impression of a figure with a continuous inward existence of which he is himself fully aware, yet cannot show, and even perhaps cannot interpret.

or, as Hamlet himself puts it:

> These indeed 'seem';
> For they are actions that a man might play.
> But I have that within which passes show –
> These but the trappings and the suits of woe.
>
> (I.ii.83–86)

In many ways it remains in Shakespeare an infuriatingly private world. Although the behaviour of the Friend, the Dark Lady and the Rival Poet often dominate the speaker's thoughts, they do not become characters and we do not know what they look like.

In that the speaker of the Sonnets often seems to be thinking aloud, the soliloquy might suggest itself as a parallel instance.[27] Yet there are important differences, especially in the syntax. The Sonnets were written to be read, perhaps discussed between friends, and were subsequently printed. They are compact and metrically correct. The plays were meant to be performed. In them the sense may strain against the metre, unsettling the line to a greater extent than in the Sonnets. True, the concluding couplet of a Shakespearean sonnet may give a false impression of resolution, but sometimes the speaker seems to be deceiving himself, and occasionally accepting deceit as the lesser evil:

> Therefore I lie with her, and she with me,
> And in our faults by lies we flattered be.
>
> (Sonnet 138, 13–14)

This rueful conclusion is achieved by the pun on *lie*, 'tell lies to' and 'make love to'. Ambiguities of this kind are everywhere in the

Sonnets. The tight structure, both metre and syntax, develops an argument: lines 5, 9 and 13 begin new metrical divisions and almost always begin new clauses too. But the progress of this argument may be puzzling and sometimes contradictory. The tight structure is made to contribute to the complexity of the poet's feelings and often to his self-doubt. Look at Sonnet 5:

> Those hours that with gentle work did frame
> The lovely gaze where every eye doth dwell
> Will play the tyrants to the very same
> And that unfair which fairly doth excel;
> For never-resting time leads summer on
> To hideous winter and confounds him there,
> Sap checked with frost and lusty leaves quite gone,
> Beauty o'ersnowed and bareness everywhere.
> Then, were not summer's distillation left
> A liquid prisoner pent in walls of glass,
> Beauty's effect with beauty were bereft,
> Nor it nor no remembrance what it was.
> > But flowers distilled, though they with winter meet,
> > Leese but their show; their substance still lives sweet.

What is *gentle work*: 'tender industry' or 'refined workmanship', and is *frame* simply 'make' or does it, as John Kerrigan argues,[28] make us think of a picture or a tapestry frame? If so, it suggests a kind of imprisonment, just as *summer's distillation* (the perfume of the flowers, as in rose-water) is preserved – yet also *pent* as *a liquid prisoner* in *walls of glass*. So the *hours* become *tyrants* which will *unfair* (it is, surprisingly at first, a verb), 'make ugly' what is beautiful now. But *unfair* may surely also imply cheating, just as *leads . . . on* may be both 'guides' and 'lures'. Time and the seasons, a natural progression, give rise to a lexical set of *tyrants, unfair, confounds, checked, prisoner, pent, bereft*. *For* in line 5 has begun the argument which *Then* (9) and *But* (13) develop. If (the third quatrain seems to say) the essence (the *distillation*) of summer did not somehow remain, beauty would have disappeared and there would not even be a reminder of what it once had been. In the context of the early sonnets, this pleads for the Friend to preserve his beauty in his offspring. The *substance* (true quality) of the flowers *still* ('nevertheless', 'always', 'unmoving' – or all of these?) remains *sweet*. It is a tightly developed argument with worrying suggestions of constraint as well as beauty, even of cheating. Soliloquies were never like this.

The full possibilities of the soliloquy seem to have dawned on Shakespeare comparatively slowly. Aaron's soliloquy at the opening of the second act of *Titus Andronicus* is simply expository; he decides to use his affair with Tamora to advance himself, but there is no self-analysis. Later he simply makes certain that the audience knows him for what he really is:

> I go, Andronicus, and for thy hand
> Look by and by to have thy sons with thee.
> [*Aside*] Their heads, I mean. O, how this villainy
> Doth fat me with the very thoughts of it!
> Let fools do good, and fair men call for grace,
> Aaron will have his soul black like his face.

(III.i.200–5)

This is no better than the later villain of melodrama who twirls his black mustachios. It demands no special syntax and the concluding couplet simply marks a neat exit. He shows no consciousness of any conflicting impulses within himself, and his sole mitigating feature – his desire to keep his illegitimate child – is really an assertion of his own individuality, and characteristically results in yet another killing, that of the nurse. There are several soliloquies in *Henry VI*, but they either merely keep us abreast of events in those three confusing plays or else flatly provide information about the character's intentions. Their usual position is at the end of a scene or, less often, at its beginning.

Richard III, however, produces the right character for soliloquising, even if it does not yet achieve a demonstration of decision making – the decisions have already been made – or of moral perturbation. Useless to protest that contemporary portraits give no hint of deformity or that Richard probably had no long-term ambitions for the crown. These are historians' quibbles; the play emphasises Richard's larger-than-life character and his personal magnetism. He is, in Peter Saccio's phrase, both "demonic jester and archetypal wicked uncle".[29] He first really comes alive in a long soliloquy in *3 Henry VI*, III.ii.124–95, where the middle-style platitudes, *golden time*, *premeditation*, *corrupt frail nature*, *envious mountain*, *disproportion*, *impaled*, together with the similes of the man gazing towards the distant shore and blundering about in the thorny wood, are brought to earth by the plain-style colloquialisms: *Ay; and all*; *And so I say*; *some bribe*; *And yet I know not*; *between me and home*, concluding with his determination to achieve the crown, the sole reality, "*Tut*, were it farther off, I'll *pluck* it down". The long soliloquy which opens *Richard III* indicates his domination of the play and continues the same technique. Even metaphors can be sardonically transformed: *grim-visaged war . . . capers nimbly in a lady's chamber*. The rhetoric consists of the elaboration of the first-person pronouns at the beginning of lines 14, 16, 18 and 24 by a series of relative, participial and noun clauses to show him as so comprehensively out of tune with the times that Machiavellianism becomes the logical alternative: *But I . . . I . . . I . . . Why I . . .*

> *And therefore*, since I cannot prove a lover
> To entertain these fair well-spoken days,
> I am determined to prove a villain
> And hate the idle pleasures of these days.
> Plots have I laid . . .
>
> (I.i.28–32)

Certainly his intrigues are so many and so involved that the audience needs to be put in the know, but the soliloquies merely reveal his aims and his relish in furthering them:

> And thus I clothe my naked villainy
> With odd old ends stolen forth of holy writ,
> And seem a saint, when most I play the devil.
>
> (I.iii.335–7)

The *odd old ends* can serve to colour a feigned reluctance to accept the crown ("Aloft, between two bishops") or, supplemented by a Petrarchan conceit or two, help to win over Anne or Elizabeth.

After the opening three scenes there is a long gap before the next soliloquy, by which time Richard is almost king. The plotting has brought tangible rewards, but also further problems:

> But I am in
> So far in blood that sin will pluck on sin.
> Tear-falling pity dwells not in this eye.
>
> (IV.ii.62–3)

So far in blood: the very words are to become Macbeth's ("I am in blood / Stepped in so far . . .") but, unlike Macbeth's, Richard's is no tortured confession. He does not see his diabolical scheming as corrupting his own nature. Only his final soliloquy, where he starts out of the dream in which the ghosts of his victims (pure morality figures employed to externalise internal debate) have appeared to him in turn, shows him faltering, and the hitherto controlled syntax correspondingly changing:

> What do I fear? Myself? There's none else by.
> Richard loves Richard: that is, I am I.
> Is there a murderer here? No. Yes, I am.
> Then fly. What, from myself? Great reason why –
> Lest I revenge. Myself upon myself?
> Alack, I love myself. Wherefore? For any good
> That I myself have done unto myself?
>
> (V.iii.183–9)

The technique of rapid question and answer was one Shakespeare was to employ in later soliloquies, but here the attempt to show Richard's panic results in a syntax so broken that the audience is hard put to it to follow the quick reversals of thought and the speech is in danger of becoming ridiculous. Towards its end, the soliloquy repeats the same arguments but in less feverish syntax.

Clemen[30] believes that in *Dr Faustus* the soliloquy is, for the first time, used to show the character thinking as he speaks. Certainly this is true of the great final soliloquy. The comparatively smooth syntax of the opening lines, with their *enjambement*, shows Faustus still in some kind of desperate control: a miracle may even yet happen. But his increasing panic is indicated by the broken lines, and other lines which are not full lines at all but only a couple of syllables, the pause allowing the terrible reality of retribution to sink in. Unlike Richard III's final soliloquy, the broken lines are interspersed with others whose greater normality (and even some subordination) suggest possibilities other than a speedy descent to hell. These are developed for a little, only to be interrupted by the striking of the clock and the resumption of a more irregular syntax:

> No, no!
> Then will I headlong run into the earth.
> Earth, gape. O no, it will not harbour me.
> You stars that reign'd at my nativity,
> Whose influence hath allotted death and hell,
> Now draw up Faustus like a foggy mist
> Into the entrails of yon labouring cloud,
> That when you vomit forth into the air
> My limbs may issue from your smoky mouths,
> So that my soul may but ascend to heaven . . .
>
> *The watch strikes.*
>
> My God, my God, look not so fierce on me.
> Adders and serpents, let me breathe awhile.
> Ugly hell, gape not; come not, Lucifer.
> I'll burn my books. Ah, Mephistophilis!
>
> *Exeunt with him.*
> (V.ii.155–64, 188–91)

Shakespeare's early tragedies and the histories take the soliloquy little if any further. Juliet's soliloquy in III.ii. introduces the paradox of tedious day and the wished-for night, since Romeo is *day in night*. Such complexities as this will develop into the difficult and distorted syntax of the later plays, where the heroine both is and is not Cressid and nothing is but what is not. Bolingbroke only once soliloquises, and does not even seem to confide in his associates. As Henry IV he cannot sleep, but his single soliloquy refuses to face the real reason, his guilt over the way he came by the crown. Richard II's only soliloquy – one of the longest Shakespeare wrote – takes place in prison. He momentarily admits his fault ("I wasted time and now doth time waste me"), but his mind immediately diverts itself with yet another conceit and the syntax reveals little of his anxiety. Falstaff's prose soliloquies, syntactically quite complex, are simply wilful evasions of his own responsibilities. He is fully capable of seeing through the posturings of honour or the boasting of Shallow, but it does not suit him to admit this publicly.

It is Brutus who first articulates the psychological condition which gives rise to the best of the later Shakespearean soliloquies:

> Between the acting of a dreadful thing
> And the first motion, all the interim is
> Like a phantasma or a hideous dream:
> The genius and the mortal instruments
> Are then in council; and the state of man,
> Like to a little kingdom, suffers then
> The nature of an insurrection.

> (*JC* II.i.62–9)

In the early seventeenth century there was a growing interest in psychology, and this, coupled with the development of satire in the later sixteenth century, most probably fostered the use of the soliloquy as a convention for the expression of a disturbed mental state. Brutus, of course, is not emotionally unbalanced, although Hamlet seems to have moments of being fascinated by what he condemns. For almost the first time in Shakespeare, Brutus makes a deliberate moral choice, visualising the consequences of what he will do before he commits himself. This in turn necessitates a means of making the audience aware of his mental conflict. As yet, however, we are not fully admitted to the recesses of his mind. He argues with Cassius rather than with himself. We see the philosophical conclusions of his deliberations rather than the deliberations themselves:

> There is a tide in the affairs of men,
> Which, taken at the flood, leads on to fortune;
> Omitted, all the voyage of their life
> Is bound in shallows and in miseries.
> On such a full sea are we now afloat.

> (IV.iii.216–20)

Twice (II.i.229, IV.iii.265) as the boy Lucius falls asleep, we are prepared for Brutus to reveal his innermost thoughts, but each time his reverie is interrupted, first by Portia and later by Caesar's ghost, before it has properly begun. In the noblest Roman of them all, the instinctive desire not to kill Caesar conflicts with his regard for the good of the state – but publicly, not privately. Later tragedies reverse this procedure: the passions of the individual cause upheavals in the state, rather than, as earlier, the public situation giving rise to private passions.

And so (inevitably) to *Hamlet*, with its seven soliloquies from the hero, plus one from Claudius. Should anyone doubt what the soliloquies contribute to *Hamlet*, let him read Marston's *Antonio's Revenge* (probably 1600 and therefore almost exactly contemporary). Antonio's father, too, has been poisoned and his mother is about to marry the murderer; the ghost of his dead father reveals the crime and calls upon his son to revenge it. Whether one play borrowed from the other or each borrowed independently from the *Ur-Hamlet*, need not concern us here. There are differences: Pandulpho is not Polonius, nor Mellida Ophelia. Although Antonio delays his revenge, there is little of the subtlety of *Hamlet*. And, as J. W. Lever points out,[31] Antonio is not alone: the isolation of Hamlet is exceptional in revenge tragedy. Whether or not Marston tempered his approach to the abilities of his child actors, we are not shown the psychological pressures upon Antonio; his hysteria fails to convince. At the close of Act I, Hamlet sees the need "to put an antic disposition on". Everybody notices the change in him, and hence the greater need of the soliloquy to inform us of the true state of affairs. In *Hamlet* the soliloquies punctuate the play at significant points. The first establishes Hamlet's immediate reaction to his father's death and his mother's o'er-hasty marriage; the second occurs after the Ghost has told him that the death was in fact murder; the third follows the Player's recital of *Aeneas's Tale to Dido* and concludes Act II; the fourth ("To be or not to be?") comes very early in Act III and is unusual in that it is pure meditation with no direct application to Hamlet's own circumstances; the fifth and shortest separates the confirmation of Claudius's guilt in the play scene and Hamlet's visit to his mother in her bedroom; in the sixth, Hamlet has stumbled upon Claudius vainly trying to pray; the last, again more philosophical and less violent than usual in its language, is occasioned by the news of Fortinbras's expedition to Poland. There are no soliloquies in Act V in which the play hastens to its bloody ending. What have they in common? First of all, Hamlet is naturally introspective, so that it seems fitting for him to soliloquise and indeed to philosophise and generalise, for, like Timon, he always reasons from the particular to the universal. Secondly, the pace may vary considerably within a soliloquy, and with it the kind of syntax employed.

Perhaps this is best illustrated by a closer examination of the first and third soliloquies. The exclamations and curses of the first simply show Hamlet's anger and disgust, but what it is that disgusts him emerges gradually through the repetitions: "But two months dead, nay, not so much, not two . . . within a month . . . A little month . . . Within a month." The parentheses, on the other hand, both reveal his habit of generalisation and, more important, show the confused thoughts bubbling to the surface of his mind, thus giving the illusion of natural, disordered mental activity, especially under stress:

> And yet *within a month* –
> Let me not think on't. Frailty, thy name is woman.
> A little month, or e'er those shoes were old
> With which she followed my poor father's body
> Like Niobe, all tears, why *she*, even she –
> O God, a beast that wants discourse of reason
> Would have mourned longer – *married with my uncle*,
> My father's brother, but no more like my father
> Than I to Hercules.
>
> (I.ii.145–53)

The third soliloquy uses different techniques. As in the final *Faustus* soliloquy, there are short lines which allow pause for reflection but which carry the burden of the argument: "For Hecuba" (the Player's feigned passion), "Yet I" (what do *I* do?), "O vengeance" (what I *should* do), "A scullion" (what I seem to be). A series of stressed nouns (*slave, player, fiction, passion, soul, conceit, tears, distraction, voice, function*) relate to comparatively weak verbs (*am, is, force, wanned, suiting* – the last two not finite verbs but participles). After the first short line, however, the verbs dominate: *weep, do, drown, cleave, make mad, appal, confound, amaze* – the player *does* something. A series of quick-fire questions:

> Am I a coward?
> Who calls me villain? Breaks my pate across?
> Plucks off my beard and blows it in my face?
> Tweaks me by the nose? Gives me the lie i'th' throat
> As deep as to the lungs? Who does me this?
>
> (II.ii.568–72)

gives way to two lines of curses:

> Bloody, bawdy villain!
> Remorseless, treacherous, lecherous, kindless villain!
>
> (577–8)

185

culminating in the next short line. Thereafter the ranting and cursing slow to a normal, far less broken syntax, in which Hamlet, with logical reasoning, decides on the next step, the use of the play to test Claudius's guilt. We can follow Hamlet's reaction to a changing situation (changing as his knowledge increases) through the soliloquies, because the soliloquy has now developed sufficiently to allow both character and audience to verbalise, in Daniel Seltzer's words, "the thoughts and feelings of the moment", that is, how much information both can be expected to be aware of at that point in the play. No longer do characters describe themselves "as though they knew the end of the plot of the play in which they were acting".[32] Through the developed syntax of the soliloquies, Hamlet is able to convey to us what he asked of the actors, "the very age and body of the time his form and pressure".

As I hope to show in the detailed discussion of *Macbeth* in the final chapter, it was there that Shakespeare developed a syntax designed to illustrate the alternatives between which the hero must choose:

> This supernatural soliciting
> Cannot be ill, cannot be good.
>
> (I.iii.129–30)

> If it were done when 'tis done, then 'twere well
> It were done quickly. If the assassination
> Could trammel up the consequence, and catch
> With his surcease success – that but this blow
> Might be the be-all and the end-all – here,
> But here, upon this bank and shoal of time,
> We'd jump the life to come.
>
> (I.vii.1–7)

In *Othello*, the divided state of the hero's mind is conveyed by the same rhythm as in *Macbeth*:

> I think my wife be honest, and think she is not;
> I think that thou art just, and think thou art not.
> I'll have some proof.
>
> (III.iii.381–3)

and these lines occur at practically the dead centre of the play. Othello's control at the beginning of the action, both in Venice and in Cyprus ("Keep up your bright swords, for the dew will rust them"; "He that stirs next to carve for his own rage / Holds his soul light: he dies upon his motion") contrasts sharply with the incoherence which, by Act IV, Iago's insinuations have produced. (To all intents this is a soliloquy, for Othello is not really conscious of Iago's presence.):

Lie with her? Lie on her? – We say lie on her when they belie
her. Lie with her! Zounds, that's fulsome! – Handkerchief – confession –
handkerchief! To confess and be hanged for his labour. First to be hanged
and then to confess! I tremble at it. Nature would not invest herself
in such shadowing passion without some instruction. It is not words that
shakes me thus! Pish! Noses, ears, and lips! Is't possible? – Confess?
Handkerchief! O devil!

(IV.i.35–43)

It communicates practically nothing directly because the normal
syntactic connectors which make isolated words into sentences are
absent. It is also in the prose often typical of a character temporarily
deranged, and it has affinities with the broken, choking syntax of the
soliloquy beside Desdemona's death-bed, just before Emilia enters:

Yes, 'tis Emilia. – By and by. – She's dead.
'Tis like she comes to speak of Cassio's death:
The noise was high. Ha! No more moving?
Still as the grave. Shall she come in? Were't good?
I think she stirs again. No. What's best to do?
If she come in, she'll sure speak to my wife –
My wife! My wife! What wife? I have no wife.
O insupportable! O heavy hour!
Methinks it should be now a huge eclipse
Of sun and moon, and that th'affrighted globe
Should yawn at alteration.

(V.ii.92–102)

In the light of outbursts like these, we are encouraged to think again
about Othello's earlier calm language: was it, after all, an imposed
control, something the soldier had trained himself to show? Even
in these earlier expressions there seems to lurk a sort of suppressed
passion and poeticism: the *bright* swords may be rusted by the dew.
"Rude am I in my speech", says Othello, but I doubt whether he really
believes it. He is more to the point five lines later:

And little of this great world can I speak
More than pertains to feats of broil and battle;
And therefore little shall I grace my cause
In speaking for myself.

(I.iii.86–9)

since, as the play demonstrates, Iago can run rings round him
philosophically and dialectically. For a professional soldier, Othello
seems oddly romantic about the pride, pomp and circumstance of
glorious war and we hear no mention of any private life until he
met Desdemona. In his soliloquy which begins V.ii ("It is the cause
. . .") the syntax is straightforward enough, but he feels the need
of figurative language to represent Desdemona's purity: *smooth as*

monumental alabaster, that Promethean heat / That can thy light relume, thy rose, balmy breath. In the last few lines of the soliloquy just quoted, after the deed is done and Emilia bangs on the door for entry, he thinks the whole world, not simply *his* world, should end with the act. Yet I cannot believe that all this is simply self-dramatisation, flamboyance, a delight in observing – or at least imagining – his own reactions. We must allow for the rhetoric thought appropriate by the Elizabethans for the description of heroes, and, at the other extreme, for our modern distaste for the heroic in drama, so that twentieth-century tragedies are apt to be about the little man lost in a world wholly alien to him. No one in the play accuses Othello of histrionics and he does not seem to be striking a pose in the manner of Richard II. Othello's grand manner never becomes ridiculous; it is part of his make-up, to love expansively and to act immediately. The pity of it is that he acts on insufficient evidence, really on no evidence at all. The soliloquies show up the cracks in the facade.

Iago, too, has his soliloquies, but they are essentially in the manner of Richard III's, explaining how he delights to make the puppets dance. There is certainly an air of spontaneity ("Let me see now . . . How? How? Let's see . . . I have't") but there is practically no self-questioning, for the *how* of the deed is all that matters to him. He is, in fact, surprisingly opportunist, giving an impression of energy (by a liberal use of compounds and colloquial idiom) and making clear the general direction of his thought, but leaving the execution until the last moment: "'Tis here, but yet confused" (II.i.302).[33] His motivation is various and unclear – Cassio's advancement? Othello's fancied adultery with Emilia? He is simply a master tactician.

One might expect Lear to soliloquise, but, as McElroy points out, the whole structure of the play differs from that of *Hamlet* and *Othello*:

> From his earliest plays onward, Shakespeare usually constructed charac-terizations sequentially; that is, the character unfolds before our eyes gradually, and we get to know a fair amount about him before he performs his most crucial actions. Thus, Hamlet soliloquises, philo-sophises, and discourses upon a variety of subjects, including himself, before he confronts the Ghost. We see Othello before he is jealous, and are shown Iago's plot developing gradually in his mind from its first inception. Nothing of the kind occurs in *King Lear*. The old monarch walks out, sits down on the throne, and without preliminaries proceeds to commit several of the most astounding blunders anywhere in world drama. At this point in the play, we know nothing of what is going on inside his mind . . . Lear's world makes sense to him, but we do not find out what kind of sense until by his own actions he has undermined its foundations.[34]

So we follow laboriously the progress of Lear's self-discovery. Technically there are no soliloquies; often it is difficult to be sure whether or not the other characters are meant to overhear him. Increasingly, Lear inhabits a world of his own creation and in it carries on a conversation with all kinds of characters, some real, some imagined. As E. A. J. Honigmann has perceptively observed:

> And when things go badly for him he retires into the inner self, where no one can follow – we hear him talking to himself but feel shut out from his inwardness, a retreat more impenetrable than Hamlet's or Othello's, because we hear only a part of a continuing private dialogue, Lear answering himself:
>
> > No, I will be the pattern of all patience;
> > I will say nothing.
> >
> > (III.ii.37–8)
>
> > No, they cannot touch me for coining; I am the King himself.
> >
> > (IV.vi.83–4)
>
> Torn open by grief and rage, pitifully exposed by madness, the quintessential Lear shrinks into a secret place and wards off the prying world with his characteristic verbal gesture, negation, which is psychologically necessary to him as he tries to maintain his identity.[35]

The repeated *No* gives the illusion of a dialogue, but it is often difficult to identify Lear's *they*.

The 'problem' comedies have their soliloquies too, but they mostly seem undeveloped in comparison with those of *Hamlet* and *Macbeth*. *Troilus and Cressida* uses soliloquies to punctuate the development of the love-affair: Troilus's opening realisation that he needs Pandarus to win Cressida's love dissolves in a conceit. Her decision ("Yet hold I off") and Troilus's fear that achievement cannot possibly measure up to expectation, generate short speeches and neither is really argued. What might have been the exploration of a paradox in the manner of *Macbeth*, Troilus's refusal in V.ii to admit that Cressida can be false ("This is, and is not, Cressid"), is not, in fact, a soliloquy at all. The Duke in *Measure for Measure* has two expository soliloquies, and Isabella's resolve to ask Claudio to sacrifice himself for her ("More than our brother is our chastity") shows that the decision has really been arrived at before the soliloquy is begun. The exception to all this is Angelo's inability to pray (at the opening of II.iv). The effect is achieved by the regular clash of antitheses in stressed positions: *words / invention* ('imagination'), *mouth / heart, gravity / plume, place / seeming*. Once more we see the mind divided against itself. Yet, in my view, the two final images, the crowd around a fainting man whom they deprive of air and the multitude who flatter and distract a king, blur rather than reinforce the effect already made which is better achieved by the irony of Isabella's immediate entrance: "I am come to know your pleasure".

It is sometimes said that, in the final plays, soliloquies are reduced in number and that exploration of character gives way to complexity of plot,[36] as fathers rediscover lost children, and husbands wives, and themselves in the process. This is only partly true. *Cymbeline* is full of soliloquies. The Queen, Imogen, Iachimo, Cloten, Posthumus, Pisanio, Belarius – in fact, almost everyone except Cymbeline himself – soliloquise. For the most part, however, these soliloquies are of the earlier expository kind which reveal to the audience either the situation or the character's future intentions and which recall most the early histories and tragedies. Perhaps the intricacy of the plots makes some of these necessary to the audience's comprehension. Wolsey, that arch-politician, seems a likely figure to soliloquise, and he has two soliloquies in *Henry VIII* III.ii. The first shows his mind racing to find explanations for his apparent sudden fall from grace and a possible *new device* to regain royal favour; it is full of rapid self-questions to which, alas, he sees no sure answers. The second, "A long farewell to all my greatness", is metaphorical, somewhat in the manner of Richard II in prison, but without the self-pity. Posthumus, wrongly believing Imogen to be unfaithful, acts not unlike Hamlet. Extravagant praise jostles with curses and heaped-up questions:

> O, vengeance, vengeance!
> Me of my lawful pleasure she restrained
> And prayed me oft forbearance – did it with
> A pudency so rosy, the sweet view on't
> Might well have warmed old Saturn – that I thought her
> As chaste as unsunned snow. O, all the devils!
> This yellow Iachimo in an hour, was't not?
> Or less? At first?

The syntax of this has more than a touch of Othello, but, like Hamlet, Posthumus generalises: Imogen is false, so must all women be. Copious lexis 'proves' his case:

> Be it lying, note it,
> The woman's; flattering hers; deceiving, hers;
> Ambitions, covetings, change of prides, disdain,
> Nice longing, slanders, mutability,
> All faults that have a name . . .

>   (II.v.8–15, 22–27)

It is, though, even more in the manner of Leontes in *The Winter's Tale* which will form part of the final chapter.

Shakespeare developed the soliloquy to show a character at odds with himself, thinking as he goes, and that is how they should be delivered in the theatre. I believe their final form, as in *Macbeth* or *The Winter's Tale*, owed something to his earlier writing of sonnets, although the extreme compression of several of the sonnets, their multiple puns, lexical sets and balanced syntax, requires more time for reflection than spoken drama can allow.

ABSOLUTE INTEGRITY

In *King Lear* Shakespeare faced (but perhaps did not completely solve) the task of creating a style to suggest absolute goodness. Other characters praise Cordelia generously; she herself speaks in only four scenes of the play and is far less prominent than in the old play of *King Leir* (1594 or earlier).[37] The Gentleman's description of her sorrow (IV.iii) is over-metaphorical, artificial and distant, the formal language of public events rather than the tone of deep concern. Cordelia sometimes states what she *cannot* do: "heave my heart into my mouth"; "show a glib and oily art / To speak and purpose not"; "counterfeit a still-soliciting eye or blown ambition". Occasionally, as with the doublets *aidant and remediate* (IV.iv.17) and *untuned and jarring senses* (IV.vii.16) or the coinage *out-frown false Fortune's frown* (V.iii. 6 – a compound and a personification more characteristic of her father), her language seems too premeditated and contrived. But by this time she is to be seen as Queen of France, a role which does not quite complement that of Lear's daughter. Twice in IV.vii. repetition ("And so I am, I am", "No cause, no cause") is used to suggest sincerity, but only once, in her first speech of any length in the play, do the simple lexis and straightforward syntax convey her utter integrity:

> Good my lord,
> You have begot me, bred me, loved me.
> I return those duties back as are right fit,
> Obey you, love you, and most honour you.
> Why have my sisters husbands, if they say
> They love you all? Haply when I shall wed,
> That lord whose hand must take my plight shall carry
> Half my love with him, half my care and duty.
> Sure I shall never marry like my sisters,
> To love my father all.
>
> (I.i.95–104)

Lear knows that plainness may conceal pride – "Let pride, which she calls plainness, marry her" – but with Cordelia, no more than with

Kent, is he able to recognise true worth when he sees it.[38] Yet, in a strange way, Lear *is* right: nothing will come of nothing. Edgar acts out his suffering and in it assumes different identities: poor Tom, the peasant who witnesses Gloucester's 'fall', a knightly champion, but Cordelia, as John Reibetanz says,[39] simply *is*.

It may well be that there is no special rhetoric to express a feeling as deep as Cordelia's. Elsewhere in Shakespeare this is stated; it cannot be easily demonstrated:

> For truth hath better deeds than words to grace it.
>
> (*TGV* II.ii.18)

> Honest plain words best pierce the ear of grief.
>
> (*LLL* V.ii.754)

> The silence often of pure innocence
> Persuades where speaking fails.
>
> (*WT* II.ii.41–2)

Octavia, of a "holy, cold and still conversation" and Virginia, too much under the domination of Volumnia, scarcely come alive as Cordelia does, despite her few appearances. The father-daughter relationship seems increasingly to have occupied Shakespeare in his later plays. Both Perdita and Marina do not appear until Act IV, although their earlier adventures have been narrated. Miranda appears much earlier, although her function in I.ii. is simply to act as a willing listener as Prospero recounts the circumstances of his exile from Milan. She is reminded of the hardships she endured as a child; she is not called upon to suffer, as Marina does, within the play itself. The simple style of her speech demonstrates her compassion for those in the shipwreck or later for Ferdinand as he toils to collect logs. Once only is *plain and holy innocence* really challenged to express itself in appropriate language:

> I am your wife, if you will marry me.
> If not, I'll die your maid. To be your fellow
> You may deny me, but I'll be your servant
> Whether you will or no.
>
> (III.i.83–6)

Perdita's inability to match Florizel's public avowal of their love:

> I cannot speak
> So well, nothing so well; no, nor mean better.
> By th'pattern of mine own thoughts I cut out
> The purity of his.
>
> (IV.iv.377–80)

achieves, by its hesitant syntax and double negatives, something of her goodness and diffidence; she is not surprised when Polixenes rejects her as a daughter-in-law (IV.iv.438–47). Florizel *describes* her, but the problem at the sheep-shearing is to show her as "something greater than herself / Too noble for this place".

Marina's speech in the brothel, as well as her behaviour, surprises Lysimachus, and her blistering accusations deflate even Boult. Twice in the play, I think, Marina comes closest of all these heroines to achieving by her style both directness and utter candour:

> Why would she have me killed?
> Now, as I can remember, by my troth,
> I never did her hurt in all my life.
> I never spake bad word nor did ill turn
> To any living creature. Believe me, law,
> I never killed a mouse, nor hurt a fly,
> I trod upon a worm against my will,
> But I wept for't. How have I offended,
> Wherin my death might yield her any profit,
> Or my life imply her any danger?
>
> (IV.i.73–82)

> But, good sir,
> Whither will you have me? Why do you weep? It may be
> You think me an imposter. No, good faith!
> I am the daughter to King Pericles,
> If good King Pericles be.
>
> (V.i.177–81)

Yet the first of these speeches almost slips into sentimentality. The linguistic problem is acute, perhaps even beyond the range of the mature Shakespeare. In *All's Well*, Helena, concealing her true identity, belies herself:

> . . . all her deserving
> Is a reserved honesty, *and that*
> *I have not heard examined.*
>
> (III.v.60–2)

Perhaps we have here reached the limits of stylistic variation.

Notes and References

1. Salmon (1967), reprinted in Salmon and Burness, pp. 37–70.
2. Berry (1988), p. xvi.
3. Vickers (1968). See also Barish (1964).
4. Greene (1980), pp. 87–8.
5. Antony Bacon's introduction to the first English translation of Tacitus (by Sir Henry Savile, 1591); quoted in Williamson (1936), p. 327.

6. *The Advancement of Learning*, ed. A. Johnston (1974), p. 25.
7. Carey (1970), p. 399.
8. Quoted from Harris (1968), p. 133. See also Eliot (1951), pp. 341–53.
9. *The Essayes or Counsels, Civill and Morall*, ed. M. Kiernan (1985), pp. 152–3 (capitalisation modernised).
10. R. Berry, *Shakespeare and Social Class* (1988), p. 13. He is actually discussing the Bastard, Fauconbridge, in *KJ*. Bennett (1976) distinguishes the Machiavel and the malcontent. The malcontent (Jaques, Bussy and, in part, Hamlet) would like to proceed peaceably but, because of the irrationality of men's behaviour, is led to adopt more active means of achieving his object.
11. 'To the Reader', *Christ's Tears Over Jerusalem* (1594), *The Works of Thomas Nashe*, ed. R. B. McKerrow (1958), II, p. 184.
12. Kernan (1982), p. 112.
13. Replogle (1969). In *The Spanish Tragedy*, however, "Soliman and Persida" is not distinguished in style from the play proper. See Hibbard (1981), p. 15.
14. Kernan (1979), p. 80. The plays are *Hamlet*, *TS*, *LLL* and *MND* respectively.
15. See the notes in the New Penguin edition (1977), pp. 164–7.
16. "[Rumour] is the tutelary spirit to the play as a whole, in which slander and false report spread through the body politic like a virulent disease.", Palmer (1982), p. 513.
17. Danson (1974), p. 176.
18. New Penguin, ed. N. Sanders (1967), p. 24. Cf. "He [Antony] used a manner of phrase in his speeche, called Asiatik, which carried the best grace and estimation at that time, and was much like to his manners and life: for it was full of ostentation, foolishe braverie, and vaine ambition." Plutarch, *Life of Marcus Antonius*.
19. Burton (1968), p. 141.
20. Burckhardt (1968), p. 282.
21. There are several discussions of the style of *Coriolanus*, e.g. Hill (1964), Calderwood (1966), Sicherman (1972), Vickers (1976), van Dyke (1977), Goldman (1981).
22. Doran (1976), p. 190.
23. "It is difficult to find one English word to cover this complex of austerity, pride, heroic virtue and public service that constitutes Romanness in Shakespeare." Cantor (1976), p. 37.
24. Baxter (1980), pp. 116–17; Hockey (1964); Potter (1974).
25. Booth (1977).
26. Ferry (1983); the quotation is on p. 210.
27. Dubrow (1981), p. 60.
28. New Penguin edition (1986), p. 177.
29. Saccio (1977), p. 159.
30. Clemen (1961), p. 50. See also Palmer (1964).
31. Lever (1971), pp. 18–26.
32. Seltzer (1977).
33. See Evans (1979), pp. 128–32.
34. McElroy (1973), p. 164.
35. Honigmann (1976), p. 136.

36. Ewbank (1980), p. 115.
37. Brennan (1986), pp. 122–5.
38. Champion (1976), p. 47. See also Leider (1970).
39. Reibetanz (1977), p. 65.

CHAPTER NINE

Four plays

In this final chapter I want to offer a reading of some very different Shakespearean plays. It is not meant to be a comprehensive reading (how could it be?) but an indication of how far some of the ideas about language and style set out earlier in this book may help to illuminate four plays which I have hitherto deliberately not referred to in very much detail. I should add that, in quotations, italics are my own.

HENRY V

Henry V, in 1599, is the culmination of the second tetralogy (*Richard II*, *1* and *2 Henry IV* and *Henry V*) but, more than that, it is, except for *Henry VIII* which may very well not be all his and *King Lear* where history seems to dissolve into myth, Shakespeare's last excursion into English history. It is not the climax historically, but it is dramatically, for the first tetralogy (*Henry VI* parts *1, 2* and *3* and *Richard III*) had been written some years before. There is a sense, therefore, of the ending of one phase of his career, the last piece slotted into this particular jigsaw. What follows *Henry V* are *Julius Caesar* and *Hamlet*.

Each act of *Henry V* is preceded by a Chorus and the same character speaks the Epilogue. Is what the Chorus says to be trusted? We might well suppose so, and yet most people today would not regard *Henry V* as unquestionably demonstrating military flamboyance and its hero–king as exhibiting unexceptionable heroism. The theatre – Shakespeare's or ours – cannot reproduce the magnificence of the Olivier film of 1944, meant for a political climate very different from our own. The recent Kenneth Branagh film was decidedly less spectacular, stressing the suffering as well as the grandeur. The play itself does not even square in all details with what the Chorus says. Chorus 4 has Henry, on the night before Agincourt, visiting his army and cheering up his troops:

> For forth he goes and visits all his host,
> Bids them good morrow with a modest smile,
> And calls them brothers, friends, and countrymen . . .
>
> That every wretch, pining and pale before,
> Beholding him, plucks comfort from his looks.
>
> (32–34, 41–42)

In fact he moves among his men incognito and another view of war begins to emerge in the disillusionment, fears and suspicions of Bates and Williams. Yet, as Antony Hammond says, "If it is not a patriotic play about a warrior-king, why does Chorus say it is?"[1] One answer might be that Chorus deliberately presents only one view, even if that is the most obvious view, of the war. Q1, admittedly a 'bad' quarto, omitted the choruses and the Epilogue. How was that read?

Not many of Shakespeare's plays have formal openings, whatever they may be called. If we exclude *Henry VIII*, whose Prologue one hopes Shakespeare did *not* write, and *Pericles*, a play not wholly by Shakespeare, with its 'Gower' prologues, there remain *Romeo and Juliet*, *2 Henry IV*, *Troilus and Cressida* and *Henry V*. Act I of *Romeo and Juliet* is preceded by a sonnet, spoken by Chorus, in which Shakespeare sets out, in the kind of language appropriate to affairs of state, the course of the play. Chorus opens Act II with another sonnet, taking the plot forward from Act I rather in the manner of *Henry V*, but the experiment is not continued and there are no further choruses. *2 Henry IV* begins with a long Induction, spoken by Rumour "in a robe painted full of tongues", who, as well as reminding the audience of the part played in politics by conjecture and surmise, recalls the situation at the close of *1 Henry IV*. The high style of the Prologue to *Troilus and Cressida* (discussed on p. 166) magnificently sets the scene of the siege of Troy. The structural formality of *Henry V*, with five choruses and an Epilogue, would therefore seem to be something special.

The style of the opening Chorus certainly promises great things: "a Muse of fire that would ascend / The brightest heaven of invention" (a technical rhetorical term); Henry assuming the *port of Mars* with famine, sword and fire *crouching* at his feet; the setting of the *vasty* fields of France; *casques* (not helmets) to *affright* the air. We have begun at the highest level. The actors are merely *ciphers to this great account*, figures of no value, nothings, with the pun on *account* as 'sum total' and 'narrative'. Our cooperation is necessary if this play is to be a success. We must

> Suppose within the girdle of these walls
> Are now confined two mighty monarchies,
> Whose high upreared and abutting fronts
> The perilous narrow ocean parts asunder.

(19–22)

It is all going to depend on our *imaginary forces* and our *imaginary puissance*. We must respond to this very visual language step by step:

> Think, when we talk of horses, that you see them
> Printing their proud hoofs i'th'receiving earth.

(26–27)

"for the which supply / Admit me Chorus" – a very Latinate construction to end on.

The second Chorus deals with preparations for the invasion of France, a report rather than a visual representation. Chorus 3 sees the English army before the gates of Harfleur. Here almost every line has its descriptive adjective, sometimes two:

> behold the threaden sails,
> Borne with th' invisible and creeping wind,
> Draw the huge bottoms through the furrowed sea,
> Breasting the lofty surge.

(10–13)

Sounds confused (10) and *fleet majestical* (16) achieve greater formality by placing their adjectives after their nouns. The appeal for the cooperation of the audience is even more insistent than in the first Chorus: *Suppose that you have seen*; *Play with your fancies*; *Hear; behold*; *do but think*; *Grapple your minds*; *Work, work your thoughts*; *Behold* (again); *Suppose* (again); concluding with

> Still be kind,
> And eke out our performance with your mind.

(34–35)

Chorus 4 presents the two armies facing each other on the long night before Agincourt, the *weary and all-watched night*, as if it too were apprehensive. Shakespeare cannot *show* all this (as the cinema of course can), but his language brings English and French into close juxtaposition: *Fire answers fire* and *Steed threatens steed*. (In the first Chorus the *high upreared and abutting fronts* of the two mighty monarchies had been parted by the *perilous narrow ocean*.) The night seems interminable as, on the one side, Henry makes the round of his troops and, on the other, the over-confident French are impatient for action. IV.ii.36–53 is not a chorus, but it finally admits to the same problem:

> Description cannot suit itself in words
> To demonstrate the life of such a battle
> In life so lifeless as it shows itself.

(IV.ii.51–53)

Here, surely, is the clue to much of the language of this play. To an extent unusual even in Shakespeare, the words themselves must show what the confines of the stage cannot. Jonson had earlier mocked not only the staging but the vocabulary of the *Henry VI* plays:

> with three rusty swords,
> And help of some few foot and half-foot words
> Fight over York and Lancaster's long jars.

(*Prologue to Every Man in His Humour*, 1598)

Jonson professed (in the same Prologue) that his comedies employed "deeds and language such as men do use". But his gibe is answered directly in the Fourth Chorus of *Henry V*:

> Where – O for pity! – we shall much disgrace
> With four or five most vile and ragged foils,
> Right ill-disposed in brawl ridiculous,
> The name of Agincourt.

(49–52)

The problem had been faced squarely from the opening Chorus:

> Suppose within the girdle of these walls
> Are now confined two mighty monarchies,
> Whose high upreared and abutting fronts
> The perilous narrow ocean parts asunder.

and it is put most succinctly, with due modesty, in the Epilogue:

> In little room confining mighty men,
> Mangling by starts the full course of their glory.

"Can this cockpit hold / The vasty fields of France?" asks Chorus at the beginning of the play. The deliberate exaggeration invites the answer No; by the end we are almost tempted to answer Yes. If *Henry V* is, in one important respect, an experiment in staging which must fail without the constant exercise of the audience's imagination which the Chorus calls for, the imagery assumes a double importance and the diction should not claim undue attention as a result of unusual Latinisms or compounds. The best of the compounds are primarily visual: "the *worm-holes* of *long-vanished* days" (II.iv.86); "Defile the locks of your *still-shrieking* daughters" (III.iii.35); that *nook-shotten* isle of Albion (III.v.14); "*lank-lean* cheeks and *war-worn* coats" (4 Chorus 26); "The gum *down-roping* from their *pale-dead* eyes" (IV.ii.46).

It has often been observed that, in the course of the two *Henry IV* plays, politics increasingly become *policy* (in the Elizabethan sense of scheming) and pragmatism replaces idealism:

> The England which is made by killing Richard, Hotspur and Falstaff is a more efficient but a less vital and less honest realm.[2]

Part II of *Henry IV* is much more sombre than Part I. In Part II the characters do not make history so much as brood on it, from the harking-back to what can now be seen as the good old days of Richard II to the near-Chekhovian scenes in Shallow's orchard in Gloucestershire. Eastcheap is no longer high-spirited so much as simply seedy – as Leggatt says, more like the London of Middleton.[3] Falstaff and Hal meet only twice in Part II, and the second meeting is the rejection scene. In *Henry V* Falstaff has nothing to say and dies off-stage. Before the play is over Bardolph and Nym are hanged, Doll Tearsheet is *dead i' th' spital* and Quickly has disappeared from the action. Only Pistol survives, to limp back to England and a life of pimping and thievery.

The development of Henry himself, from madcap Prince to heroic King, has however been carefully planned from the beginning of *1 Henry IV* through to *Henry V*. From the soliloquy which closes I.ii. of the first play, the audience, at least, has known that Hal is *redeeming time*, waiting for the proper occasion to throw off *this loose behaviour* and (unlike Falstaff) *pay the debt I never promised*. He is not directly involved in the more shady business of Eastcheap. In the Gadshill robbery he and Poins do not rob the travellers, they later rob the thieves. We hear, but do not see, that he has boxed the Lord Chief Justice's ears. The coldness, which some critics have seen as characterising Hal, emerges in some mercantile imagery in which honour becomes a matter of book-keeping:

> Percy is but my factor, good my lord,
> To engross up glorious deeds on my behalf.
>
> (*1 Henry IV*, III.ii.147–8)

Before Agincourt, it is true, Henry remembers "the fault / My father made in compassing the crown" (IV.i.285) and speaks of the poor whom he supports and the chantry-chapels he has founded in Richard's memory. But, for the most part, he seems to have few of his father's scruples about the succession:

> You won it, wore it, kept it, gave it me;
> Then plain and right must my possession be.
>
> (*2 Henry IV*, IV.v.220–1)

The nature of kingship has evidently suffered a sea-change:

> One implication is that kingship now has to be *earned*; and the mastery
> of appearances is recognised by both Henry and his son as a principal
> means of earning it. After the débâcle of *Richard II* it may no longer
> be possible to *be* a king; the best you can do is look like one. The
> acting skill Richard II called on in moments of crisis is now simply
> part of the job.[4]

And in role-playing manipulation of language is no mean
accomplishment.

When he ascends the throne, Henry comes to see his destiny as the
efficient ruler England so obviously needs. In his first long speech he
sounds like a king, demanding royal respect and supporting his case
by using religious imagery. Ralph Berry notices how Canterbury
and Ely, his advisers at the beginning of *Henry V*, open their
discussion in I.i. colloquially: "My lord, I'll tell you"; "But how,
my lord, shall we resist it now?"; "It must be thought on". They
soon pass, however, even between themselves, to public oratory and
public rhetoric: "heady currance scouring faults"; "The air, a chartered
libertine, is still" (which Dr Johnson thought 'exquisitely beautiful');
"Unseen, yet crescive in his faculty". They argue by analogy, for
example the strawberry growing underneath the nettle (60–66) and
the lengthy simile of the honey-bees (187–204) in which the emperor
– Henry – replaces the usual queen. Yet they return – especially Ely –
to everyday speech for the real bargaining of money and titles: "Doth
his majesty / Incline to it or no?"; "How did this offer seem received?"
The manner is opportunist and cynical: these churchmen-politicians
expound the Salic Law and invoke the Book of Numbers to bolster
a doubtful claim to the throne of France.[5] *They* make the argument
to which Henry simply has to agree. *Henry V*, in fact, paces the
development of its hero very carefully. If, in the opening Chorus, he
does assume the port of Mars, even so famine, sword and fire crouch
at his heels, as they are to be so vividly pictured later by Burgundy
in V.ii. He recognises that the Dauphin may have misunderstood his
earlier way of life (which Canterbury has already told us has been
miraculously reformed):

> And we understand him well,
> How he comes o'er us with our wilder days,
> Not measuring what use we made of them.
>
> (I.ii.267–9)

Before committing himself to invade France he is careful to secure his Scottish border. This advance planning is a feature already noted by Shakespeare's source, Holinshed:

> He never enterprised anything before he had fully debated and forecast all the main chances that might happen, which done, with all diligence and courage he set his purpose forward.[6]

He grieves over the three traitors, Cambridge, Scroop and Grey, but is decisive in his despatch of them to instant death. He consequently crosses the Channel not only with all the youth of England now on fire but with a set of leaders unbelievably united if we think back to the quarrels of *Henry IV*. By contrast, all we see of the *confident and over-lusty French* is the high command, no other ranks at all, and even the generals bicker over their private concerns. Theirs is the unacceptable face of feudal chivalry.

The war in France, however, turns into something far removed from the exhilaration of the first three choruses. The Henry before the gates of Harfleur, with winter coming on and sickness rife among his troops, speaks very differently:

> What is it then to me, if impious war,
> Arrayed in flames, like to the prince of fiends,
> Do, with his smirched complexion, all fell feats
> Enlinked to waste and desolation?
>
> (III. iii. 15–18)

and threatens to let loose upon the unfortunate city the *licentious wickedness* of his soldiers. He recovers his composure, however, with the sentence of death on Bardolph:

> We would have all such offenders so cut off: and we give express charge, that in our marches through the country there be nothing com-
> pelled from the villages, nothing taken but paid for, none of the French upbraided or abused in disdainful language; for when lenity and cruelty play for a kingdom, the gentler gamester is the soonest winner.
>
> (III. vi. 104–10)

Unexceptionable, of course, and in the balanced prose Henry often employs, yet with no expression of regret that this particular offender was one of his Eastcheap cronies. Chorus 4, on the night before Agincourt, begins to recognise that war can be a dirty business. After Agincourt the English kill their French prisoners and the French kill the boys guarding the baggage.

Yet it never had been all heroics. Act I is all about justification for the war with France and getting the preparations under way. Act II opens with Bardolph and Nym in Eastcheap, soon joined by Mistress

Quickly and Pistol. Pistol, too, sets out for France, but with a very different aim from Henry's:

> Let us to France, like horse-leeches, my boys,
> To suck, to suck, the very blood to suck!

> (II.iii.52–53)

In the opening line of III.ii., Bardolph echoes his commander's words in the previous scene:

> On, on, on! To the breach, to the breach!

only to be immediately rebuked by Nym:

> Pray thee, Corporal, stay – the knocks are too hot, and,
> for mine own part, I have not a case of lives.

and they have to be driven forward by Fluellen:

> Up to the breach, you dogs! Avaunt, you cullions!

Chorus is prodigal with words. But as the Boy knows all too well, in Eastcheap great words do not issue in great deeds:

> For Bardolph, he is white-livered and red-faced; by the means whereof
> 'a faces it out, but fights not. For Pistol, he hath a killing tongue,
> and a quiet sword; by the means whereof 'a breaks words, and keeps
> whole weapons. For Nym, he hath heard that men of few words are
> the best men; and therefore he scorns to say his prayers, lest 'a should
> be thought a coward; but his few bad words are matched with as few
> good deeds.

> (III.ii.32–39)

Act IV begins with Henry once more encouraging his soldiers, this time before Agincourt, but, as he makes the rounds of his troops, the first man he meets is Pistol. At the close of IV.iii., Henry dismisses the final offer of ransom by the French, and waves his soldiers forward to the battle:

> Now, soldiers, march away:
> And how Thou pleasest, God, dispose the day!

> (IV.iii.132–3)

but the stage direction immediately following is "Alarum. Excursions. Enter Pistol, French Soldier, Boy." It is as if heroism regularly needs to be qualified by sordid reality. The extreme plain style lessens the danger of the high style, and what it represents, becoming pretentious. *All* aspects of war are shown: the exhilaration and ferocity of it, as well as occasional cowardice, the destruction and the sorrow, as well as the glory.

So what of Henry himself? He is clearly a hero to Chorus, as he had been to Holinshed. Does he represent a brief period of English glory before the country once more relapses into civil war, as the Epilogue seems to suggest?

> Small time, but in that small most greatly lived
> This star of England. Fortune made his sword.

(5–6)

Or is he simply a hypocrite? In that case much of his language, and that of Chorus, is good stirring stuff, but Henry is using it to smother the deeper questions about the nature and responsibilities of kingship which he cannot – or will not – answer.[7] In a play which dabbles in stage dialect (Fluellen, Macmorris and Jamy) and the franglais of Henry and Katherine, the surface would then be glittering but it would remain surface only. Tension, ambiguity, open-endedness are convenient and fashionable late twentieth-century critical concepts, but as this play proceeds both it and its hero do seem to veer between triumphalist rhetoric and an undercurrent of cynicism. Not, perhaps, quite so pointedly as Antony Hammond puts it:

> The only intelligible conclusion is that the duality is built into the play: Henry is a great hero, and a cold, conniving bastard.[8]

Of course we conspire to write our own history. To Tillyard and Olivier (and to most Elizabethans?) little England took on and comprehensively defeated an over-mighty and apparently invincible enemy. Our danger, fifty years later, is that we may perhaps go to the other extreme and read a play which subtly questions its own premises through the simplifying spectacles of *Oh, What a Lovely War!*

AS YOU LIKE IT

A letter to the Earl of Pembroke in 1603 asks him to bring James I from Salisbury – where the Court was, to avoid the plague in London – to nearby Wilton House, the seat of the Pembroke family, since "we have the man Shakespeare with us". The Royal Bedchamber accounts for December of the same year record a payment to John Heminges (who was later to be one of the editors of the First Folio) on behalf of the Chamberlain's Company, for coming to Wilton House "and there presenting before His Maiestie an playe".[9] The play is not named, although it is tempting to think that it may have been *As You Like*

It. As You Like It had been entered in the Stationers' Register (a kind of copyright) in 1600, "to be staied", which usually meant there was a fear of piracy by unauthorised people. We now have only the F1 text which is clear and orderly, carefully divided into acts and scenes with brief stage directions, perhaps derived from the theatre prompt-book. But it is likely that the play was composed in 1599, the year of the opening of the Globe Theatre. As Orlando comes upon the banished Duke (Duke Senior) and his followers in the Forest of Arden, the Duke welcomes him with a theatrical 'conceit':

> Thou seest we are not all alone unhappy.
> This wide and universal theatre
> Presents more woeful pageants than the scene
> Wherein we play in.
>
> (II. vii. 137–40)

The best-known passage in the whole play, Jaques's "All the world's a stage", immediately follows. Its equivalent in Latin, *Totus mundus agit histrionem*, was the motto of the new Globe Theatre. 1599 was also the year in which Robert Armin succeeded Will Kempe as the leading clown in Shakespeare's company. Armin was an educated man who had himself written minor plays and pamphlets. His speciality was wit and mock-logic, the very qualities on which Touchstone prides himself. His fools know they are licensed jesters, unlike the earlier Dogberry who is unconscious of the effect he creates. He also possessed a good singing voice and may have doubled the parts of Touchstone and Amiens. Later Armin would play parts like Feste in *Twelfth Night* and the Fool in *King Lear*. If *As You Like It* was his first major performance with the company, Shakespeare may have written (or adapted) the part of Touchstone for him.[10] Touchstone first speaks at I.ii.55 when Celia addresses him, yet the Folio marks his entry at line 41. He is referred to as *this fool* at 46, but if he entered up-stage a little earlier he could move down-stage to respond to the audience's welcome to a new actor in a new theatre. But that must be speculation only.

In Shakespeare's middle comedies (*Much Ado*, *As You Like It*, *Twelfth Night*, all three written between 1599 and 1602) the plots are complex but we know the difficulties will all be ironed out in the final scene. This is not always the case elsewhere: the endings of *The Taming of the Shrew* and *Measure for Measure*, for instance, allow different interpretations. At the opening of *As You Like It* we see Orlando, with a paltry inheritance from his father, kept at home by his older brother, Oliver, in conditions – in Orlando's eyes, anyway – no better than a servant's, while the third brother is sent to university:

My father charged you in his will to give me good education: you
have trained me like a peasant, obscuring and hiding from me all
gentleman-like qualities. The spirit of my father grows strong in me,
and I will no longer endure it. Therefore allow me such exercises as
may become a gentleman, or give me the poor allottery my father left
me by testament; with that I will go buy my fortunes.

(I.i.62–69)

In this way Elizabethan younger sons turned into angry young men.[11]
Rosalind is the daughter of Duke Senior, banished from the court
by *his* brother, Frederick. She leaves for Arden, accompanied by
Frederick's daughter, Celia. In the forest both Orlando and Rosalind
move from oppression to independence and they marry at the end of
the play. Frederick eventually sends Orlando's older brother Oliver
into Arden to pursue Orlando, which allows Oliver to meet and
marry Celia, a convenient and apparently instant passion which takes
place off-stage:

ROSALIND   For your brother and my sister no sooner met but
            they looked; no sooner looked but they loved; no
            sooner loved but they sighed; no sooner sighed
            but they asked one another the reason; no sooner
            knew the reason but they sought the remedy: and
            in these degrees have they made a pair of stairs to
            marriage which they will climb incontinent or else
            be incontinent before marriage. They are in the very
            wrath of love and they will together; clubs cannot
            part them.

(V.ii.31–39)

At the end of the play, too, Jaques de Boys, Orlando's second brother,
is wheeled in to relate how the usurping Duke Frederick, setting out
for the forest to apprehend Duke Senior, improbably met an *old
religious man*, was converted, and, restoring his lands to Rosalind's
father, plans to retire from the world. In comedy we have to accept
this old religious man, just as we accept the old religious uncle who
taught Rosalind to speak well (III.ii.331), the magician who showed
her how to perform strange things (V.ii.56) and the convenient
lioness from which Orlando rescues Oliver. All this might seem
unnecessarily complex and difficult, but, as Richard Dutton says, we
are kept in the know:

Shakespeare never 'cheats' his audience, *we* always know who is in
disguise and why, and we enjoy sharing vicariously in the fantasy
of their advantage over the other characters on stage . . . the final
'revelations' come to us in the working-out of careful processes, not as
ironic surprises.[12]

In *As You Like It*, then, we are led through a complex plot which finally synthesises several divergent perspectives. The complexity is reflected much more in the patterning of the syntax than in any unusual vocabulary. This was also true of *Love's Labour's Lost*, although there the Latin words, newly arrived in the language and sometimes misunderstood by the clowns, were an additional source of amusement. There are, in *As You Like It*, a few instances of copious lexis: "*Firm and irrevocable* is my doom" says Duke Frederick to his daughter Celia (I.iii.81); Adam reminds Orlando that it is a harsh world where "your virtues, gentle master / Are *sanctified and holy* traitors to you" (II.iii.12–13); and Silvius defines love as

> It is to be all made of fantasy,
> All made of passion, and all made of wishes,
> All adoration, duty and observance,
> All humbleness, all patience, and impatience,
> All purity, all trial, all observance.
>
> (V.ii.89–93)

But Silvius is a courtly lover and they are never shy of elaborating the delights of the passion or the virtues of their mistress. Elsewhere *allottery* (I.i.68), *intendment* (I.i.125), *unquestionable* (III.ii.356) and *recountments* (IV.iii.141) are rare words, or at least rare affixes, but their number or difficulty is in no way remarkable and they need not detain us for long.

From the beginning a good deal of *As You Like It* is in prose. In Act I, all of scene one, the first two-thirds of scene two, and the beginning of scene three adopt the typical prose of some earlier Elizabethan writing, full of balance and antithesis, reflecting the need to make distinctions in the middle style of conversation between courtiers. Even Oliver and Charles the wrestler speak this kind of prose to each other. Once in Arden, the banished Duke and his followers speak in verse: "Hath not old custom made this life more sweet?" Yet if the new existence is sweeter, free from the flattery and danger of the court which they have left, their view of life in the Forest of Arden veers towards the unrealistic approach of much pastoral writing. Those other characters in the play – and there are several of them – who need to discover their true natures, to make distinctions between competing ideologies, usually speak prose which, however balanced and even artificial its syntax may seem, nevertheless anchors the play in a sharper, more 'real' world. Rosalind, Celia and Touchstone, as they travel into Arden, speak prose among themselves, although they soon encounter Corin and Silvius who employ verse. Corin is a shepherd, and so maybe initially a creature from pastoral;

his 'reality' does not become apparent until his conversation with Touchstone in III. ii. which is in prose. Silvius is scarcely developed as a character. He hardly needs to be; the typical courtly lover can never believe that there is, or was, or ever could be, anyone to compete with his mistress. But in Act III, conversations between Corin and Touchstone; Rosalind and Touchstone; Celia and Rosalind; Orlando and Jaques; Orlando and Rosalind; and Touchstone, Audrey, Jaques and Sir Oliver Martext are all in prose. This is the centre of the play, the place where truth begins to throw off its covering of fiction.

This, however, is no easy or sudden matter. Distinctions need to be made and argued out, and this is the function of this kind of prose which may at first seem too self-conscious. Two instances from several[13] will serve for illustration:

> A lean cheek, which you have not; a blue eye and sunken, which you have not; a beard neglected, which you have not – but I pardon you for that, for simply your having in beard is a younger brother's revenue. Then your hose should be ungartered, your bonnet unbanded, your sleeve unbuttoned, your shoe untied, and everything about you demonstrating a careless desolation. But you are no such man: you are rather point-device in your accoutrements, as loving yourself, than seeming the lover of any other.
>
> (III.ii.358–68)

> I have neither the scholar's melancholy, which is emulation; nor the musician's, which is fantastical; nor the courtier's, which is proud; nor the soldier's, which is ambitious; nor the lawyer's which is politic; nor the lady's, which is nice; nor the lover's, which is all these: but it is a melancholy of mine own, compounded of many simples, extracted from many objects, and indeed the sundry contemplation of my travels, in which my often rumination wraps me in a most humorous sadness.
>
> (IV.i.10–18)

In the first Rosalind instructs Orlando how to recognise a man in love. These are the literary conventions of fashionable Renaissance poetry. The fact that Orlando has none of these demonstrates that his love for Rosalind is true, although she cannot yet admit that openly. The balance of the speech is evident: "a lean cheek . . . a blue eye and sunken . . . a beard neglected", all foregrounded to the head of the clause, and the repetition of *which you have not*. The parenthesis, "but I pardon . . . revenue" and the later colloquialism "But you are no such man" prevent the speech from becoming too stylised. Balance is resumed with "your hose should be ungartered, your bonnet unbanded, your sleeve unbuttoned, your shoe untied", once more to be partially offset by the conclusion "and everything about you demonstrating a careless desolation". This short speech ends with a neat paradox: "as loving yourself, than seeming the lover of any other". The second is Jaques's own idea of his individual brand of melancholy. This needs less analysis since the symmetry is even more obvious – *which* is seven times repeated and *compounded of* neatly matched by *extracted from*. Perhaps significantly it lacks the saving grace of Rosalind's occasional lapses into a more 'natural' style; Jaques is captivated by his own cleverness. Comedy such as *As You Like It* involves much role-playing and disguise. Characters frequently need to demonstrate to the audience or to other characters 'I am not *that*, I am really *this*'. The symmetrical syntax consequently serves the demands of the plot. Yet the grammatical units, the balanced clauses and phrases, are not here so complex as those of Lyly's comedies referred to earlier or, indeed, those of *Love's Labour's Lost* which uses much more verse, for undue complexity might suggest insincerity.

Although the love-affair between Rosalind and Orlando does not begin in earnest until III.ii., by which time we are domiciled in Arden, it is carefully prepared for. Oliver has to admit, however reluctantly, Orlando's virtues:

> Yet he's gentle, never schooled and yet learned, full of noble device, of all sorts enchantingly beloved, and indeed so much in the heart of the world, and especially of my own people, who best know him, that I am altogether misprized.

> (I.i.154–59)

Orlando's own balanced prose at I.ii.171–80 (quoted earlier, p. 75) establishes him as a thoughtful and intelligent character ("O excellent young man!", as Rosalind says in an aside to Celia shortly afterwards). The poems which are in honour of Rosalind and which he hangs from the bushes in Arden are pretty poor efforts, but he still has to be educated by Rosalind out of a literary approach to loving:

ORLANDO   Then in mine own person, I die.
ROSALIND   No, faith, die by attorney. The poor world is almost
           six thousand years old, and in all this time there was
           not any man died in his own person, videlicet, in a
           love-cause. Troilus had his brains dashed out with a
           Grecian club, yet he did what he could to die before,
           and he is one of the patterns of love. Leander, he
           would have lived many a fair year though Hero had
           turned nun, if it had not been for a hot midsummer
           night: for, good youth, he went but forth to wash him
           in the Hellespont and being taken with the cramp was
           drowned, and the foolish chroniclers of that age found
           it was 'Hero of Sestos'. But these are all lies; men have

> died from time to time and worms have eaten them,
> but not for love.
>
> (IV.i.84–98)

Phoebe, too, demolishes the stock image of the lover wounded by a glance from his mistress's eyes:

> but now mine eyes,
> Which I have darted at thee, hurt thee not,
> Nor, I am sure, there is no force in eyes
> That can do hurt.
>
> (III.v.24–27)

As Jaques remarks, at first Orlando is *Full of pretty answers* (III.ii.263). Immediately after this Rosalind tries out her wit on Orlando who is so overwhelmed that he is almost reduced to a feed. This dialogue on Time (287–322) might well later on – in *Twelfth Night*, say – be between heroine and clown rather than heroine and hero, and even in this passage Rosalind says she will speak like *a saucy lackey*. For much of the time she walks a difficult tightrope and we sometimes feel that she is in danger of falling off.[14] Celia plays her part in restoring the balance by teasing her friend. In reply to Rosalind's inability to admit (even in private) Orlando's attraction for her, Celia pretends to take the request literally:

ROSALIND	What did he when thou sawest him? What said he? How looked he? Wherein went he? What makes he here? Did he ask for me? Where remains he? How parted he with thee? And when shalt thou see him again? Answer me in one word.
CELIA	You must borrow me Garguantua's mouth first: 'tis a word too great for any mouth of this age's size. To say 'ay' and 'no' to these particulars is more than to answer in a catechism.
ROSALIND	But doth he know that I am in this forest and in man's apparel? Looks he as freshly as he did the day he wrestled?
CELIA	It is as easy to count atomies as to resolve the propositions of a lover; but take a taste of my finding him, and relish it with good observance. I found him under a tree like a dropped acorn.

> (III.ii.213–28)

Celia continues in this vein for the next few lines. She needs to bring Rosalind down to earth, just as Rosalind herself has already made fun of Orlando's verses and will later appear to ridicule Orlando himself (not to mention Silvius and Phoebe). The heroine must not seem too perfect, too superior. Rosalind knows, of course, that her public manner is all a disguise (just as the boy-actor is playing a girl disguised as a boy) but she needs Celia, now and again, to make fun of *her*, as she does once more in the closing lines of IV.i. Literary attitudes, as well as literary characters, must fail when confronted with real life.

But where, in this play, is real life to be found? Hardly in Arden where Duke Senior regrets that the deer ("native burghers of this desert city") have to be killed for their venison. The situation is a mixture of pastoral idyll and boy-scout camp, but is presented in typical pastoral verse:

> Today my lord of Amiens and myself
> Did steal behind him as he lay along
> Under an oak whose antick root peeps out
> Upon the brook that brawls along this wood,
> To the which place a poor sequestered stag
> That from the hunter's aim had ta'en a hurt
> Did come to languish; and indeed, my lord,
> The wretched animal heaved forth such groans
> That their discharge did stretch his leathern coat
> Almost to bursting, and the big round tears
> Coursed one another down his innocent nose
> In piteous chase; and thus the hairy fool,
> Much marked of the melancholy Jaques,
> Stood on th' extremest verge of the swift brook
> Augmenting it with tears.
>
> (II.i.29–43)

The oak with antick root, the brook that brawls along the wood, the sequestered stag, with its leathern coat and big round tears coursing down its innocent nose, are all idealised, seen in a sort of middle distance. Lodge's *Rosalynde* (1590) gave Shakespeare his plot but is more complex, more determinedly polished, more moral, and often more obviously pastoral than *As You Like It*. Nevertheless, Silvius and Phoebe, shepherd and shepherdess, attempt to live out a fashionable view of loving, although Corin seems to know rather better and Audrey has her goats to look after.

It is left to the two commentators, Jaques and Touchstone, each of them Shakespeare's addition to his source, in some way to set matters right. Touchstone follows one of Silvius's rhapsodies on Phoebe by the bathos of his love for Jane Smile ("We that are *true* lovers . . ."), and Rosalind's offer that Orlando should woo her (as Ganymede, pretending to be Rosalind) is succeeded in the next scene (III.iii) by Touchstone wooing Audrey and starting the old classical and Renaissance argument about whether poets are liars:

TOUCHSTONE Truly, I would the gods had made thee poetical.

AUDREY   I do not know what 'poetical' is. Is it honest in
deed and word? Is it a true thing?
TOUCHSTONE No, truly: for the truest poetry is the most feigning;
and lovers are given to poetry; and what they swear
in poetry may be said as lovers they do feign.

(III.iii.13–19)

Audrey is a moral girl, and her honesty outdoes Touchstone's
learning. Juxtaposition of conflicting attitudes is an important way in
which *As You Like It* achieves its desired effects. Initially Touchstone
is simply the *natural* (I.ii.47), the congenital idiot who is licensed to be
witty within the court, to provide material for the linguistic cleverness
of his betters ("for always the dullness of the fool is the whetstone of
the wits"). As the *clownish fool* (I.iii.128) he is amusing company, and
perhaps also some measure of protection for Rosalind and Celia as
they set out in disguise for Arden. Touchstone's forte is punning:

CELIA   I pray you, bear with me, I cannot go no further.
TOUCHSTONE For my part, I had rather bear with you than bear
you: yet I should bear no cross if I did bear you,
for I think you have no money in your purse.

(II.iv.8–11)

Jaques admires his ability to rail "in good set terms", and Touchstone is far from averse to displaying his learning, as he does in his
demonstration of the dialectic of quarrelling in V.iv. Linguistically he
has now clearly progressed beyond the original *natural* and even the
clever punster. Perhaps Shakespeare was writing his way into a part
for Armin who would eventually play the Fool in *King Lear* with
his strange comparisons which nevertheless provide a comment on
Lear's own situation. Jaques may wonder that "fools should be so deep
contemplative" (II.vii.31) but *As You Like It* is a comedy and this is only
one of Touchstone's poses. Elsewhere he says that "It is meat and drink
to me to see a clown" – which is what he is himself. It is no great feat for
him to put down Audrey's William, and in general he regards himself
as infinitely superior to the *country copulatives*, a decidedly Latinate word
which he has used earlier (at III.ii.76). Yet Corin's common sense almost
defeats him and he needs Jaques to extract him from the clutches of Sir
Oliver Martext. Corin has the truth of the matter:

Those that are good manners at the court are as ridiculous in the
country as the behaviour of the country is most mockable at the court.

(II.ii.43–46)

As Agnes Latham appositely remarks,[15] Touchstone never fully
develops a character; amongst courtly people he appears awkward
and amongst country people he appears courtly.

Jaques, too, is not quite what he seems. He is first heard of in his romanticised vignette of the wounded deer, as retailed by the "First Lord" (quoted earlier). He, too, can find sermons in stones, if not good in everything. "All the world's a stage . . ." is a set-piece, arising from Duke Senior's mannered comparison of the world to this "wide and universal theatre". It passes the time before Orlando returns with Adam. No doubt it went down well in the Globe in 1599, as indeed it still can. Jaques is an Elizabethan malcontent, acting more in sorrow than in anger, arguing for the reform of society even as he despises the task. But does he really believe that all conventions are fictions in which men wrap themselves in order to hide their true emotions ("All the world's a stage / And all the men and women merely *players*") or is his cynicism a pose? He is treated quite well in Arden where he shares the belief of Duke Senior that "these woods [are] / More free from peril than the envious court" (II.i.3–4), a court in which he was once himself a libertine. He says he pines for motley, to be a *licensed* fool, and his comment on Touchstone is perhaps revealing of his own unwillingness to commit himself: "Is not this a rare fellow, my lord? He's as good as anything, and yet a *fool*" (V.iv.101–2). These commentators have their own hang-ups. No more than Touchstone can Jaques finally give us a considered, mature view of life. He can simply contrive his own brand of melancholy, which clearly gives him great satisfaction. With him the smooth, balanced syntax perhaps measures the tensions in his own character, but their resolution may finally appear too contrived, too 'literary', the pose of the amused, cynical outsider who is somehow himself inadequate.

At the end of the play we see the pairing-off characteristic of comedy, brought about formally under the auspices of Hymen and with Rosalind as mistress of ceremonies. Rosalind marries Orlando, as we had known all along she would; Celia marries Oliver, a perhaps contrived solution for two characters who would otherwise have been left over (compare Olivia and Sebastian in *Twelfth Night*); Phoebe has to marry Silvius, as she had agreed; Touchstone marries Audrey, a union which does not inspire much confidence in its future. Rosalind has carried out her promise "To make these doubts all even" (V.iv.25). In terms of plot, certainly, but I can well imagine some twentieth-century readers, impatient of the artifice, viewing the language of the play as too self-conscious and too knowing. A more rewarding approach might be to read its message as stressing not only the improbabilities in love (and hence in life) but also the need for tolerance to match its high spirits. There may well be no clear-cut solution on offer and the play has one last surprise for us. The 'bad'

Duke Frederick finally repents, restores his lands to the 'good' Duke
Senior, is converted by the old religious man, and opts to remain in
the forest where Jaques says he will join him, to experience yet another
life-style, for "out of these convertites / There is much matter to be
heard and learned". And what becomes of the others? Why, they all
troop back to the court.

MACBETH

I don't think we consider *Macbeth* in quite the same way as we
consider the other three major tragedies. The title page of all three
texts of *Hamlet* (Fl and both quartos) all mention Hamlet only,
and the title of *Othello*, written about 1604 but first published
after Shakespeare's death, is simply "The Tragedie of Othello,
the moore of Venice". The quarto text of *King Lear* tries to
include everybody except Edmund: "M. William Shakespeare his
True Chronicle History of the life and death of King Lear and
his three daughters. With the unfortunate life of Edgar, son and
heir to the Earl of Gloucester, and his sullen and assumed humour
of Tom of Bedlam". *Macbeth*, probably 1606, is the shortest of
the tragedies and first appeared in the First Folio of 1623. My
point is that nobody thinks of 'Hamlet and Ophelia', 'Othello and
Desdemona' or 'Lear and Cordelia' as possible titles. Although
Macbeth begins and ends the play – technically he first appears
in I.iii. although we hear about him before that – it is impossible,
I think, to exclude Lady Macbeth as his almost-equal partner.
He himself calls her "my dearest partner of greatness", "My
dearest love", "dearest chuck". Macbeth, then, is not alone. Lady
Macbeth carries on where the Witches leave off. The Witches
were Shakespeare's addition to his source, Holinshed's *Chronicle*.
Their exact status is deliberately left unclear and they consequently
become even more menacing. They do not mention murder to
Macbeth. They prophesy what he will become (Thane of Glamis,
Thane of Cawdor and king hereafter) but they do not will the
means to these ends. It is left to his wife to show him that
to achieve the throne of Scotland he must change his whole
nature.

My approach to the play is influenced by one of the best books on
the tragedies, in my view, Bernard McElroy's *Shakespeare's Mature
Tragedies* (1973). McElroy says:

Macbeth and his lady have the makings of one murderer between
them. She is capable of contemplating the crime with something that
borders upon exaltation, but is not, it turns out, capable of dealing the
fatal stroke herself. He is quite capable of doing that, but cannot even
think of the moral quality of the act without horror and aversion. He
would, no doubt, be capable of resisting the temptation to strike were
it not for the devastating attack she launches against the foundation
of his world-view, his concept of what it means to be a man. Thus,
the great confrontation between them in Act 1, scene vii, presents the
disconcerting picture of two people inciting each other to crime, for
the presence of each makes crime possible for the other.[16]

Unlike Hamlet, then, Macbeth is not alone. No reader, I imagine,
doubts the rapport between husband and wife at the beginning of the
play. But, like many reasonably happily married husbands and wives,
one has plans for the other, wants to push him further and faster than
he is initially prepared to go. He, too, has his own thoughts, his own
idea of where he is going and the obstacles in the way of getting there;
these thoughts may not completely coincide with her views and are
therefore sometimes going to be concealed from her. All this is, I
suppose, a fairly common state of affairs, even if the marital plans
do not normally extend to ascending the throne of Scotland. But it
is, if you think about it, a fairly complex state of affairs, especially
if you have to communicate it to a theatre audience by what the
actors actually *say*. How do the Macbeths talk to each other, and,
perhaps more important still, to themselves? When each thinks his
own thoughts, how far is the other conscious of being excluded?
How can *that* be shown, for language – especially in the Elizabethan
theatre with its comparatively little scenery – is almost all we have?

Now the device for conveying the Shakespearean character's
thoughts to the audience, and sometimes for making him realise
for himself the true significance of his actions, was, of course, the
soliloquy. As I have indicated in an earlier chapter, Shakespeare
seems to have spent some time developing the soliloquy as a
method of showing the conflicting impulses within the hero's
mind. This reaches a climax in *Hamlet* which was written some
five or six years before *Macbeth*. *Macbeth* is a concentrated play:
there is no sub-plot, no comic scenes (unless we include the Porter).
We need, even more than in *Hamlet*, the breathing-space of the
soliloquies to take stock of the hero's and heroine's reactions to
the developments of the play.

Macbeth's first soliloquy comes quite early in the action, before
we have seen him in Duncan's presence, before, indeed, Macbeth

and Lady Macbeth have been on stage together. It is quite short, but it begins with a very characteristic syntax of Macbeth's, a kind of see-saw between opposites:

> This supernatural soliciting
> Cannot be ill, cannot be good. If ill,
> Why hath it given me earnest of success
> Commencing in a truth? I am Thane of Cawdor.
> If good, why do I yield to that suggestion
> Whose horrid image doth unfix my hair,
> And make my seated heart knock at my ribs
> Against the use of nature? Present fears
> Are less than horrible imaginings.
> My thought, whose murder yet is but fantastical,
> Shakes so my single state of man
> That function is smothered in surmise,
> And nothing is but what is not.
>
> (I.iii.129–41)

Each proposition is considered logically: "If ill . . . If good . . ." and the antithesis runs throughout: "Present fears / Are less than horrible imaginings". It concludes with another characteristic figure of speech in *Macbeth*, paradox: "And nothing is but what is not". Macbeth's very first words in the play had been paradoxical: "So foul and fair a day I have not seen" (I.iii.37) which in turn echo the Witches' earlier "Fair is foul and foul is fair" (I.i.9). In one sense the whole play is Macbeth's attempt to prove the paradox true.[17]

Act I, scene v introduces us to Lady Macbeth, but without her husband present: "Enter Macbeth's Wife alone with a letter" runs the stage direction. The letter begins "They met *me* in the day of success". There is no mention that Banquo was also present and that the Witches prophesied to him too. Her mind runs ahead from the contents of the letter to a recognition of the dilemma in Macbeth's make-up which may prevent their good fortune – as she sees it – from coming true. From now on the play concentrates on the two of them. Her own ambition is subsumed in her plans for Macbeth's advancement. Here she speaks of *his* greatness, just as she will later taunt him with his lack of manhood.[18] He needs her to drive him on towards the throne of Scotland, but it is he who is to be King rather than she Queen. In I.v. she expresses her thoughts in a syntax we have already seen to be characteristic of him:

> What thou wouldst highly
> That wouldst thou holily, wouldst not play false,
> And yet wouldst wrongly win.
>
> (I.v.18–20)

Already it is clear that she knows her man. Yet her style in the first part of this scene is largely uncharacteristic of her. She tells us what she intends to do, the line she means to take with her husband, in a much higher style than she usually uses:

> Hie thee hither
> That I may pour my spirits in thine ear,
> And chastise with the valour of my tongue
> All that impedes thee from the golden round
> Which fate and metaphysical aid doth seem
> To have thee crowned withal.
>
> (23–27)

The later Lady Macbeth hardly ever uses this sort of language. Further on in the same soliloquy (interrupted only by the Messenger who brings the news of Duncan's impending visit) she speaks of *compunctuous visitings of nature, sightless substances*, and even essays a metaphor, the one which so displeased Dr Johnson, *the blanket of the dark*. Similarly in the next scene, I.vi., her public welcome to Duncan is in a syntax far more elaborate than her usual speech. Only when Macbeth arrives at the castle and they are alone together do we see two features which are to become characteristic of her language. The first is her constant imperatives: "*Look* like the time", "*bear* welcome in your eye", "*Look* like the innocent flower / But *be* the serpent under it". She gives the commands and ends the scene with yet another one – "*leave* all the rest to me". The second feature, less prominent and seemingly almost the direct opposite of the first, is her occasional habit of circumlocution:

> He that's coming
> Must be *provided for*, and you shall put
> *This night's great business* into my dispatch.
>
> (I.v.64–66)

If this means that even *she* cannot yet name directly what it is she means them to do, it may be the first clue that she is subsequently not to prove as strong and remorseless as she imagines herself to be.

Macbeth's great soliloquy in the last scene of Act I[19] begins with what we now recognise as "his" syntax:

> If it were done when 'tis done, then 'twere well
> It were done quickly. If the assassination
> Could trammel up the consequence, and catch
> With his surcease success – that but this blow
> Might be the be-all and the end-all! – here,
> But here, upon this bank and shoal of time,
> We'd jump the life to come. But in these cases

> We still have judgement here – that we but teach
> Bloody instructions, which, being taught, return
> To plague the inventor. This even-handed justice
> Commends the ingredience of our poisoned chalice
> To our own lips. He's here in double trust:
> First, as I am his kinsman and his subject,
> Strong both against the deed; then, as his host,
> Who should against his murderer shut the door,
> Not bear the knife myself. Besides, this Duncan
> Hath borne his faculties so meek, hath been
> So clear in his great office, that his virtues
> Will plead like angels, trumpet-tongued against
> The deep damnation of his taking-off.

Again, the progress is logical: *If . . . But . . . First . . . then . . . Besides . . .*, as he weighs up the pros and cons. For the first time he admits to himself what it is he intends – *assassination*, interestingly the only use of the word in Shakespeare, as if the enormity of the deed necessitated an unusual Latinate word to express it fully. Another characteristic of Macbeth's soliloquies is that he is apt to begin them in the middle style suitable to educated argument, as in the lines just quoted, with even a plain style phrase or two interspersed: "the be-all and the end-all", "we'd jump the life to come", "his taking-off", but, as they proceed, they soar into the much higher style of the similes and metaphors. Only with the mention of the *angels trumpet-tongued* does the soliloquy begin to slip out of control. Macbeth's vivid imagination is seen in the images of the naked newborn babe, heaven's cherubin, and the tears drowning the wind; only the entrance of Lady Macbeth interrupts the mounting hysteria. For Macbeth, then, the murder and still more the consequences of the murder, are far from simple. He has not yet managed to quieten his strong moral convictions which express themselves first through the inexorable logic and then through the rhetorical panic at what might follow Duncan's *taking-off*. He begins the soliloquy prepared to murder Duncan; he ends with a number of arguments why he shouldn't. He concludes "We will proceed no further in this business", a conclusion hardly won but expressing his better nature.

This of course will not do for Lady Macbeth. She apparently has no doubts. To her earlier imperatives she now adds interrogatives, short, sharp questions intended to pull him together, first to commit the murder and then not to go to pieces after he has done it:

> Was the hope drunk
> Wherein you dressed yourself? Hath it slept since?
> And wakes it now to look so green and pale
> At what it did so freely? From this time

Such I account thy love. Art thou afeard
To be the same in thine own act and valour
As thou art in desire?

(I.vii.35–41)

Such questions are incapable of an answer. "If we should fail?", asks
Macbeth tentatively, but his wife will not admit of failure:

. . . screw your courage to the sticking place
And we'll not fail.

(60–61)

She has a foolproof plan by which Duncan can be murdered by
his two chamberlains and the way thus made clear for Macbeth to
take his place as king. At the close of Act I Macbeth is convinced
that she is right, the throne is within his grasp. But once again he
hesitates. The dagger, at the beginning of the next soliloquy, very
soon afterwards, is another manifestation of his mental torment.
Again he swings between thinking of it as palpable and a dagger
"Proceeding from the heat-oppressed brain". Repetition ("I see thee
yet . . . I see thee still") helps to bind together the first half of the
soliloquy, but once more logic gives way to imagination: the wolf
arouses withered murder which, thus personified, stalks, ghostlike, its
destined prey. In his soliloquies, then, Macbeth drifts off into higher
style generalities and personifications. It is his way of postponing
the consequences of reality. "Words to the heat of deeds", or, as his
wife disdainfully calls it, "the very painting of your fear". But the
soliloquy ends with the plain style "Whiles I threat, he lives". *That*
remains the reality. And he proceeds on his way to kill Duncan.

Yet he cannot stand the sight of Duncan's blood on his hands nor
the fact that he could not say Amen to Malcolm and Donalbain's
prayers as they stirred in their sleep. This will never do. The deed is
done, but the benefits for which it has been done are in grave danger
of being thrown away. Macbeth is typically lost in a reverie about his
murder, not of Duncan but of *sleep* which he proceeds to characterise
in a series of apparently endless noun phrases:

Macbeth does murder sleep – the innocent sleep,
Sleep that knits up the ravelled sleave of care,
The death of each day's life, sore labour's bath,
Balm of hurt minds, great nature's second course,
Chief nourisher in life's feast . . .

(II.ii.36–40)

Lady Macbeth must restore sanity with yet more down–to–earth
questions and commands: "What do you mean?', "Who was it that
thus cried?" and the directives, as if speaking to a child:

219

> *Go get* some water,
> And *wash* this filthy witness from your hand.
> *Why* did you bring these daggers from the place?
> They must lie there. *Go carry* them and *smear*
> The sleepy grooms with blood.
>
> (II.ii.46–50)

> *Retire* we to our chamber.
> A little water clears us of this deed;
> How easy is it then. Your constancy
> Hath left you unattended. *Hark*! more knocking.
> *Get on* your nightgown, lest occasion call us
> And show us to be watchers. *Be not lost*
> So poorly in your thoughts.
>
> (II.ii.66–72)

The knocking at the outer gate comes to her aid and wrenches Macbeth back to everyday common courtesies and later to pretended horror and outrage when the murder is discovered.

Macbeth makes quite a good hand at welcoming Macduff and Lennox. His laconic reply to Lennox's exaggerated description of the night's storm and destruction ("'Twas a rough night"); his pretence that the whole of life has come to an end with Duncan's murder; his eventual revelation that his fury led him to kill the grooms; and his tableaux-like account of the dead king and the dead assassins:

> Who can be wise, amazed, temp'rate and furious,
> Loyal and neutral in a moment? No man.
> The expedition of my violent love
> Outrun the pauser, reason. Here lay Duncan,
> His silver skin laced with his golden blood,
> And his gashed stabs looked like a breach in nature
> For ruin's wasteful entrance: there the murderers,
> Steeped in the colors of their trade, their daggers
> Unmannerly breeched with gore. Who could refrain
> That had a heart to love, and in that heart
> Courage to make's love known?
>
> (II.iii.110–20)

This speech is meant to strike just the right public note. It is one Macbeth cannot keep up for long, and, moreover, one which does not convince Malcolm ("To show an unfelt sorrow is an office / Which the false man does easy") or Donalbain, or indeed Banquo (". . . question this most bloody piece of work / To know it further"). Macbeth's language has been rather *too* studied, *too* contrived for the man who was only such a short time ago the apologetic host to the King. Some time later, after Banquo's death has followed Duncan's, Lennox (III.vi.) gives us the clue: it was all too pat. On the one hand

"Things have been strangely borne", but on the other "He [Macbeth] has borne all things well". Macbeth, whom we first heard of as a soldier, has found that the calculated attempt to kill Duncan was a very different matter from the slaughter of the battlefield which had been much more impersonal. His soliloquies show him wrestling with this problem: the one kind of killing cannot be made into the other. Foul cannot be made fair. Lady Macbeth has presumably never experienced the reality of battle. She can *imagine* what she *might* do – dash her baby's brains out – and can confidently assert that "The sleeping and the dead / Are but as pictures", but when it comes to the murder, although she makes the preparations she is unable to carry out the deed herself:

> I laid their daggers ready;
> He could not miss 'em. Had he not resembled
> My father as he slept, I had done't.
>
> (II.ii.11–13)[20]

I am not sure whether her swoon at the discovery of the murder (II.iii.115) is real or assumed.

Once the deed is done and the murder proclaimed, the tone alters. The plain style simplicity of Banquo's "Thou hast it now" which begins Act III signals the change. From Act III onwards the couple begin to drift slowly apart. He plans the killing of Banquo and makes all the arrangements for it without telling her. When she does get to know, her reception of the news, "What's to be done?" (III.ii.44) is strangely muted and hesitant after her earlier show of decisiveness. His soliloquy immediately before he gives the murderers their final instructions (he had sounded them out the previous day) begins with the genuine Macbeth antithesis: "To be thus is nothing: / But to be *safely* thus . . ." and it ends with the typical metaphorical "Put rancours in the vessel of my peace, / Only for them; and mine eternal jewel / Given to the common enemy of man." But the bulk of the soliloquy is unusually expository. Perhaps the audience needs to be reminded of the Witches' prophecy – two whole acts ago – that Banquo's children should be kings. Perhaps Macbeth needs to remind himself that Banquo is the sole remaining threat to him and, as eyewitness to what the Witches originally said, a very real one. It is the last detailed planning Macbeth does. Later he becomes capable of further and unnecessary murders, like the killing of Macduff's family in which he plays no direct part and which he appears to think of no consequence. Increasingly he acts quickly in order to blot out feeling, to silence that imagination which still plagues him nightly: "Strange things I have in head, that will to hand; / Which must be acted ere they may be scanned" (III.iv.138–9). Macduff himself is the exact opposite. He pauses after the murder of his wife and children because, as he says, in order to dispute it like a man he must first feel it like a man.

Not only do Macbeth and Lady Macbeth seem far less united than they did, their conversation begins to take on the other's style. In his scene with the assassins of Banquo, Macbeth once speaks of Banquo's *death* but never of murder. Instead, he talks of *that business, his fall, the business* (again), *it, the work, absence, the fate of that dark hour.* He has caught an earlier trick of hers: *that which rather thou dost fear to do, This night's great business, this enterprise, the deed.* But for her, still, *what's done is done*; for him the snake is merely scotched. He needs to articulate his fears, but he cannot come right out with the reality, and so he turns to euphemism.[21] In her own mind Lady Macbeth begins to realise the irony of the situation:

> Naught's had, all's spent,
> Where our desire is got without content.

> (III.ii.4–5)

What has now happened, the throne of Scotland but without the peace of mind to enjoy it, would have seemed impossible to her before, but almost natural to Macbeth, for it is exactly what he had feared. The *assassination* of Duncan cannot be the *be-all* and the *end-all.* But she still needs to keep up appearances in front of him, to act the pragmatist:

> Things without all remedy
> Should be without regard; *what's done is done.*

> (III.iv.11–12)

just as she has to persuade him to "Be bright and jovial among your guests tonight", and, when the Ghost of Banquo puts a stop to that, to hustle her guests away with whatever semblance of social etiquette she can muster. Lady Macbeth has not been involved in Banquo's murder and therefore she does not see the Ghost of Banquo in the banquet scene. She is terribly puzzled because she senses that something dreadful is wrong, but she does not know what. So she switches between her private style to Macbeth and her public style to her guests. For the last time, as it turns out, she tries to jerk Macbeth back to reality, taunting him with the earlier vision of the dagger, challenging him to be a *man*:

> O proper stuff.
> This is the very painting of your fear.
> This is the air-drawn dagger which you said

> Led you to Duncan. O these flaws and starts,
> Impostors to true fear, would well become
> A *woman*'s story at a winter's fire,
> Authorized by her grandam. Shame itself.
> Why do you make such faces? When all's done
> You look but on a stool.
>   . . . What, quite *unmanned* in folly?
>
> (III.iv.59–67, 72)

But Macbeth begins to take his stand on the terrible reality he sees. It may bear no relation to the terrible reality everyone else sees, but it is all he has. After all, stones have been known to move and trees to speak. And he does this in a plain, simple style, pared down to essentials, more characteristic of her than of him:

> The time has been
> That, when the brains were out, the man would die,
> And there an end. But now they rise again
> With twenty mortal murders on their crowns,
> And push us from our stools. This is more strange
> Than such a murder is.
>
> (III.iv.77–82)

He resolves to seek out the witches in order to learn more. At the beginning of the play *they* sought out *him*.

Macbeth appears only in the first scene of the fourth act and Lady Macbeth not at all. Ironically, she disappears commending to him "the season of all natures, sleep" and reappears in V.i. sleep-walking. Time must elapse for Lennox, "another Lord", Ross, and also Malcolm and Macduff to signify, in the high style appropriate to affairs of state, the condition of Scotland under the usurper. In Acts IV and V flashes of the old antithetical style linger: "From this moment / The very firstlings of my heart shall be / The firstlings of my hand"; "This push / Will chair me ever or dis-seat me now"; and, most clearly, to the unfortunate messenger who brings him news that the wood of Birnam is apparently beginning to move:

> If thou speak'st false,
> Upon the next tree shalt thou hang alive
> Till famine cling thee. If thy speech be sooth,
> I care not if thou dost for me as much.
>
> (V.v.38–41)

but the resignation of *the sere, the yellow leaf* and *tomorrow and tomorrow and tomorrow* increasingly take their place. The early violent images of the naked babe and the wolf give way to the passive walking shadow, the poor player, the bear tethered to his stake.[22] Macbeth has done his best to make himself into an automaton. He cannot quite sustain the role: he has *almost* supped full of horrors, *almost* forgot the taste of fears, is uneasily aware of the loss of sustaining honour and friendship, unwilling to fight with Macduff whose family he has murdered, conscious of the response his wife's death ought to – but somehow no longer can – draw from him ("There would have been a time for such a word"). But essentially Macbeth and his Lady have changed places. For her now "All the perfumes of Arabia will not sweeten this little hand" (whereas earlier "A little water clears us of this deed") and now she, not he, is troubled with *thick-coming fancies*.

Yet everything in the first half of the play had shown us how inter-dependent the Macbeths once were: the murder of Duncan would have been impossible for either without the close support of the other. The rapport between husband and wife may be even closer than the play actually states. She hints that he once spoke to her about murdering Duncan:

> What beast was't then
> That made you break this enterprise to me?
> When you durst do it, then you were a man;
> And to be more than what you were, you would
> Be so much more the man. Nor time nor place
> Did then adhere, and yet you would make both,
> They have made themselves, and that their fitness now
> Does unmake you.
>
> (I. vii. 47–54)

I do not think this merely refers to the letter to her which precedes his arrival at the castle – the first lines, perhaps, but not the rest. Have they thought about the killing of Duncan independently? Do they even believe that each did it for the other?[23] Part of her later taunting of him at the banquet is

> This is the very painting of your fear.
> This is the air-drawn dagger *which you said*
> Led you to Duncan.
>
> (III. iv. 60–62)

but this information has been given to us in a soliloquy.

We have, however, been less than properly attentive if we have not noticed how the Witches' temptations have shown up moral scruples which he did not think he possessed. Initially, Ross praises Macbeth's valour on the battlefield:

> Nothing afeard of what thyself didst make,
> Strange images of death.
>
> (I. iii. 95–6)

but, as he muses on what the Witches have told him, that rapidly gives way to

> Present fears
> Are less than horrible imaginings.
>
> (I.iii.136–7)

Late in the play, Menteth, more psychologically aware than his associates, recognises what has been Macbeth's dilemma throughout:

> Who then shall blame
> His pestered senses to recoil and start,
> When all that is within him does condemn
> Itself for being there?
>
> (V.ii.22–5)

In the last act Macbeth reverts to being once more the brave soldier, the fighting machine he was at the beginning of the play ("I'll fight till from my bones my flesh be hacked", V.iii.32), comfortable only when he is in armour, but still secure because, as he believes, the impossible cannot happen: he will not be harmed until he is attacked by one not born of woman and until Birnam Wood comes to Dunsinane. But too much has happened in this play for us to be sure any more of what is or is not possible. The Witches had in fact prophesised true, but Macbeth no longer believes them:

> And be these juggling fiends no more believed
> That palter with us in a double sense,
> That keep the word of promise to our ear
> And break it to our hope.
>
> (V.vi.58–61)

Now Birnam Wood has indeed come to Dunsinane and Malcolm was not born of woman but was untimely ripped from his mother. The play is full of echoes:[24]

> I go and it is done. (II.i.62) – Macbeth
> What's done is done. (III.ii.12) – Lady Macbeth
> What's to be done? (III.ii.44) – Lady Macbeth
> What's done cannot be undone.(V.i.63) – Lady Macbeth

The early battle, as a result of which Macbeth was created Thane of Cawdor, was ended by Macbeth fixing the traitor's head "upon our battlements". The play ends with Macbeth's own head fixed on the battlements. Macduff had once advised Malcolm "the time you may so hoodwink" (IV.iii.72), but that same Macduff, as he enters with Macbeth's severed head and proclaims Malcolm King of Scotland, joyfully exclaims "The time is free" (V.vi.94). We are constantly being invited to compare and re-evaluate. But for the Macbeths themselves foul cannot, after all, be made fair, and paradox and equivocation have been demonstrated to be no answer.

Here, it seems to me, is the importance of the Porter at the gate of Macbeth's castle. Certainly, as is often said, he represents the world outside, continuing to talk about farmers and Jesuits and English tailors and drink and lechery, while within Duncan lies murdered by his host. But the Porter sees that society is, like Macbeth, bent on *equivocation*, using vague or ambiguous language in order to avoid giving an honest answer. It is a way of life, but you cannot equivocate yourself into heaven or out of hell. I said earlier that *assassination* is found only in *Macbeth* amongst Shakespeare's plays. *Equivocator*, too, is rare, although not unique in this play: three times in *Macbeth*, with the verb *equivocate* twice and the related noun *equivocation* once. Elsewhere *equivocation* appears once (in *Hamlet*) and *equivocal* twice. If the play is obviously about assassination it is even more about equivocation. The Macbeths try to equivocate to each other and, more importantly, to themselves. For some time this works: they support and complement each other. But their end comes separately, his in battle and hers in the madness of sleep-walking and eventual suicide. But while they remained together, perhaps they were not really, as we might put it today, 'good for each other'. The simile of the Captain at the beginning of the play (who is, of course, describing the state of the battle) might also apply to the royal couple:

> Doubtful it stood,
> As two spent swimmers that do cling together
> And choke their art.

(I.ii.7–9)

THE WINTER'S TALE

The Winter's Tale is a late play (c. 1611). What on earth do you write after the four great tragedies, not to mention *Antony and Cleopatra*? What Shakespeare wrote were romances. Romances deal with marvels. They often work through unexpected 'discoveries', like the *fardel* which the Old Shepherd has kept since he found it on the 'coast' of Bohemia with the letters attached to it. In V.ii. this is revealed and the true parentage of Perdita becomes known. The statue of Hermione comes alive. In the earlier plays wonders frequently occur off-stage and are reported; this one happens before the characters' very eyes. Florizel and Perdita, 'the lost one' ("for the babe / Is counted lost for ever, Perdita / I prithee call't",

III.iii.31) are romance-sounding names. Perdita is born in prison and later survives both the tempest and the bear (Antigonus isn't so lucky: he manages the first but not the second). In romances the characters are often disguised or pretend to be what they aren't. Yet *The Winter's Tale*, with three major women's parts, all played by boys of course, has no cross-dressing, unlike *As You Like It* or *Twelfth Night*[25] Time itself, the passing of sixteen years, sees to it that the shepherdess is not recognised as Perdita. Another romance convention operates here, however: if the characters are noble-born, their nobility shows through their humble surroundings, as Polixenes remarks at the sheep-shearing:

> This is the prettiest low-born lass that ever
> Ran on the greensward: nothing she does or seems
> But smacks of something greater than herself,
> Too noble for this place.

(IV.iv.156–9)

although she sees herself as "Most goddess-like pranked up".

But it isn't quite so simple as that. True worth has to prove itself against misguided opposition. Happy-ever-after can't come quite yet. Events take an ugly turn when Polixenes opposes his son's marriage to Perdita and threatens to disinherit him. This begins to look like real, 'political' life breaking the romance spell. Once again Camillo puts things right with his common-sense perception of the true state of affairs, just as he had recognised the corrupting force of Leontes's jealousy back in Act I. Romance always needs one of these loyal characters who suffers for his loyalty; Camillo is here in Bohemia because he had to flee from Sicilia. In romance, too, youth shows age where it has gone wrong; if the new generation is inevitably different from the old, it won't be inferior. When the Old Shepherd discovers the shipwrecked baby he has his own ideas about its parentage and expresses them in the kind of colloquial compounds Shakespeare had used earlier to help characterise the language of (say) Hal and Falstaff:

> What have we here? Mercy on's, a barne! A very pretty barne. A boy or a child, I wonder? A pretty one, a very pretty one. Sure, some scape. Though I am not bookish, yet I can read waiting gentlewoman in the scape: this has been *some stair-work, some trunk-work, some behind-door work.* They were warmer that got this than the poor thing is here. I'll take it up for pity – yet I'll tarry till my son come.

(III.iii.68–75)

When his son does come he brings news of the shipwreck and of Antigonus pursued and gobbled up by the bear, but the father has found something even more marvellous:

227

> . . . look thee here, boy. Now bless thyself: thou met'st with things
> dying, I with things new-born.
>
> (III.iii.109–10)

The young do eventually put things right. Shakespeare is interested
in fathers and daughters, especially in the last plays: Prospero and
Miranda, Pericles and Marina. Quite another view of the relationship
had occurred in *King Lear*.

Things dying and things new-born. This play is called *The Winter's
Tale*. "A sad tale's best for winter", says little Mamillius as his mother
asks him to tell her a story (another reversal of the usual parent–child
situation). And the 'Gentlemen' of V.ii. know that our initial disbelief
at such unlikely events must be made to give way to the demonstrable
fact that these things are true:

> This news, which is called true, is so like an old tale that the verity of
> it is in strong suspicion.

> Like an old tale still, which will have matter to rehearse, though credit
> be asleep and not an ear open: he was torn to pieces by *a bear*.
>
> (V.ii.27–29, 59–61)

And of course the seasons do pass in *The Winter's Tale*. At IV.iv.
114–16 Perdita refers to the classical myth in which Proserpina was
carried off from the fields by Pluto (Dis) who kept her underground
for six months of the year but allowed her to return to earth for the
other six months – clearly winter and summer. Leontes's jealousy
plumbs the depths of winter. The sheep-shearing of Act IV takes
place in summer and in a different country, in the good fresh open air
of Bohemia rather than in the closed, jaundiced court of Sicilia. The
years pass too. At the opening of Act IV, Time, the Chorus, comes
on stage and says, in effect, 'Sixteen years have passed and we're
now in Bohemia'. Not very dramatic or very subtle, but, as it turns
out, there is more to it than that. Mamillius, the image of Leontes,
has died, but Perdita, Hermione's image, has survived. In terms of
plot and character, then, we have a highly improbable tale of exile,
shipwreck and rebirth, culminating in a 'dead' queen miraculously
restored to life sixteen years later. We need some counter-weight to
all these marvels and Shakespeare supplies it, from the beginning of
the play, in his probing of Leontes's jealousy and especially in the
language through which it is expressed.

In fairy tales, if a king is jealous he is jealous because the story
requires him to be and that is all there is to it. Leontes is more subtle
than that. Shakespeare had written a play about jealousy before, of
course: *Othello*. But *Othello* is essentially a confidence trick. Iago says,

in effect: 'Look, I can't give you absolute *proof*, but if you'll accept the next best thing, you shall have it'. Othello does, and is convinced that Desdemona did indeed give the all–important handkerchief to Cassio. But here there is no Iago to play upon an initial suspicion and make it grow into a cancer; Leontes convinces himself. In one way it is the reverse of Othello, since Leontes tries – but fails – to persuade Camillo that Hermione is guilty of adultery with his best friend Polixenes. And in *The Winter's Tale* it happens much more quickly. By the end of I.ii., Leontes is convinced that Hermione and Polixenes are lovers. Camillo has told Polixenes of this and by so doing has committed himself to exile. Polixenes leaves Sicilia, which simply convinces Leontes he was right all along. In fact the real damage is done within about twenty lines, earlier in I.ii. Leontes has been anxious to persuade his friend from boyhood, Polixenes, to extend his stay in Sicilia, but Polixenes has refused. So, at Leontes's request, Hermione tries. At first Polixenes refuses her too, but eventually he gives in, out of politeness to a lady as much as anything else. So she goes back to her husband to report her success:

> LEONTES   Is he won yet?
> HERMIONE   He'll stay, my lord.
> LEONTES   At my request he would not.
>
>   (I.ii.86–87)

When Leontes makes Camillo repeat this, later in the same scene, he has already built in the innuendo:

> CAMILLO   Bohemia stays here longer.
> LEONTES   Ha?
> CAMILLO   Stays here longer.
> LEONTES   Ay, but why?
> CAMILLO   To satisfy your highness, and the entreaties
>   Of our most gracious mistress.
> LEONTES   Satisfy?
>   The entreaties of your mistress? Satisfy?
>   Let that suffice.
>
>   (230–35)

But to go back to the passage which immediately precedes the first of these quotations: suppose Leontes had overheard the last part of the conversation between Hermione and Polixenes?

> HERMIONE   Yet go on:
>   Th' offences we have made you do we'll answer,
>   If you first sinned with us, and that with us
>   You did continue fault, and that you slipped not
>   With any but with us.

LEONTES   (*approaching*) Is he won yet?

                                                              (82–86)

Hermione's use of *offences . . . sinned . . . continue fault . . . slipped* is all clever language, dependent upon what Polixenes had been saying about how courtship inevitably makes a man give up some of the freedom of bachelorhood, and her *us* is plural ('your queen and me') not singular (the royal *we*). But Leontes understands the words in quite another, sexual, sense. And so, shortly afterwards, the most innocent action between Hermione and Polixenes becomes suspect:

> *She gives her hand to Polixenes*
> LEONTES   (*aside*)   Too hot, too hot.
> To mingle friendship far is mingling bloods.
> I have *tremor cordis* on me: my heart dances,
> But not for joy, not joy. This entertainment
> May a free face put on, derive a liberty
> From heartiness, from bounty, fertile bosom,
> And well become the agent – 't may, I grant.
> But to be paddling palms and pinching fingers,
> As now they are, and making practised smiles
> As in a looking glass; and then to sigh, as 'twere
> The mort o' th' deer – O that is entertainment
> My bosom likes not.
>
>   (108–19)

The passage is very like Iago's deliberate misconstruction of a meeting between Desdemona and Cassio:

> IAGO   Didst thou not see her paddle with the palm of his
>   hand? Didst not mark that?
> RODERIGO   Yes, that I did: but that was but courtesy.
> IAGO   Lechery, by this hand: an index and obscure
>   prologue to the history of lust and foul thoughts.
>   (*Oth*, II.i.245–50)[26]

It is the first time of many in *The Winter's Tale* that Leontes takes up a word (here *entertainment*), savours it, and spits it out with quite another meaning.

He does it in the following lines with little Mamillius, who of course cannot understand what his father is about:

>   Come, captain,
> We must be neat – not neat but cleanly, captain.
> And yet the steer, the heifer, and the calf
> Are all called neat. Still virginalling
> Upon his palm? – How now, you wanton calf.
> Art thou my calf?
> MAMILLIUS   Yes, if you will, my lord.
>
>   (122–27)

Neat are horned cattle – but cuckolds have horns too; *virginalling* – playing with her fingers as if on the *virginals*, a musical instrument with keys, perhaps so called because it was originally made for young ladies. *Wanton* is 'frisky'/'frolicsome', either in an innocent or a sexual sense. In the next lines logic flies right out of the window:

> Thou want'st a rough pash and the shoots that I have
> To be full like me; yet they say we are
> Almost as like as eggs. Women say so,
> That will say anything. But were they false
> As dice are to be wished by one that fixes
> No bourn 'twixt his and mine, yet were it true
> To say this boy were like me. Come, sir page,
> Look on me with your welkin eye. Sweet villain.
> Most dear'st! My collop! Can thy dam? May't be?
> Affection, thy intention stabs the centre.
> Thou dost make possible things not so held,
> Communicat'st with dreams – how can this be? –
> With what's unreal thou coactive art,
> And fellow'st nothing. Then, 'tis very credent
> Thou mayst co-join with something; and thou dost,
> And that beyond commission, and I find it,
> And that to the infection of my brains
> And hardening of my brows.
>
> (128–46)

His vocabulary is an odd mixture of the colloquial (*rough pash*, *like as eggs*, *false as dice*, *collop*) and, in the second half of the passage, such Latinisms as *coactive*, *credent*, *co-join*. (*Co-join* occurs only there; *coact* is found in *Troilus and Cressida* only; *credent* appears on three other occasions. They thus draw attention to themselves.) But more difficult than his vocabulary is his syntax, the putting together of words into sentences. Leontes's syntax is disjointed, associative, as his diseased mind leaps from one idea to another, with sometimes only a tenuous connection between them, and the connection is what we have to tease out. *Women say so/That will say anything . . . But were they false . . . yet were it* [still] *true / To say this boy were like me . . .* [So how] *Can thy dam* [carry on like this]? *Affection* ('sexual desire') *. . . dost make possible things not so held . . . Then, 'tis very credent . . . and thou dost . . . and I find it*. Starting with a facial resemblance between father and son, Leontes has proved, to his own satisfaction, that Hermione is an adulteress.

As Polixenes and Hermione go off to walk in the garden, Leontes is in a tormented world of his own:

> Inch-thick, knee-deep, o'er head and ears a forked one!
> Go play, boy, play: thy mother plays, and I

> Play too – but so disgraced a part, whose issue
> Will hiss me to my grave. Contempt and clamour
> Will be my knell. Go play, boy, play. There have been,
> Or I am much deceived, cuckolds ere now;
> And many a man there is, even at this present,
> Now while I speak this, holds his wife by th' arm,
> That little thinks she has been sluiced in's absence,
> And his pond fished by his next neighbour, by
> Sir Smile, his neighbour. Nay, there's comfort in't
> Whiles other men have gates, and those gates opened,
> As mine, against their will. Should all despair
> That have revolted wives, the tenth of mankind
> Would hang themselves.

> (I.ii.186–200)

The Latinate vocabulary has disappeared and the colloquial dominates. This passage is deliberately, revoltingly, obscene in its choice of words: *sluiced*, *his pond fished*, *gates*. And he is convinced it happens all the time – "even at this present / Now, while I speak this" – maybe with you out there in the audience?

He plays with the different senses of words and always chooses the worst sense, or else he replaces a comparatively innocent word with a more blunt, unambiguous one:

> I have said
> She's an *adult'ress*; I have said with whom.
> More, she's a *traitor*, and Camillo is
> A *fedary* with her, and one that knows
> What she should shame to know herself
> But with her most vile *principal* – that she's
> A *bed-swerver*.

> (II.i.88–93)

By II.i. *adult'ress*, *fedary*, *principal* are terms too grand for the supposed conspirators Hermione, Camillo and Polixenes. The colloquial compound *bed-swerver* is much more emphatic and to Leontes much more appropriate. In earlier conversation with Camillo, *cogitation* and *impudently negative* jostle with *slippery*, *hobby-horse* and *puts to*.

> Ha'not you seen, Camillo –
> But that's past doubt, you have, or your eye-glass
> Is thicker than a cuckold's horn – or heard –
> For to a vision so apparent rumour
> Cannot be mute – or thought – for cogitation
> Resides not in that man that does not think –
> My wife is slippery? If thou wilt confess –
> Or else be impudently negative
> To have nor eyes, nor ears, nor thought – then say
> My wife's a hobby-horse, deserves a name

As rank as any flax-wench that puts to
Before her troth-plight: say't and justify't.

(I.ii.267–78)

If you haven't *seen*, then you must have *heard*, or, at the very least, *thought* "my wife's a hobby-horse", that is, promiscuous. All those parentheses are not a bad way of making us see into the recesses of Leontes's mind. They justify his own actions to himself.

So Hermione is condemned and imprisoned and Polixenes leaves for his own country, Camillo going with him. II.iii. begins where II.ii. left off, with another passage of apparently casual syntax ("Nor night nor day no rest!"), once more giving the impression of thought being turned immediately into speech. Antigonus protests gently and Paulina vigorously, but all to no avail. The baby Perdita makes no impression on Leontes because he has already persuaded himself that the child is Polixenes', not his. He has agreed, though, to send to the oracle at Delphi for what he believes will simply be confirmation of his own views.

The trial of Hermione begins at III.ii. Leontes has insisted on going ahead, even though he is told that the messengers are on their way back to the court with Apollo's answer. Her language is movingly simple, as it had been when she was led away to prison (II.i.116–24). In her defence at the trial she demonstrates a natural colloquialism with her piling up of adjunct phrases:

Both disobedience and ingratitude
To you and toward your friend, whose love had spoke
Even since it could speak, *from an infant, freely*
That it was yours.

lastly, hurried

Here to this place, i' th' open air, before
I have got strength of limit.

(III.ii.67–70, 103–5)

But perhaps she is already partially linguistically compromised by the deliberately flirtatious *double entendres* she has exchanged with Polixenes in the first act? They are eventually proved innocent, but have their words not been liable to misconstruction?[27] Leontes at first refuses to believe the message from the oracle that

Hermione is chaste; Polixenes blameless; Camillo a true subject;
Leontes a jealous tyrant; his innocent babe truly begotten; and the
King shall live without an heir, if that which is lost be not found.

Then news is brought to him of his son's death and Hermione collapses, apparently dead. He suddenly realises that everything he

233

has said and done is absolutely wrong, so he goes slap into reverse:

> Apollo, pardon
> My great profaneness 'gainst thine oracle!
> I'll reconcile me to Polixenes;
> New woo my queen; recall the good Camillo –
> Whom I proclaim a man of truth, of mercy:
> For, being transported by my jealousies
> To bloody thoughts and to revenge, I chose
> Camillo for the minister to poison
> My friend Polixenes; which had been done,
> But that the good mind of Camillo tardied
> My swift command, though I with death and with
> Reward did threaten and encourage him,
> Not doing it and being done. He, most humane,
> And filled with honour, to my kingly guest
> Unclasped my practice, quit his fortunes here –
> Which you knew great – and to the hazard
> Of all incertainties himself commended,
> No richer than his honour. How he glisters
> Through my rust. And how his piety
> Does my deeds make the blacker!
>
> (III.ii.151–70)

He begins with a series of resolutions, expounded by parallel infinitives: *reconcile, woo, recall*. But the mention of Camillo leads him to remember, in parenthesis, the plot to use Camillo to poison Polixenes. This in turn gives rise to further subordination (*which had been done*/*But that . . .*). The first sentence ends with a compressed conditional clause involving two pairs, each with three components: 'I threatened him with death if he didn't do it, and encouraged him with reward if he did.' The second, shorter sentence, containing two brief parentheses, resumes the verbal parallelism of the opening of the speech: *Unclasped, quit, commended*. He is still thinking as he goes, although he is now thinking to some purpose. But it isn't so easy to change his whole world around. And the strain is beginning to tell, on us as well as on him. So Leontes is offstage for the whole of Act IV, and things begin to sort themselves out, not in Sicilia but in Bohemia.

Act IV, scene i, spoken by Chorus, records the passing of time and the change of scene. IV.ii., a relatively short scene between Polixenes and Camillo, is in prose, just as the opening scene of the play, at the court of Bohemia, is a prose conversation between Camillo and Archidamus, a visiting Bohemian courtier. We have the sense of a new beginning, with Camillo now anxious to return home and Polixenes reluctant to let him go. But it is the new character, Autolycus, once a servant to Florizel but now out of favour and living on his wits, who provides the sense of life the play has lately been so lacking. In the *Odyssey*, Autolycus is called "one who excelled all men in thievery and in oaths" and in William Golding's translation of Ovid (which Shakespeare knew) "a wily pie / And such a fellow as in theft and filching had no peer".[28] Nor has he; he darts all over the place, he thieves and cheats but at the same time indulges our wish to cock a snook at society. His knavery prevents the sheep-shearing from becoming too much of an idyll. *As You Like It* had already shown that straight pastoral was not for Shakespeare. His vocabulary includes several of the canting terms popularised by writers like Greene or Harman, as we have seen earlier: *doxy* ('beggar's girl'); *pugging* ('pulling', 'tugging', and by extension 'stealing'); *aunts* ('loose women'); *silly cheat* ('simple trickery'); *troll-my-dames* (the name of a game, probably with a pun on the *dames*, his 'aunts'). But he also knows the recent French borrowing *caparison*, literally 'trappings for a horse' and presumably equivalent to our 'get-up'. From straight thief he turns pedlar and later still disguises himself as a courtier. He is as excellent at one as at the other. When he says "I can bear my part: you must know 'tis my occupation", he is referring to singing; we, the audience, can take it in the acting sense.

We last saw Perdita as a baby. Florizel we have heard mentioned but have not seen until now. As befits aristocrats – even if unrecognised – Florizel and Perdita speak verse. Florizel's style is usually the more complex, and occasionally rhetorical, as in his marvellous tribute to Perdita at the feast (IV.iv.135–46): "What you do. . .When you speak. . .When you dance . . ." and concluding with the involved and paradoxical:

> Each your doing,
> So singular in each particular,
> Crowns what you are doing in the present deeds,
> That all your acts are queens.
>
> (IV.iv.143–6)

Perdita's language is more varied. Her modesty, her essential 'niceness', must be evident. She herself says that, in comparison with Florizel:

> I cannot speak
> So well, nothing so well; no, nor mean better.
> By th' pattern of mine own thoughts I cut out
> The purity of his.
>
> (IV.iv.377–80)

When Polixenes and Camillo reveal themselves, her fears surface in a speech (438–47) which is plain style in both its vocabulary and

235

syntax. On the other hand, she is a princess (although she does not yet know it). The syntax of IV.iv.79–85 is rather more involved, with its opening participial construction and the correlatives *Not. . .nor*:

> Sir, the year growing ancient,
> Not yet on summer's death nor on the birth
> Of trembling winter, the fairest flowers o' th' season
> Are our carnations and streaked gillyvors,
> Which some call Nature's bastards; of that kind
> Our rustic garden's barren, and I care not
> To get slips of them.

She has classical references for all the spring flowers and she knows a word like *auspicious*. And she has a mind of her own, as she shows Polixenes in the discussion about *gillyvors*.

The link between the earlier jealous hysteria of Leontes (with the consequent 'death' of Hermione) and the apparent incredibility of romance (with her 'resurrection' in the final scene) is Paulina. There is no equivalent to Paulina in the source, Greene's *Pandosto*. In Shakespeare she brings the baby to Leontes in a despairing attempt to make him see the truth. When the courtiers try to stop her, she turns on them and argues that only she is honest. She alone can take on Leontes, can throw his own mocking words right back at him:

> PAULINA   I say I come
> From your good queen.
> LEONTES   Good queen?
> PAULINA   Good queen, my lord, good queen, I say good
> queen;
> And would by combat make her good, so were I
> A man, the worst about you.
>
>   (II.iii.57–61)

She too can probe for the most damning word, just like Leontes:

> I'll not call you tyrant;
> But this most cruel usage of your queen –
> Not able to produce more accusation
> Than your own weak-hinged fancy – something savours
> Of *tyrrany*, and will *ignoble* make you,
> Yea, *scandalous* to the world.
>
>   (II.iii.115–20)

It is Paulina who announces Hermione's death as the climax of all that Leontes has done and she has no scrap of comfort or excuse for him. So it is fitting that Paulina produces the statue in Act V.

In several ways this final scene is different. It is different from the source, *Pandosto*, where there is no resurrection: Hermione dies and stays dead. Leontes's language, on his return, has become much

simpler (as Lear's did when he regained *his* sanity) and he now
fully recognises the terrible nature of what he has done. Paulina,
although initially unforgiving (V.i.34–49), gradually becomes more
accommodating as she prepares to reveal the statue. It is different,
too, in that the reunions which usually conclude a play have here
taken place before the final scene for which something special has
obviously been reserved.[29] And it is different in that, for once,
Shakespeare hasn't taken the audience into his confidence. As we
sit in the theatre, we suspect that something will happen to this
statue, but we don't know what. Our surprise and wonder when
it comes alive coincides with that of the characters on stage. We
have to be made to see through their eyes, especially through the
eyes of Leontes. It is Paulina who directs him – and us – how to
respond: "Paulina manages the reunion like a stage show, drawing a
curtain, calling for music, and requesting silence."[30] This was surely
better performed in the private Blackfriars theatre.

The process has in fact begun before the final scene. In V.i. we learn
that Leontes has done regular penance since Hermione's death, but
even so Paulina is not completely satisfied. She makes him promise
that he will marry again only if *another Hermione* should appear and
that she, Paulina, shall choose the new queen. By this time she is
addressing him colloquially, as an equal, almost an inferior:

> Yet if my lord will marry – if you will, sir,
> No remedy, but you will – give me the office
> To choose you a queen: she shall not be so young
> As was your former, but she shall be such
> As, walked your first queen's ghost, it should take
> joy
> To see her in your arms.

LEONTES My true Paulina,
We shall not marry till thou bid'st us.

PAULINA That
Shall be when your first queen's again in breath;
Never till then.

> (76–84)

The first evidence of the statue is reported (by Third Gentleman, V.ii.
92–100) as the work of "that rare Italian master Julio Romano"). We
are gradually being prepared for the final scene which takes place in
Paulina's house where Leontes, Perdita, Polixenes and Camillo have
all gathered:

> But here it is: prepare
> To see the life as lively mocked as ever
> Still sleep mocked death. Behold, and say 'tis well!

And Paulina draws the curtain. Leontes, like everyone else, is impressed by the lifelike quality, but protests that Hermione was not so much wrinkled as this face seems. So she wasn't, Paulina replies, but you are thinking of sixteen years ago, so the statue now is even more lifelike than you thought at first. Perdita wants to kiss it, but Paulina prevents her. She says that soon they will believe it *moves* (61) and *lives* (70). And then it *can* and it *does*:

> If you can behold it,
> I'll make the statue move indeed, descend
> And take you by the hand.
>
> (87–89)

But the movement depends on the co-operation of the assembled company ("It is required / You do awake your faith", with its formality and its religious language). And, to the accompaniment of music, Hermione descends. Paulina's language is now straightforward, with simple directives and short sense units: nothing must detract from the miracle:

> 'Tis time: descend; be stone no more; approach;
> Strike all that look upon with marvel. Come,
> I'll fill your grave up. Stir; nay, come away.
> Bequeath to death your numbness, for from him
> Dear life redeems you. You perceive she stirs.
> Start not: her actions shall be holy as
> You hear my spell is lawful.
>
> (99–106)

And Hermione finally *speaks* (121). Paulina herself comments on the marvel she has presented:

> That she is living
> Were it but told you, should be hooted at
> Like an old tale: but it appears she lives.
>
> (115–17)

We too have seen and have been made to share the characters' amazement. We do not need to be informed about how and when it was all managed, and the play rapidly comes to an end. There is no more to be done: we believe this winter's tale.

In *The Winter's Tale* Shakespeare employed almost the whole of his linguistic armoury: synonyms, compounds, occasional Latinisms, both rhetorical and colloquial syntax, but developed and refined these to illuminate the pathological obsession of Leontes, the innocence of Perdita and eventually of Hermione, the sturdy common sense of Paulina. The basis of both diction and syntax is colloquial usage, but if this is 'natural' in Perdita and Paulina, with Leontes it is flawed, 'artful', rather like the carnations and gillyvors Perdita would not admit into her country garden. The art has come to seem like nature.

Yet it remains true that, in his last plays, Shakespeare seems less concerned to show the mind turned against itself and more interested in – what? The language which suggests true pathos or the serenity of reconcilement? The true pastoral of the Welsh mountains in *Cymbeline* or of Bohemia (with its rogue Autolycus but no melancholy Jaques)? Whatever it was, there are signs in the last plays of yet further experimentation with language, a willingness to revive old techniques occasionally but a refusal to stand pat on what had already been achieved. Man had always been infinite in his faculties, in form and moving express and admirable. There was still so much to do.

But perhaps I am wrong about this, and it might be instructive, even if fanciful, to imagine Shakespeare taking another view of his writing around 1612–13. The final plays work through a relative simplicity of lexis to the alternation of colloquial and deliberately complex syntax. The peal of ordnance which set fire to the Globe in 1613 and burnt down the theatre might have had its linguistic counterpart. Perhaps Shakespeare not altogether unwillingly put off the amazing technicolour dreamcoat of literary language to return to Stratford, to at least semi-retirement, to just about the best house in the town (with its second-best bed). The time is free. He can pass his days once more in speaking that 'real' language which, in the last resort, we can never really know.

Notes and References

1. Hammond (1985), p. 133. See also Brennan (1979). I cannot detect the self-conscious exaggeration of Chorus suggested by Danson (1983).
2. Kernan (1975), p. 288.
3. Leggatt (1988b), p. 104. See also Wharton (1983).
4. Leggatt (1988b), p. 78.
5. Berry (1978), pp. 49–59.
6. Quoted in the Notes to the New Penguin edition (1968), p. 174.
7. As suggested by Kernan (1975) and Calderwood (1979).
8. Hammond, p. 144. The portrait in the National Portrait Gallery has something of the same coldness.
9. Quoted by Agnes Latham, Arden edition (1975), pp. ix–x.
10. For Armin, see Latham, pp. li–lv, and Dutton (1989), pp. 113–15.
11. Montrose (1981).
12. Dutton (1989), p. 104.
13. Further instances are I.i.154–59, I.ii.171–80, III.iii.391–402, IV.i.135–45.

14. "Rosalind teases Orlando because she loves him, and because she is absurdly happy, and because she knows that swinging on the branches can't possibly break the tree, or if she isn't perfectly sure of it she's going the best way towards finding out." Latham, p. lxxviii.
15. Latham, p. lxxv.
16. McElroy (1973), p. 221.
17. Burrell (1954).
18. Novy (1984), pp. 87–88.
19. There is an excellent discussion of this soliloquy (also pointing out its contrast with the soliloquy which opens *Richard III*) in Scragg (1988), pp. 186–88.
20. Foakes (1982), pp. 7–27.
21. Jorgensen (1971), p. 49.
22. Scragg (1988), pp. 192–3.
23. Professor S. Cavell in a lecture at Lausanne, August 1989.
24. Doran (1983).
25. Overton (1989), p. 46.
26. Quoted in the Notes to the New Penguin edition of *The Winter's Tale* (1960).
27. See further, Felperin (1985).
28. Note to New Penguin edition (1969).
29. Gurr (1983), p. 420.
30. Brown, in Andrews (1985), II, p. 545.

Select Bibliography

A small collection of introductory books (all in paperback) might include:

BRIGGS, J. *This Stage-Play World: English Literature and Its Background, 1580–1625* (1983).

CLARK, S. *Hutchinson Shakespeare Dictionary* (1986).

DUTTON, R. *William Shakespeare: A Literary Life* (1989).

EDWARDS, P. *Shakespeare: A Writer's Progress* (1986).

WELLS, S. (ed.) *The Cambridge Companion to Shakespeare Studies* (1986).

Other reference works:

ANDREWS, J. F. (ed.) *William Shakespeare: His World, His Work, His Influence*, 3 vols (New York, 1985).

BROOK, G. L. *The Language of Shakespeare* (1976).

BULLOUGH, G. *Narrative and Dramatic Sources of Shakespeare*, I–VIII (1957–75).

ONIONS, C. T. *The Oxford Dictionary of English Etymology* (1966).

ONIONS, C. T. *A Shakespeare Glossary* (rev. R. D. Eagleson, 1986).

The Oxford English Dictionary (2nd edn, 1989).

SCHMIDT, A. *Shakespeare-Lexicon*, 2 vols (rev. G. Sarrazin, 1962).

SPEVACK, M. *The Harvard Concordance to Shakespeare* (Cambridge, Mass., 1973).

WELLS, S. *Shakespeare: A Bibliographical Guide* (1990).

The standard edition must now be

WELLS, S. and TAYLOR, G. *William Shakespeare: The Complete Works* (1986). (Also, by the same authors, a compact edition (1988),

an Original Spelling edition (1987) and detailed discussion of individual readings in *William Shakespeare: A Textual Companion* (1987).
Two other editions are frequently quoted:
ALEXANDER, P. *William Shakespeare: The Complete Works* (1951).
EVANS, G. B. *The Riverside Shakespeare* (Boston, 1974).

In this book reference is to the New Penguin edition, except for *Cymbeline* and *Titus Andronicus* which are quoted from Signet. The New Arden edition, especially the later volumes, is often useful.

Abbreviations used in the following section of this Bibliography:

E&S.	*Essays and Studies by Members of the English Association*
EC	*Essays in Criticism*
ELH	*ELH, A Journal of English Literary History*
PQ	*Philological Quarterly*
SEL	*Studies in English Literature*
SQ	*Shakespeare Quarterly*
S on A St.	*Stratford on Avon Studies*
S St.	*Shakespeare Studies*
SS	*Shakespeare Survey*

Citations are by author, title, place of publication (if outside England) and date.
ANDERSON, J. J. "The morality of *Love's Labour's Lost*", *SS* 24 (1971), pp. 55–62.
BARBER, C. *Early Modern English* (1976).
BARBER, C. "'You' and 'Thou' in Shakespeare's *Richard III*", *Leeds Studies in English 12* (1981), pp. 273–89 (reprinted in SALMON and BURNESS (1987), pp. 163–80)
BARISH, J. A. *Ben Jonson and the Language of Prose Comedy* (Harvard, 1960).
BARISH, J. A. "Shakespeare's Prose", in *Approaches to Shakespeare*, ed. N. Rabkin (New York, 1964), pp. 245–63.
BARISH, J. A. "*The Spanish Tragedy* or the pleasures and perils of rhetoric", *S on A St.* 9 (1966), pp. 59–86.
BARISH, J. A. "Pattern and purpose in the prose of *Much Ado About Nothing*", *Rice University Studies* 60 (1974), pp. 19–30.
BAXTER, J. *Shakespeare's Poetic Styles* (1980).
BENNETT, R. B. "The reform of the malcontent: Jaques and the meaning of *As You Like It*", *S St.* 9 (1976), pp. 183–204.
BENTLEY, G. A. *The Profession of Player in Shakespeare's Time, 1590–1640* (Princeton, 1984).

BERRY, R. *The Shakespearean Metaphor* (1978).

BERRY, R. *Shakespeare and Social Class* (Atlantic Highlands, NJ, 1988).

BLAKE, N. F. *The Language of Shakespeare* (1988).

BLAKE, N. "Negation in Shakespeare" in *An Historic Tongue, Studies in English Language in Memory of Barbara Strang*, eds G. Nixon and J. Honey (1988), pp. 89–111.

BLANPIED, J. W. *Time and the Artist in Shakespeare's English Histories* (1983).

BOOTH, S. *An Essay on Shakespeare's Sonnets* (1969).

BOOTH, S. "Syntax and rhetoric in *Richard II*", *Mosaic* 10 (1977), pp. 87–103.

BRADBROOK, M. C. *Shakespeare and Elizabethan Poetry* (1951).

BRENNAN, A. S. "'That Within Which Passes Show': The Function of the Chorus in *Henry V*", *PQ* 58 (1979), pp. 40–52.

BRENNAN, A. *Shakespeare's Dramatic Structures* (1986).

BROOKS, H. F. *A Midsummer Night's Dream* (Arden edn, 1979).

BROWN, J. R. *The White Devil* (Revels Plays, 1960).

BROWN, R. and GILMAN, A. "Politeness Theory and Shakespeare's Major Tragedies", *Language in Society* 18 (1989), pp. 159–212.

BURCKHARDT, S. *Shakespearean Meanings* (Princeton, 1968).

BURRELL, M. D. "*Macbeth*: a study in paradox", *Shakespeare Jahrbuch* 90 (1954), pp. 167–90.

BURTON, D. M. *Shakespeare's Grammatical Style* (1968).

BURTON, D. M. "Discourse and Decorum in the First Act of *Richard III*", *S St.* 14 (1981), pp. 55–84.

CALDERWOOD, J. L. "*Love's Labour's Lost*: a wantoning with words", *SEL* 5 (1965), pp. 317–32.

CALDERWOOD, J. L. "*Coriolanus*: wordless meanings and meaningless words", *SEL* 6 (1966), pp. 211–24.

CALDERWOOD, J. L. *Metadrama in Shakespeare's Henriad* (Berkeley and Los Angeles (1979).

CANTOR, P. A. *Shakespeare's Rome: Republic and Empire* (Cornell, 1976).

CAREY, J. "Sixteenth and seventeenth–century prose", in *English Poetry and Prose, 1570–1674*, ed. C. Ricks (1970), pp. 339–431.

CARROLL, W. C. *The Great Feast of Languages in "Love's Labour's Lost"* (Princeton, 1976).

CHAMPION, L. *Shakespeare's Tragic Perspective* (Athens, Georgia, 1976).

CLEMEN, W. *English Tragedy before Shakespeare* (1961).

CLEMEN, W. *Shakespeare's Dramatic Art* (1972).

CLEMEN, W. *The Development of Shakespeare's Imagery* (2nd edn, 1977).

CLEMEN, W. "Some aspects of style in the *Henry VI* plays", in EDWARDS *et al.* (1980), pp. 9–24.

COLMAN, E. A. M. *The Dramatic Use of Bawdy in Shakespeare* (1974).

COOK, A. J. *The Privileged Playgoers of Shakespeare's London* (Princeton, 1981).

CRUTWELL, P. *The Shakespearean Moment* (1954).

CUSACK, B. "Shakespeare and the tune of the time", *SS* 23 (1970), pp. 1–12 (reprinted in SALMON and BURNESS (1987), pp. 23–34).

DANSON, L. P. *Tragic Alphabet, Shakespeare's Drama of Language* (1974).

DANSON, L. P. *The Harmonies of the Merchant of Venice* (1978).

DANSON, L. P. "*Henry V*: King, Chorus and Critics", *SQ* 34 (1983), pp. 27–43.

DE GRAZIA, M. "Shakespeare's view of language: an historical perspective", *SQ* 29 (1978), pp. 374–88 (reprinted in SALMON and BURNESS (1987), pp. 473–88).

DIXON, P. *Rhetoric* (1971).

DONAWERTH, J. *Shakespeare and the Sixteenth-Century Study of Language* (Urbana and Chicago, 1984).

DONNER, M. "Derived words in Chaucer's language", *Chaucer Review* 13 (1978), pp. 1–15.

DORAN, M. *Shakespeare's Dramatic Language* (1976).

DORAN, M. "The *Macbeth* Music", *S St.*, 16 (1983), pp. 153–73.

DUBROW, H. "Shakespeare's Undramatic Monologues: Towards a Reading of the Sonnets", *SQ* 32 (1981), pp. 55–68.

EAGLESON, R. D. "'Propertied in All the Tuned Spheres': Aspects of Shakespeare's Language", *The Teaching of English* 20 (1971), pp. 4–15 (reprinted in SALMON and BURNESS (1987), pp. 133–44).

EDWARDS, P., EWBANK, I–S. and HUNTER, G. K. *Shakespeare's Styles, Essays in Honour of Kenneth Muir* (1980).

ELAM, K. *Shakespeare's Universe of Discourse* (1984).

ELIOT, T. S. *Selected Essays* (1951).

EVANS, B. *Shakespeare's Tragic Practice* (1979).

EWBANK, I–S. "'Were man but constant, he were perfect': constancy and consistency in *The Two Gentlemen of Verona*", *S on A St.* 14 (1972), pp. 31–57.

EWBANK, I–S. "'My name is Marina': the language of recognition", in EDWARDS *et al.* (1980), pp. 111–30.

FELPERIN, H. "'Tongue-tied our queen?': the deconstruction of presence in *The Winter's Tale*", in *Shakespeare and the Question of Theory*, eds P. Parker and G. Hartman (1985), pp. 3–18.

FERRY, A. *The "Inward" Language: Sonnets of Wyatt, Sidney, Shakespeare, Donne* (Chicago, 1983).

FOAKES, R. A. "Images of Death: ambition in *Macbeth*", in *Focus on Macbeth*, ed. J. R. Brown (1982), pp. 7–27.

FOWLER, R. *Style and Structure in Literature* (1975).

GARNER, B. A. "Shakespeare's Latin Neologisms", *S St.* 15 (1982), pp. 149–70 (reprinted in SALMON and BURNESS (1987), pp. 207–28).

GARNER, B. A. "Latin-Saxon Hybrids in Shakespeare and the Bible", *Studies in the Humanities* 10 (1983), pp. 39–44 (reprinted in SALMON and BURNESS (1987), pp. 229–34).

GILBERT, A. J. *Literary Language from Chaucer to Johnson* (1979a).

GILBERT, A. J. "Techniques of Focus in Shakespeare's sonnets", *Language and Style* 12 (1979b), pp. 245–67.

GOLDMAN, M. "Characterizing Coriolanus", *SS* 34 (1981), pp. 73–84.

GORDON, G. "Shakespeare's English", *Society for Pure English*, Tract XXIX (1928) (reprinted in *Shakespearian Comedy and Other Studies* (1944)).

GRAY, J. C. (ed.) *Mirror Up to Shakespeare: Essays in Honour of G.R. Hibbard* (1984).

GREENE, G. "'The Power of Speech/To Stir Men's Blood', The Language of Tragedy in Shakespeare's *Julius Caesar*", *Renaissance Drama* 11 (1980), pp. 67–93.

GREENE, G. "Language and value in Shakespeare's *Troilus and Gressida*", *SEL* 21 (1981), pp. 271–85.

GURR, A. *The Shakespearean Stage, 1574–1642* (2nd edn, 1980).

GURR, A. "*You* and *Thou* in Shakespeare's Sonnets", *EC* 32 (1982), pp. 9–25.

GURR, A. "The Bear, the Statue, and Hysteria in *The Winter's Tale*", *SQ* 34 (1983), pp. 420–25.

GURR, A. "Theaters and the Dramatic Profession", in ANDREWS (1985), II, pp. 107–28.

GURR, A. and ORRELL, J. *Rebuilding Shakespeare's Globe* (1989).

HALL, A. D. "Tudor prose style: English humanists and the problem of a standard", *English Literary Renaissance* 7 (1977), pp.267–96.

HAMMOND, A. "'It must be your imagination then': the Prologue and the Plural Text in *Henry V* and Elsewhere" in MAHON and PENDLETON, (1985), pp. 133–50.

HARRIS, D. J. *Elizabethan Prose* (1968).

HART, A. "Vocabularies of Shakespeare's plays", *Review of English Studies* 19 (1943), pp. 128–40.

HEILMAN, R. B. "'To know himself': an aspect of tragic structure", *Review of English Literature* 5 (1964), pp. 36–57.

HENIGER, S. K. "The pattern of *Love's Labour's Lost*", *S St.* 7 (1974), pp. 25–33.

HIBBARD, G. R. "The forced gait of a shuffling nag", in *Shakespeare 1971*, eds. C. Leech and J. M. R. Margeson (Toronto, 1972).

HIBBARD, G. R. *The Making of Shakespeare's Dramatic Poetry* (1981).

HILL, R. F. "*Coriolanus*: violentest contrariety", *E&S* 17 (1964), pp. 12–23.

HOCKEY, D. C. "A world of rhetoric in *Richard II*", *SQ* 15 (1964), pp. 179–91.

HOLMES, E. *Aspects of Elizabethan Imagery* (1929).

HONIGMANN, E. A. J. *Shakespeare: Seven Tragedies* (1976).

HONIGMANN, E. A. J. *Shakespeare: The "Lost Years"* (1985).

HOUSTON, J. P. *Shakespearean Sentences: A Study in Style and Syntax* (1988).

HULME, H. M. *Explorations in Shakespeare's Language* (1962).

HUNTER, G. K. "The dramatic technique of Shakespeare's sonnets", *Essays in Criticism* 3 (1953), pp. 152–64.

HUNTER, G. K. *All's Well That Ends Well* (Arden edn, 1959).

HUNTER, G. K. *John Lyly: The Humanist as Courtier* (1962).

ISER, W. "The Dramatisation of Double Meaning in Shakespeare's *As You Like It*", *Theatre Journal* 35 (1983), pp. 307–32.

IVES, E. W. "Shakespeare and History: Divergencies and Agreements", *SS* 38 (1985), pp. 19–35.

JARDINE, L. *Still Harping on Daughters: Women and Drama in the Age of Shakespeare* (1983).

JENKINS, H. *Hamlet* (Arden edn, 1982).

JONES, R. F. *The Triumph of the English Language* (Stanford, 1953).

JORGENSEN, P. *Redeeming Shakespeare's Words* (Berkeley and Los Angeles, 1962).

JORGENSEN, P. *Our Naked Frailties: Sensational Art and Meaning in Macbeth* (Berkeley and Los Angeles, 1971).

JOSEPH, M. *Shakespeare's Use of the Arts of Language* (New York, 1947).

KERNAN, A. "The plays and the playwrights", in *The Revels History of Drama in English*, eds C. Leech and T. W. Craik (1975), III, pp. 269–99.

KERNAN, A. *The Playwright as Magician* (1979).

KERNAN, A. B. "Courtly Servants and Public Players: Shakespeare's Image of Theatre in the Court at Elsinore and Whitehall", in *Poetic Traditions of the English Renaissance*, eds M. Mack and G. de F. Lord (New Haven, 1982), pp. 103–21.

KING, A. H. *The Language of Satirized Characters in Poetaster, Lund Studies in English* 10 (Lund, 1941).

LANHAM, R. A. *The Motives of Eloquence* (1976).

LATHAM, A. *As You Like It* (Arden edn, 1975).

LEGGATT, A. *King Lear* (Harvester New Critical Introductions to Shakespeare, 1988a).

LEGGATT, A. *Shakespeare's Political Drama* (1988b).

LEGGATT, A. *English Drama, Shakespeare to the Restoration, 1590–1660* (1988c).

LEIDER, E. W. "Plainness of style in *King Lear*", *SQ* 21 (1970), pp. 45–53.

LEVER, J. W. *The Tragedy of State* (1971).

MacALINDON, T. P. "Language, style and meaning in *Troilus and Cressida*", *Publications of the Modern Language Association of America* (*PMLA*) 84 (1969), pp. 29–43.

McELROY, B. *Shakespeare's Mature Tragedies* (Princeton, 1973).

McINTOSH, A. "*As You Like It*: a grammatical clue to character", *Review of English Literature* 4 (1963), pp. 68–79.

MAHON, J. W. and PENDLETON, T. A. (ed.), "*Fanned and Winnowed Opinions*", *Shakespearean Essays presented to Harold Jenkins* (1985).

MATTHEWS, W. "Language in *Love's Labour's Lost*", *E&S* 17 (1964), pp. 1–11 (reprinted in SALMON and BURNESS (1987), pp. 499–509).

MONTROSE, L. A. "'The Place of A Brother' In *As You Like It*: Social Process and Comic Form," *SQ* 32 (1981), pp. 28–54.

MUIR, K. *Shakespeare's Sonnets* (1979).

MULHOLLAND, J. "'Thou' and 'You' in Shakespeare: a study in the second person pronoun", *English Studies* 48 (1967), pp. 34–43 (reprinted in SALMON and BURNESS (1987), pp. 153–62.

MULRYNE, J. R. "*The White Devil* and *The Duchess of Malfi*", *S on A St.* 1 (1960), pp. 201–25.

NASH, W. *Rhetoric: The Wit of Persuasion* (1989).

NEELY, C. T. "*The Winter's Tale*: the triumph of speech", *SEL* 15 (1975), pp. 321–38.

NEWMAN, K. *Shakespeare's Rhetoric of Comic Characters* (1985).

NOVY, M. *Love's Argument: Gender Relations in Shakespeare* (Chapel Hill, NC, 1984).

NOWOTTNY, W. "Formal elements in Shakespeare's sonnets", *EC* 2 (1952), pp. 76–84.

NOWOTTNY, W. *The Language Poets Use* (1962).

OLIVER, H. J. *The Merry Wives of Windsor* (Arden edn, 1971).

OVERTON, Bill *The Winter's Tale* (The Critics' Debate Series, 1989).

OWEN, C. A. "Comic awareness, style and dramatic technique in *Much Ado About Nothing*", *Boston University Studies in English* 5 (1961), pp. 193–207.

PALMER, D. J. "Magic and poetry in *Doctor Faustus*", *Critical Quarterly* 6 (1964), pp. 56–67.

PALMER, D. J. "Elizabethan tragic heroes", *S on A. St.* 9 (1966), pp. 11–36.

PALMER, D. J. "Tragic error in *Julius Caesar*", *SQ* 21 (1970), pp. 399–410.

PALMER, D. J. "'We shall know by this Fellow': Prologue and Chorus in Shakespeare", *Bulletin of the John Rylands Library* 64 (1982), pp. 501–21.

PALMER, K. *Troilus and Cressida* (Arden edn, 1982).

PALMER, K. "Iago's questionable shapes", in MAHON and PENDLETON (1985), pp. 184–201.

PARTRIDGE, A. C. *The Language of Renaissance Poetry* (1971).

PEARSALL, D. A. *John Lydgate* (1970).

PEET, D. "The rhetoric of *Tamburlaine*", *ELH* 26 (1959), pp. 137–55.

POTTER, L. "The antic disposition of Richard II", *SS* 27 (1974), pp. 33–41.

QUIRK, R. "Shakespeare and the English Language", in *A New Companion to Shakespeare Studies*, ed. K. Muir and S. Schoenbaum (1971), pp. 67–82 (reprinted in SALMON and BURNESS (1987), pp. 3–23).

RAMSEY, P. *The Fickle Glass: A Study of Shakespeare's Sonnets* (New York, 1979).

REIBETANZ, J. *The Lear World* (1977).

REPLOGLE, C. "Not parody, not burlesque: the play within the play in *Hamlet*," *Modern Philology* 67 (1969), pp. 150–59.

ROBERTS, J. "King Lear and the Prefixes of Inversion", *Neuphilologische Mitteilungen* 79 (1978), pp. 384–90.

SACCIO, P. *Shakespeare's English Kings* (1977).

SACCIO, P. "Shakespeare's Treatment of English History", in ANDREWS (1985) II, pp. 453–71.

SALMON, V. "Sentence structures in colloquial Shakespearean English", *Transactions of the Philological Society*, 1965, pp. 105–40.

(reprinted in SALMON and BURNESS (1987), pp. 265–300).

SALMON, V. "Elizabethan colloquial English in the Falstaff plays", *Leeds Studies in English* 1 (1967), pp. 37–70 (reprinted in SALMON and BURNESS (1987), pp. 37–70).

SALMON, V. "Some functions of Shakespearean word-formation", *SS* 23 (1970), pp. 13–26 (reprinted in SALMON and BURNESS (1987), pp. 193–206).

SALMON, V. and BURNESS, E. *A Reader in the Language of Shakespearean Drama* (Amsterdam and Philadelphia, 1987).

SAMUELS, M. L. "The role of functional selection in the history of English", *Transactions of the Philological Society* (1965), pp. 15–40 (reprinted in R. Lass, *Approaches to English Historical Linguistics* (1969), pp. 325–44).

SAMUELS, M. L. *Linguistic Evolution* (1972).

SCHOENBAUM, S. "The Life: A Survey", in ANDREWS (1985), II, pp. 281–90.

SCRAGG, L. *Discovering Shakespeare's Meaning* (1988).

SELTZER, D. "Prince Hal and the tragic style", *SS* 30 (1977), pp. 13–27.

SICHERMAN, C. M. "*Coriolanus*: the failure of words", *ELH* 39 (1972), pp. 189–207.

SMALLWOOD, R. W. "Shakespeare's Use of History", in WELLS (1986), pp. 143–61.

SMITH, J. "The Language of Leontes", *SQ* 19 (1968), pp. 317–27.

SPEVACK, M. "Shakespeare's Language", in ANDREWS (1985), II, pp. 343–6.

STARNES, D. T. and NOYES, G. E. *The English Dictionary from Cawdrey to Johnson, 1604–1755* (Chapel Hill, NC, 1946).

STURGESS, K. *Jacobean Private Theatre* (1987).

TAYLOR, E. W. "Shakespeare's use of *-eth* and *-es* endings of verbs in the First Folio", *CLA Journal* 19 (1976), pp. 437–57 (reprinted in SALMON and BURNESS (1987), pp. 371–90).

THOMPSON, A. and THOMPSON, J. O. *Shakespeare: Meaning and Metaphor* (1987).

THOMSON, P. "Rant and cant in *Troilus and Cressida*", *E&S* 22 (1976), pp. 33–56.

THORNE, J. P. "The grammar of jealousy: a note on the character of Leontes", in *Edinburgh Studies in English and Scots*, eds A. J. Aitken, A. McIntosh and H. Palsson (1971), pp. 55–65.

TILLYARD, E. M. W. *Shakespeare's History Plays* (1944).

TURNER, R. Y. "Characterization in Shakespeare's early history plays", *ELH* 31 (1964), pp. 241–58.

URKOWITZ, S. *Shakespeare's Revision of "King Lear"* (Princeton, 1980).

VAN DYKE, J. "Making a scene: language and gesture in *Coriolanus*", *SS* 30 (1977), pp. 135–46.

VICKERS, B. *The Artistry of Shakespeare's Prose* (1968).

VICKERS, B. "Shakespeare's use of rhetoric", in *A New Companion to Shakespeare Studies*, eds K. Muir and S. Schoenbaum (1971), pp. 83–98 (reprinted in SALMON and BURNESS (1987), pp. 391–406).

VICKERS, B. *Shakespeare: The Critical Heritage* (1974).

VICKERS, B. *Shakespeare: Coriolanus* (1976).

VICKERS, B. "Shakespeare's Use of Prose", in ANDREWS (1985), II, pp. 389–95.

WALDRON, R. A. *Sense and Sense-Development* (1967).

WALES, K. "An aspect of Shakespeare's dynamic language: A Note on The Interpretation of *King Lear* III.vii.113: "He Childed as I Father'd", *English Studies* 59 (1978), pp. 395–404 (reprinted in SALMON and BURNESS (1987), pp. 181–90).

WALES, K. *A Dictionary of Stylistics* (1989).

WALES, K. M. "*Thou* and *You* in Early Modern English: Brown and Gilman Re-Appraised", *Studia Linguistica* 37 (1983), pp. 107–25.

WALL, S. "Shakespeare: his later plays", in *English Drama to 1710*, ed. C. Ricks (1971), pp. 253–73.

WATKINS, W. B. C. *Shakespeare and Spenser* (Princeton, 1950).

WHARTON, T. F. *Henry the Fourth, Parts 1 and 2* (Shakespeare: Text and Performance, 1983).

WHITAKER, V. K. *The Mirror Up to Nature* (San Marino, 1965).

WILLIAMSON, G. "Senecan style in the seventeenth century", *PQ* 15 (1936), pp. 321–51 (reprinted in S. Fish, *Seventeenth Century Prose* (1971), pp. 112–46).

WILSON, F. P. "Shakespeare and the diction of common life", *Proceedings of the British Academy* 27 (1941), pp. 167–97 (reprinted in H. Gardner, *Shakespearean and Other Studies* (1969), pp. 100–29).

WRIGHT, G. T. "Shakespeare's Poetic Techniques", in ANDREWS (1985), II, pp. 363–87.

Index